The Frank W. Angel Report on the Death of John H. Tunstall

First Edition

David G. Thomas

Mesilla Valley History Series, Vol 8

Doc45 Publishing, P. O. Box 5044, Las Cruces, N. M. 88003
books@doc45.com

To obtain books, visit:
doc45.com

YouTube Channel
youtube.com/c/Doc45Publications

Cover artwork by Dusan Arsenic.

ISBN 978-1-952580-05-5

000

DOC45 PUBLISHING

Mesilla Valley History Series

La Posta – From the Founding of Mesilla, to Corn Exchange Hotel, to Billy the Kid Museum, to Famous Landmark – by David G. Thomas

Giovanni Maria de Agostini, Wonder of The Century – The Astonishing World Traveler Who Was A Hermit – by David G. Thomas

Screen with a Voice – A History of Moving Pictures in Las Cruces, New Mexico – by David G. Thomas

Billy the Kid's Grave – A History of the Wild West's Most Famous Death Marker – by David G. Thomas

Killing Garrett, The Wild West's Most Famous Lawman – Murder or Self-Defense? – by David G. Thomas

The Stolen Pinkerton Reports of Colonel Albert J. Fountain Investigation – David G. Thomas, Editor

The Trial of Billy the Kid – by David G. Thomas

The Frank W. Angel Report on the Death of John H. Tunstall by David G. Thomas

Mesilla Valley Reprints

When New Mexico Was Young – by Harry H. Bailey

Doc 45

Buenas noches boys,
A social call no doubt –
Do we talk it over,
Or do we shoot it out?

I'm Doc 45,
Toughest man alive.
Hand over those golden bills
Or I'll dose you up with dirty leaden pills.

Acknowledgments

For essential help in transcribing the Angel Report, I thank Sally Kading.

I thank Dan Aranda, Lanty Wylie, and Josh Slatten for proofing the manuscript and making corrections and suggestions.

Special thanks to the many who sought out source materials and provided invaluable help in my research efforts: Dennis Daily, Elizabeth Villa, and Teddie Moreno, Library Archives & Special Collections, NMSU; Evan Davies, Institute of Historical Survey Foundation; Rick Hendricks, New Mexico State Records Administrator; Josh Slatten, Historical Billy the Kid's Coalition; Tomas Jaehn, Special Collections, UNM; Dena Hunt, Senior Archivist, State Archives of New Mexico; Julie Mayle, Curator of Manuscripts, Rutherford B. Hayes Presidential Library & Museums.

For the Lincoln County area map, I thank Billy Roberts, oldwestmaps.com.

Unattributed photos are from the author's collection.

Contents

List of Images

Chapter 1 | Preface

"In the matter of the cause and circumstances of the death of John H. Tunstall a British subject to the honorable Charles Devens, Attorney General...."

So begins the single most important contemporary document recounting the origins of the Lincoln County War. That document – really, a set of documents – is the "Report of Special Agent Frank Warner Angel on the Death of John Henry Tunstall," known today to historians as the "Angel Report."

Frank Warner Angel was born May 28, 1845, in Watertown, New York. In June, 1868, Angel graduated from The Free Academy, now City College, of New York. A year later, after interning with the law firm of Barney, Humphrey, & Butler, Angel was admitted to the New York bar, permitting him to practice law in the state.

On April 15, 1878, Angel was appointed a Special Agent by U.S. Attorney General Charles Devens. He was given credentials by both the Departments of Justice and the Interior. His charges were to investigate: the killing of John Henry Tunstall; alleged corruption by New Mexico Territorial officials, especially Governor Samuel Axtell and U.S. Attorney Thomas Catron; violence in Lincoln County; and alleged land grant frauds in Colfax County, NM.

The event that triggered Angel's appointment as Special Agent was the unprovoked, sadistic murder of John Henry Tunstall in Lincoln, New Mexico, on February 18, 1878.

Angel travelled to New Mexico and began his official investigation on May 4, 1878. His investigative process was to take sworn statements from every witness he could who had information on the events related to his charges as Special Agent.

The 395-page, hand-written Report that Angel submitted to Attorney General Devens on October 3, 1878, on the *"cause and circumstances"* of Tunstall's killing is published for the first time in this book. (Only Angel's investigations of Tunstall's killing and the roles Governor Axell and U.S. Attorney Catron played in the subsequent events are covered in this book. Angel submitted accounts of his non-Tunstall related investigations in separate reports. Those reports are outside of the scope of this book.)

The Report consists of 40 sworn witness statements, two with exhibits (in the case of Alexander A. McSween's statement, 21 exhibits), and Angel's conclusions regarding his investigations.

These sworn statements are of immense value to historians. They are the primary sources for Tunstall's killing and the initiating events of the Lincoln County War. Both sides of the conflict are reflected in the Report – by named participants – in their own words:

- For the Murphy-Dolan side – statements by James J. Dolan and Lawrence G. Murphy.

- For the McSween-Tunstall side – statements by Alexander A. McSween, Florencio Gonzales, Jose F. Montaño, Juan B. Patron, John B. Wilson, and others.

- For the posse that chased and killed Tunstall – statements by Jacob B. Mathews, Robert W. Beckwith, Pantaleón Gallegos, John C. Galvin, John Hurley, "Dutch Charley" Kruling, and others.

- For the men who were with Tunstall when he was killed – statements by Billy the Kid, Henry N. Brown, Fred T. Waite, and Robert A. Widenmann.

- For the condition of Tunstall's body – the statement and autopsy by Dr. Daniel M. Appel.

- For the killers of Tunstall, Tom Hill and William "Buck" Morton, I have added the statements they made on the killing that are not included in the Report.

- For the military authorities and their role in the conflict – statements by Lt. Millard F. Goodwin, Col. George A. Purington, and others.

This book is divided into a preface, six chapters and two appendices. This is the Preface. Chapter One is a narrative account of Tunstall's killing and the events surrounding the killing. The details in this chapter are taken to the extent possible from the Report statements, and are referenced to the appropriate statement(s).

Chapter Two gives the 31 interrogatories (formal questions) that Angel demanded that Governor Axtell answer on August 11, 1878, and Axtell's (belated) reply.

Chapter Three gives the 12 formal charges Angel made against Governor Axtell and Angel's conclusions as to whether a charge was sustained by his investigation.

Chapter Four is the complete, never before published Report, with editorial annotations and supplementary information supplied by the author (enclosed in brackets).

Chapter Five prints contemporary correspondence filed with the Report which are essential to understanding the genesis and consequences of the Report.

Chapter Six gives the history of the Report after it was submitted and the details of the attempt to destroy it by Thomas Catron and Stephen Elkins.

Appendix A gives biographies of 71 men and women who have important roles in the Report events. Providing this information in an appendix makes it possible to avoid interrupting the flow of the narrative in Chapter Two with repeated biographical asides.

Appendix B provides a timeline of the most important events related to the Report. Following Appendix B are footnotes and an index. See the publisher's website doc45. com for a bibliography.

All places not otherwise identified are in New Mexico.

Frank Warner Angel. Graduation photo taken in June, 1868. The photo, which bears Angel's signature, shows him to be a member of Phi Gamma Delta, a social fraternity founded in 1848. Courtesy Lewis A. Ketring Papers, Archives and Special Collections, NMSU.

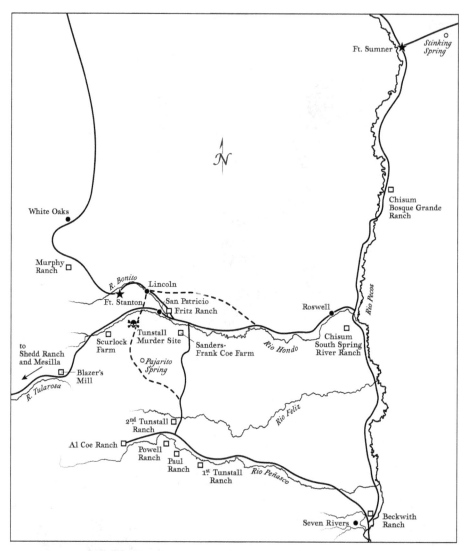

Map of portion of LIncoln County, New Mexico, showing the location of events described in the Angel Report. Among the sites marked are: Town of Lincoln, Fort Stanton, Tunstall's Murder Site, San Patricio, Blazer's Mill, Tunstall's Rio Feliz Ranch, Tunstall's Rio Penasco Ranch, Seven Rivers, Beckwith's Ranch, Chisum's South Spring River Ranch, Chisum's Bosque Grande Ranch, Stinking Springs, and Fort Sumner. The dotted lines mark trails, the solid lines mark roads. Courtesy oldwestmaps.com.

Chapter 1 | Genesis of the "Angel Report"

The event that led to the "Angel Report," was the murder of John Henry Tunstall.

Tunstall was an Englishman who arrived in Lincoln, New Mexico, on November 6, 1876, with hopes of building a profitable cattle empire. Lincoln at the time was divided into two antagonistic factions, one headed by Lawrence G. Murphy and one headed by Alexander A. McSween. Allied with Murphy were business associates Emil A. Fritz, John H. Riley, and James J. Dolan.

Murphy, who settled in Lincoln in 1866, controlled the town and county politically and economically. He owned the town's primary mercantile; but the real basis of his power was the exclusive contract he held to sell cattle and supplies to the U.S. Army based at Fort Stanton. The Army needed the cattle to fulfill the Federal Government's treaty obligation to supply food to Native Americans on the Mescalero Apache Reservation. That contract gave Murphy a stranglehold on Lincoln County. It meant that Murphy owned the only forage and livestock market in the county, and he set prices that kept the local ranchers indebted to him.[1]

Florencio Gonzales, a resident of Lincoln County since 1863, gave the following account of affairs under Murphy:

> *"Murphy's power in the County was absolute. It was almost impossible for any one who did not do his bidding and aid him in his corruption to live in said County, as he and those allied with him in business had absolute sway, and those who did not do as they bid, were kept so poor that they could not do anything, and if they undertook to oppose L. G. Murphy & Co., they were either killed or run out of the County." (Gonzales, p 81.)*

Emil Fritz's Life Insurance Policy

McSween came to Lincoln in 1875 as a young lawyer. Initially, he was a Murphy ally. That changed when Murphy's partner Emil Fritz died unexpectedly on a visit to his family home in Germany. McSween was hired to collect Fritz's $10,000 life insurance policy benefit from the Merchants Life Assurance Company, which was bankrupt and in receivership. McSween's efforts to obtain the money from a firm in Santa Fe failed, necessitating a trip to New York, where the company had its office. Here is his account of the difficulties he encountered:

> *"I went to New York to ascertain the real condition of the policy on Col. Fritz's life. Whilst there... efforts were made by certain parties to compel me to accept fifty cents on the dollar in full for the policy. When it was found I would not compromise, it was said that the whole claim was lost through my obstinacy. In order to get the policy out of the hands of the party having it, seven to eight hundred dollars had to be paid. Upon payment of this sum the policy was reluctantly surrendered.... I was absent on this business trip two months. I paid all the expenses of the trip out of my own pocket."[2]*

John Henry Tunstall. Undated photo. Courtesy Palace of the Governors Photo
Archives (NMHM/DCA), 066009.

Lawrence Gustave Murphy. Undated photo. Courtesy Center for Southwest Research and Special Collections, UNM.

Emil Adolf Fritz. Undated photo. Courtesy Center for Southwest Research and Special Collections, UNM.

James Joseph Dolan. Undated photo. Courtesy Center for Southwest Research and Special Collections, UNM.

John Henry Riley. Undated photo. Courtesy Center for Southwest Research and Special Collections, UNM.

Alexander Anderson McSween, undated photo. Courtesy Maurice G. Fulton Papers, Special Collections, UA.

McSween succeeded in collecting $7,148.49 of the $10,000 death value of the policy. (McSween, Ex. 7, p 123.) On his return to Lincoln, McSween submitted to the Probate Court a detailed claim of expenses and commissions against the insurance proceeds totaling $3,815.50. (McSween, Ex. 3, p 119.) The Probate Court approved the claim, meaning that the amount left for the estate was only $3332.99, one third of the value of the policy.

Naturally, this reduced sum did not sit well with the heirs of the estate, Emil's brother Carl Phillip Friedrich Fritz, known in Lincoln as "Charles" Fritz, and Emilie Scholand, Emil's sister. However, it was Murphy partner John H. Riley who was most vociferously upset at this amount. McSween noted:

"On my return to Lincoln, I found J. H. Riley was exceedingly angry and was trying to cause trouble. During my absence he had broken into my office and destroyed some of my furniture grossly insulted my wife and vowed that he would run me out of the County." (McSween, p 101.)

Riley, Dolan, and Murphy hoped to get some of the insurance funds by claiming that Emil owed them money from when he was their partner, and therefore they were entitled to a share of his insurance proceeds. Dolan in his statement to Angel explained:

"[My] interest in said money arose out of the fact that L. G. Murphy & Co. had a claim against the estate." (Dolan, p 75.)

After the ruling of the Probate Court, McSween said he was ready to pay the heirs their portion, but he was unwilling to pay it all to Charles Fritz, as Fritz was demanding. McSween insisted that Emilie Scholand, who lived in Las Cruces, come to Lincoln to receive her share, or designate a legal representative to do so.

"That deponent [McSween] informed said Fritz then and there that as soon as he or any other person was authorized by said Emilie Scholand to receive and receipt deponent for the money, the money would be paid." (McSween, p 102.)

Dolan's reaction was:

"I & others informed him [McSween] that the parties were very much troubled about the situation & wanted the money and requested him in order to quiet every one to deposit the money with the court subject to the order of the court. This he refused to do." (Dolan, p 74.)

While waiting for Emilie to act, McSween was hired by John S. Chisum to accompany him to St. Louis, Missouri, as his legal representative.

"I left Lincoln on the 18th of Dec. 1877 in company with my wife and John S. Chisum my client and on whose business I was then going to St. Louis to attend to." (McSween, p 103.)

Following the Probate Court ruling, about two weeks before McSween left for St. Louis, Dolan traveled to Las Cruces to meet with Emilie Scholand, with the intention of manipulating her into supporting his claim to the some of the insurance proceeds. While there, he learned that McSween had left for St. Louis. That played into his hands beautifully. He persuaded Emilie that McSween had left Lincoln for good, intending to keep all the insurance money for himself. (Dolan, p 75.)

Territory of New Mexico Third Judicial District Judge Warren Henry Bristol.

Based on Dolan's lies, Emilie cheerfully signed an affidavit claiming McSween was stealing the insurance money. Dolan took the affidavit to District Attorney William L. Rynerson, a stanch ally of Dolan, who issued arrest warrants for McSween and Chisum. McSween was charged with embezzling. Chisum, who had no connection to the inheritance conflict, was charged with *"fleeing the jurisdiction,"* a ruse. The details of the warrants were telegraphed to Las Vegas, where McSween and Chisum were arrested and jailed (the three had only got that far on their trip). (McSween, p 103.)

After 48 hours in jail, the physical warrants had not arrived, so the two men were released, as required by law. They hired an ambulance to continue their trip (an ambulance was a wagon with leather rather than steel shocks, providing an easier ride). They were only a half mile out of town when they were violently arrested by a posse of over thirty men led by the county sheriff.

"Chisum was jerked out [of the ambulance] head foremost & fell upon his face on the hard road and [was] seized by the throat.... McSween also was jerked out of the ambulanch [sic] and drug off by a lot of the gang & Mrs. McSween was left sitting all alone crying.... Chisum and McSween were then marched to the Court house and [locked up]" [3]

McSween was refused bail and ordered transported to Mesilla to appear before the District Judge, Judge Warren Henry Bristol. Chisum chose to stay in the Las Vegas jail, not trusting the courts in Lincoln. Deputies Adolph P. Barrier and Antonio Campos were ordered to take McSween to Mesilla, by way of Lincoln, a distance of about 350 miles. (Barrier, p 65.)

Adolph P. Barrier. 1901 Photo. Courtesy
NARA.

At Lincoln, McSween and Barrier were joined by Tunstall, John B. Wilson, and David P. Shield. Wilson was the Lincoln Justice of the Peace. Shield was McSween's law partner and brother in law. (Deputy Campos returned to Las Vegas.) (Barrier, p 65.)

McSween was extremely lucky that Barrier was in charge of transporting him to Mesilla, as Barrier, who was a remarkably fair and honorable man, undoubtedly saved McSween's life several times. (Barrier, p 66; McSween, p 109-110.)

At Mesilla, Judge Bristol was sick, so the hearing on the embezzlement charge was held in his home, not in the court-house.

The hearing was irregular and shame-lessly biased. No witnesses were sworn, no legal record taken, and Judge Bristol's courtroom statements showed he wholeheartedly supported the prosecution. He ruled that the case should go to the grand jury for indict-ment and McSween needed to post a bond of $8,000 if he wanted to be released on bail. (McSween, p 104.)

The *Cimarron News and Press*, commenting on Judge Bristol, wrote that he made:

"...one of the most partisan charges we ever heard from the bench and which sounds much more like the argument of an attorney seeking to convict McSween of a crime than an address of a judge before whom the facts are likely to come for trial, and who from his high office, is presumed to be impartial and disinterested." [4]

Barrier reported:

"I was present during the entire examination and had McSween in my charge. The examination commenced on the 2nd day of Feb. and closed on the 4th. William L. Rynerson, the District Attorney, while said examination was in progress, frequently used insulting language towards said McSween, while he was a prisoner which I regarded as unbecoming in an officer."

"After the examination was continued & the amount of bail fixed, the Judge delivered a lecture to McSween, which was very unbecoming and showed himself to be a bitter partisan. He ordered that the bond should be approved by W. L. Rynerson Dist Atty." (Barrier, p 65-66.)

McSween, escorted by Barrier, left Mesilla with Tunstall, Wilson, and Shield to return to Lincoln to raise the $8,000 bail. The first night out of Mesilla, they camped at Shedd's Ranch on the east side of the Organ Mountains. There they were violently confronted by Dolan, Frank Baker, Jessie Evans, and Jack Long. (McSween, p 104; Barrier, p 66. See Dolan, p 73, for Dolan's version.)

Tunstall Entangled in Fritz Insurance Conflict

The day McSween's party left Mesilla, Judge Bristol issued a writ of attachment against McSween's property, ordering that the writ encompassed Tunstall's property also. The basis for including Tunstall's property was the assertion that the two were partners, an assertion that both men had strenuously denied during the Mesilla hearing. (McSween, p 108; Shield, p 155.) The writ gave the sheriff of Lincoln the authority to:

> "...attach all the right title and interest of Alex A. McSween in and to the goods, chattels, effects and provisions pertinent to the store of Tunstall & Co. in the town of Lincoln, Territory of New Mexico." [5]

Judge Bristol gave the writ to McSween's worst enemy, Dolan, who sped it to Lincoln.

> "I brought the attachment papers against McSween's property at the suit of Charles Fritz & Emile [Emilie] Scholand from Mesilla & delivered it to Sheriff Brady." (Dolan, p 73.)

McSween noted:

> "[The Writ was] sent a distance of about 154 miles in an almost unprecedented short time for this Territory. That [it] not only attached my personal property but also my real, together with the property of J. H. Tunstall and others, even pictures of the family of the latter as also a notarial seal belonging to D. P. Shield." (McSween, p 106.)

When McSween and Tunstall arrived in Lincoln, they found Lincoln County Sheriff William Brady in possession of Tunstall's store, based on Judge Bristol's writ. (McSween, pp 106, 234; Longwell, pp 90-91; Mathews, p 95; Widenmann, p 162.)

Tunstall was a close friend and ally of McSween, and was his business manager, but the two were not legal partners.

> "At this time I [McSween] was not Mr. Tunstall's partner though I would become such by articles of agreement in May 1878. I was his attorney and took an active part in the management of his business. For this I was to have one half the profits of the business up to May 1878 after the deduction of 8 per cent on the capital invested."

> "In May 1878 articles of co-ownership were to be signed by us by which Mr. Tunstall was to furnish the capital, I to pay 8 per cent interest per annum for my share. At the time (February 1878) Mr. Tunstall owed me over $4000 as appears by the copy of account hereto attached marked [Exhibit] 11, being a true and full account of all money transactions had by and between us from the time indicated until his death other than that stated. I had no other financial interest in Mr. Tunstall's business. (McSween, p 106.)

Given the detailed proof that they were not partners provided in McSween's statement, it is not believable that he and Tunstall would have testified before Judge Bristol that they were partners. The only plausible interpretation of Bristol's decision to

William Brady. Undated photo.
Courtesy Maurice G. Fulton Papers,
Special Collections, UA.

Jacob Basil Mathews. Undated photo.
Courtesy Maurice G. Fulton Papers,
Special Collections, UA.

Robert Adolph Widenmann. Undated
photo. Courtesy Maurice G. Fulton
Papers, Special Collections, UA.

William Logan Rynerson. Undated
photo. Courtesy Archives and Special
Collections, NMSU.

add Tunstall as a co-party on McSween's writ of attachment was a willful and malicious desire to harm Tunstall.

In naming McSween's bail amount, Judge Bristol specified that it had to be approved by District Attorney Rynerson, not the Lincoln Probate Court, as would have been usual. Rynerson was an extreme partisan of the Murphy-Dolan side of the conflict in Lincoln, although publicly he pretended otherwise. His secret views were accidentally revealed when a letter from him to *"Friends Riley and Dolan"* was inadvertently left in McSween's house by John Riley. (McSween, p 113; McSween, Ex. 19, p 134.) (More on this letter later in this chapter.)

When McSween reached Lincoln, he quickly found bondsmen willing to guarantee his $8,000 bail requirement. Tunstall, James West, John N. Copeland, Isaac Ellis, Francisco Romero y Valencia, and Jose Montaño pledged between them $34,500, more than four times the required amount. (McSween, Ex. 15, p 129-131.)

McSween sent Rynerson at Las Cruces a registered letter listing the bond sureties and the amount they had pledged, amounts sworn to under oath that were *"over and above [each person's] just debts and liabilities and property exempt by law from execution and forced sale."* (McSween, Ex. 15, p 130.)

Rynerson responded to McSween's letter by refusing to approve the bond:

> *"The within Bond is not approved for reasons as follows. Before approving the within Bond the sureties must justify before the undersigned as I have reason to doubt that the sureties for the most part are worth the amount set opposite their names. One of the parties had informed me that he is not worth more than one dollar and I think that some of the others on examination and upon fully understanding the justification may find they are mistaken." (McSween, Ex. 15, p 131.)*

This is an absurd ruling. The pledged amount was many times the bail; even if one bondsman was worth only one dollar, the bond guarantees well exceeded the $8,000. And note that Rynerson does not name who he claimed was worth only one dollar (it was a lie). Moreover, Rynerson had not left Mesilla, so how could he have talked with one of the bondsmen?

Before Rynerson had replied to McSween's letter on the bond, Rynerson's proxy, Sheriff Brady, doing Rynerson's muscle work, visited Montaño and potential bondsman Dr. Joseph Hoy Blazer and ordered them not to make bond guarantees. Montaño was told he would be ruined if he did. Blazer was told that he if he did, Rynerson would prosecute him for cutting lumber on public lands. (McSween, p 109; Montaño, p 138.)

Events Leading to Tunstall's Murder

Judge Bristol's writ of attachment, which was issued after McSween and his party had left Mesilla (so he would not know about it), arrived in Lincoln on February 8th. The next morning, as reported by Robert Widenmann:

> *"...Sheriff Brady entered the business house of J. H. Tunstall of which I was there in charge and read to me a writ of attachment attaching the property of A. A. McSween.... I told him that the property belonged to J. H. Tunstall,*

Gottfried Gauss. Undated photograph. Courtesy Courtesy Archives and Special
Collections, NMSU.

that I protested against any attachment & would hold him and his bonds men responsible for any loss or damages."

"Sheriff Brady said that he knew better, that the property belonged to A. A. McSween [and] he would attach it as such. He proceeded to take an inventory, without placing a value on any article or thing attached. He demanded the keys of different doors, leading from the store and upon my refusal to deliver the same had me arrested and searched without warrant or legal process and forcibly took the keys from me. He was at the time accompanied by G. W. Peppin, Jack Long, James Longwill [Longwell], and F. G. Christie." (Widenmann, p 162.)

By not recording a value for anything, Brady was able to justify attaching everything. McSween estimated the value of the seized property at $40,000. (McSween, p 106.)

Two days later, McSween and Tunstall arrived from Mesilla. Tunstall immediately confronted the men who were occupying his store, which was also his home. He had with him William Henry Antrim (Billy the Kid), Frederick Waite, and Robert Widenmann.

Here is Deputy James J. Longwell's account of the resulting, nearly-violent face-off:

"[Tunstall] came into the store while we were making the inventory with a man named Widderman [Widenmann] and made threats against the sheriff [Brady] telling the sheriff that he was taking his Tunstall's property for McSween's debts. That he would make all of the party suffer for it hereafter and that they had better look out. Both Tunstall and Widdermann were armed with revolvers, and two of Tunstall's party called 'Kid' & 'Waite' came up to the door with them and stood there with Winchester rifles and pistols and acted in a threatening manner." (Longwell, p 94.)

Tunstall had two mules and six horses at his store. Sheriff Brady told Tunstall they were impounded also. After some argument, Brady accepted that they belonged solely to Tunstall and agreed to release them. Tunstall immediately sent three of the horses to his ranch with Godfrey Gauss. A bit later, he sent two more to the ranch with William McCloskey, John Middleton, Fred Waite, Widenmann, and Billy. All of these men were Tunstall employees. (Widenmann, p 162.)

Tunstall's ranch, which he had homesteaded under the provisions of the U.S. Desert Land Act, was located on the Rio Feliz and consisted of approximately 2,400 acres.[6] The ranch was located about 80 miles southeast of Lincoln.

The next day, February 12, Sheriff Brady dispatched Jacob B. Mathews, who he had just sworn as a deputy, to Tunstall's ranch with a posse of between 4 and 18 men, depending on whose account you credit. (Bonney, p 68; Hurley, p 87; Mathews, p 95; Middleton, p 136; Widenmann, p 163) The posse arrived at the ranch the next morning.

"On the morning of the 13th of February, J. B. Mathews (claiming to be Deputy Sheriff) rode up to the ranch of Tunstall's on the Rio Feliz in company with George Hindman, John Hurley, and Indian, Roberts, Evans, Baker and Hill. ...I stepped out and asked the party to stop where they were (which was about 50 yards from the house) and asked Mathews to come forward and state his business. Mathews said he was Deputy Sheriff and had come to attach the

Richard M. Brewer. Undated photo. Courtesy Palace of the Governors Photo Archives (NMHM/DCA), 105400.

cattle of A. A. McSween, to which I answered that McSween had no cattle there but if there were any he might take them. I offered no resistance nor did the people with me. Nor did we make any threats." (Widenmann, p 163.)

Billy in his account states:

"Before the arrival of said J. B. Mathews, Deputy Sheriff, and his posse, having been informed that said Deputy Sheriff and posse were going to round up all the cattle and drive them off and kill the persons at the ranch, the persons at the ranch cut portholes into the walls of the house and filled sacks with earth, so that they, the persons at the ranch, should they be attacked or their murder attempted, could defend themselves. This course being thought necessary as the sheriff's posse was composed of thieves and murderers, outlaws and desperate characters, none of whom had any interest at stake in the County nor being residents of said County." (Bonney, p 68.)

Both Widenmann and Billy state that Mathews was told no cattle of McSween's were there, but if there were, Mathews could round them up and leave a man to guard them. Mathews denied he was told that:

"Widenmann positively refused to allow me to attach the cattle. I told Brewer privately that if he would allow me to attach the cattle I would come to the ranch with only one man. I never told this to Widenmann and after Widenmann's refusal to allow me to attach we left for Lincoln to obtain instructions." (Mathews, p 96.)

While Mathews and his posse were at the ranch, Widenmann, a deputy U.S. Marshal, seeing Frank Baker, Jesse Evans, and Tom Hill in the posse, told his companions he intended to arrest the three men for livestock stealing and breaking jail. Given the danger of the situation, and the violent reputation of the three men, he was talked out of that action by Billy and others. (Bonney, pp 68-69; Widenman, p 163; for details of their jail break, see McSween, p 100.)

Foiled in his efforts to attach the cattle, Mathews left for Lincoln to get further instructions from Sheriff Brady. Widenman, Billy and Waite also left for Lincoln, to tell Tunstall what was happening. (Bonney, p 69; Matthews, p 96; Middleton, p 136; Widenmann, p 163.)

After informing Tunstall of Mathews' failed attempt to impound the cattle, Widenmann, Billy, and Waite returned to the ranch, reaching there on the evening of February 14. (Bonney p 69; Widenmann, p 164.) Tunstall arrived three days later:

> "... on the night of the 17th of February... Tunstall arrived at the ranch and informed all the persons there, that reliable information had reached him that J. B. Mathews was gathering a large party of outlaws and desperadoes as a posse and that said posse was coming to the ranch, the Mexicans in the party to gather up the cattle and the balance of the posse to kill the persons at the ranch."

> "It was therefore decided that all persons at the ranch, excepting G. Gauss, were to leave and Wm. McCloskey was that night sent to the Rio Penasco to inform the posse, who were camped there that they could come over and round up the cattle, count them and leave a man there to take care of them, and that Mr. Tunstall would also leave a man there to help round up and count the cattle and help to take care of them...." (Bonney, p 69.)

The next morning, February 18, after only a few hours of sleep, Tunstall left the ranch with Billy, Widenmann, Brewer, Waite, and John Middleton. Waite was driving a supply wagon and the others were on horseback. The plan was to go to Lincoln, where Tunstall felt he would be safe. (Bonney, pp 69-70; Gauss, p 79; Middleton, pp 136-137; Widenmann, p 164.)

> "[The five men] started for the plaza about 8 o'clock.... Waite driving the waggon [British spelling], the rest of us driving about eight horses besides those we were riding. The horses were the property of J. H. Tunstall, R. M. Brewer and myself. None of the horses then or ever belonged to A. A. McSween and all but three had been released by the sheriff and of those three horses one belonged to Brewer, one to Bonney and the third was traded by Brewer to Tunstall for one of the horses which the sheriff had not attached here." (Widenmann, p 164.)

Tunstall Killed

Several hours after Tunstall left, Mathews arrived at the ranch with a posse of over 30 men. Brady (who was not present) later testified under oath that it included only John Hurley, Manuel Segovia, George Hindman, Pantaleón Gallegos, John W. Olinger, Robert W. Beckwith, Ramon Montoya, Thomas Green, Thomas Cochrane, Charles Kruling, George Kitt, Charles Marshall, Sam Perry, and William "Buck" Morton. He did not list posse leader Mathews, nor did he list known members Andrew "Buckshot" Roberts, Ham Mills, Tom Moore, Juan Silva, Felipe Mes, E. H. Wakefield, Pablo Pino [Y Pino], Charles Woltz, Albert Howe, and Ponciacho. Most significantly, he did not list the jail escapees Jessie Evans, Frank Baker, Tom Hill, and George Davis. (Brown, p 71; Gallegos, p 76; Gauss, p 78; Kruling, p 89; Mathews, p 97; Perry, p 144.)

When Mathews found only Gauss at the ranch, he was furious. Mathews demanded, "Why did not someone remain to turn over the property?" Gauss said he was there to do just that. Then, according to Gauss:

> "[Dolan] came about this time, and he picked out the men to follow after Tunstall's party to bring them back if they caught them before they reached the [Lincoln] Plaza. From their actions I thought that some of the party of Tunstall's

John Hurley. Undated photo. Courtesy Center for Southwest Research and Special Collections, UNM.

would be killed. I heard, I think it was Morton, cry out, 'Hurry up, boys, my knife is sharp and I feel like scalping some one.' They were all excited and seemed as though they were agoing to kill someone." (Gauss, p 80.)

Pantaleón Gallegos began writing down the names of the men Dolan designated for the chase posse. When Mathews noted that he was including Evans, Baker, Hill, and Davis, he told Gallegos, "Don't put those 'boys' down at all." (Gauss, p 80.)

Mathews deputized Buck Morton to lead the posse. (Mathews, p 96.)

Because Tunstall and his men were driving horses, it was a simple matter to follow their tracks. Billy recounted what happened next:

"Deponist [deponent] further says that when he and party had reached to within about 30 miles from the Rio Penasco, he and John Middleton were riding in the rear of the balance of the party and just upon reaching the brow of a hill they saw a large party of men coming towards them from the rear at full speed and that he and Middleton at once rode forward to inform the balance of the party of the fact."

"Deponist had not more than barely reached Brewer and Widenmann who were some 200 or 300 yards to the left of the trail when the attacking party cleared the brow of the hill and commenced firing at [them]. Deponist, Widenmann and Brewer rode over a hill towards another which was covered with large rocks and trees in order to defend themselves and make a stand. But the attacking party, undoubtedly seeing Tunstall, left off pursuing deponist and the two with him and turned back to the canyon in which the trail was."

"Shortly afterwards we heard two or three separate and distinct shots and the remark then made by Middleton that they the attacking party must have killed Tunstall. Middleton had in the meantime joined deponist, Widenmann and Brewer. Deponist then made the rest of his way to Lincoln in company with Widenmann, Brewer, Waite and Middleton, stopping on the Rio Penasco in order to get men to look for the body of J. H. Tunstall." (Bonney, p 70.)

Nobody saw the close-up details of the killing of Tunstall except the men who did it, Buck Morton and Tom Hill. Albert Howe, who was in the chase posse, gave the following account under oath, based on what he learned from posse members:

Tunstall's 4-room, adobe ranch house today. When Tunstall owned the house, it had a flat roof. Undated photo. Courtesy Billy Roberts.

"Tunstall was some distance off from the road, and when he found he had been deserted by his party, he turned and rode toward Hill and Morton; that when he came in sight of them he seemed very much surprised and hesitated; that Hill called to him to come up and said that he would not be hurt; at the same time both Hill and Morton threw up their guns, resting their stocks on their knees; that after Tunstall came nearer, Morton fired and shot Tunstall through the breast, and then Hill fired and shot Tunstall through the head; someone else fired and wounded or killed Tunstall's horse at the time Tunstall was shot through the head by Hill; that two barrels of Tunstall's revolver were emptied after he was killed; that Tunstall fired no shots, and that Tunstall was killed in cold blood." (Howe, p 87.)

The other posse members who gave accounts, all claimed that Tunstall had fired first:

"Morton told me that Tunstall had fired two shots at him & that he, Hill & Evans, fired back & killed him and his horse. (Cochrane, p 71.)"

"When we got up to our party, Billy Morton told us that Tunstall was killed. He said he rode up to Tunstall and called on him to surrender holding the papers in his left hand, and that Tunstall pulled his pistol out and fired twice at him, one shot going over his mare's neck, and that he Morton then fired & shot Tunstall." (Kruling, p 90.)

George Coe standing next to the marker erected by the U.S. Forest Service in December, 1929, to mark the location of Tunstall's murder. For details see *"The Trial of Billy the Kid"* by the author. Courtesy Maurice G. Fulton Papers, Special Collections, UA.

"I was informed by George Hindman, who was with the Deputy Sheriff's posse, that Morton who was at that time in command of the posse came up to Tunstall, who was driving the horses, and waived the attachment and called upon him to halt & Tunstall & his men ran & scattered & then Tunstall turned back & fired." (Longwell, p 92)

"[Morton] said that he had followed after Tunstall whereupon Tunstall turned & came riding up to him. He (Morton) commenced to read the warrant, whereupon Tunstall drew his pistol and fired two shots at him. Before Tunstall had fired, Jesse Evans called to him to throw up his hands & he would not be hurt. Tunstall disregarded this and fired as above set forth whereupon he (Morton), Jesse Evans, & Hill fired at him and the result of the firing was that Tunstall and his horse were killed...."

"When we reached the top of the hill, we saw the horses rounded up & some of our party rounding up some of the horses. When we reached the horses, Morton came up and said Tunstall was killed. I said it could not be, for I did not believe that Tunstall was there. He said that he had followed after Tunstall whereupon Tunstall turned & came riding up to him. He (Morton) commenced to read the warrant, whereupon Tunstall drew his pistol and fired two shots at him. Before Tunstall had fired, Jesse Evans called to him to throw up his hands & he would not be hurt. Tunstall disregarded this and fired as above set forth whereupon he (Morton), Jesse Evans, & Hill fired at him and the result of the firing was that Tunstall and his horse were killed." (Perry, pp 144-145.)

That Tunstall fired first was the party line, and everyone but Howe duly repeated it.

The only account the killers ever gave was given by Morton in a letter written and mailed to a friend just before he was killed:

"The 6th of March I was arrested by a constables posse accused of the murder of Tunstall. Nearly all the Sheriff's posse fired at him [Tunstall] and it is impossible for any one to say who killed him." (Morton letter, pp 175-176.)
(See page 32 for more details on this letter.)

For the only account given by Evans, see page 158.

On their flight to Lincoln, following Tunstall's killing, Billy and the others stopped at John Newcomb's place and asked him to recover Tunstall's body. The next morning Newcomb and four others found the body:

"The corpse had evidently been carried by some persons and laid in the position in which we found it; a blanket was found under the corpse and one over it. Tunstall's overcoat was placed under his head, and his hat placed under the head of his dead horse. By the apparent naturalness of the scene we were forced to conclude that the murderers of Mr. Tunstall placed his dead horse in the position indicated, considering the whole affair a burlesque...."

"We found his revolver quite close to the scabbard on the corpse.... We found two chambers empty, but there were no hulls or cartridge shells in the empty chambers; the other four chambers had cartridges in them...."

Taylor F. Ealy, undated photo. Courtesy Center for Southwest Research and Special Collections, UNM.

"The corpse of Mr. Tunstall was found over 100 yards off the trail on which the horses travelled, in advance of those said to have been driven by Mr. Tunstall, showing clearly, by fresh horse tracks which were seen by us distinctly and plainly, that the horses the posse claimed to have been trying to recover from Mr. Tunstall must have been quite a distance behind Mr. Tunstall, and must have been passed by the posse before they could get Mr. Tunstall." (Gonzales, p 83.)

A number of writers have wondered why Tunstall's horse was shot and posed as it was. The answer is, the murderers knew about Tunstall's deep love of horses, and especially of one horse named "Colonel." The gruesome death-scene posing was a final, depraved act of mockery and contempt.

Tunstall first saw Colonel in a butcher pen at Fort Stanton among cattle that were there to be slaughtered. Appalled, Tunstall asked why the horse was to be killed. He was told the horse was an army cavalry horse that was "condemned" because it had gone blind.

Tunstall wrote about Colonel to his parents:

"I gave 27 1/2 dollars for him, & I think I never saw a prettier horse, & I never threw my leg over a finer saddle horse, he walks fast enough to keep my Long Tom horse in a slow job trot, he paces, trots, & goes a single foot gait, that I never saw in England, he can canter on a cabbage leaf & gallop very finely, he is coal black, his mane & tail are as fine as I ever saw, I should think he is nearly thoroughbred, he is not over 7 years old."

"He has never had his eyes doctored, & I think I may cure him, if I could do that, he could not be bought." [7]

"I have taught him to pick up his feet when I tell him we are coming to a bad place in the road, so that he does not strike it, & I can make him understand whether it is an up or down grade we are coming to; he can walk 25 miles in five hours & a half, without any urging, which is all that can be desired of a road horse. He will come when I call, & follow me around just as if he could see." [8]

Although he was not, Tunstall could easily have been riding Colonel when he was killed; Colonel was among the horses he was herding.

Tunstall's body was brought to McSween's house *"strapped to a burro,"* [9] according to Mrs. McSween's account. Other sources say it was transferred to a wagon before it was delivered. The next day, the coroner's jury met over Tunstall's body and concluded:

> *"... the deceased came to his death on the 18th day of February, 1878 by means of divers bullets shot and sent forth out of and from deadly weapons, and upon the head and body of the said John H. Tunstall, which said weapons were held by one or more of the men whose names are herewith written: Jessie Evans, Frank Baker, Thomas Hill, George Hindman, J. J. Dolan, William Morton and others not identified by witnesses that testified before the coroner's jury."* (McSween, Ex. 12, p 126.)

U.S. Army Assistant Surgeon Daniel Appel in his autopsy report stated that Tunstall was shot in the shoulder and the back of the head. He found no powder burns, indicating Tunstall was shot from at least six feet away. (Appel, pp 64-65.)

Gonzales in his statement reported:

> *"...we found the skull broken; we found that a rifle or carbine bullet had entered his breast, and a pistol bullet entered the back of his head, coming out in the forehead."* (Gonzales, p 83.)

(For a description of Tunstall's murder site and details on how it was relocated and marked 49 years later, see *"The Trial of Billy the Kid"* by the author.)

Sheriff Brady responded to the news of Tunstall's death at the hands of his posse by sending Rynerson an official report to which he attached a statement by Mathews which claimed:

> *"...while a portion of the posse were in pursuit of the party, J. H. Tunstall fired on the posse and in the return fire he was shot and killed. It has been falsely aversed (sic) that attached to my Deputy's posse were men against whom U.S. warrants has (sic) been issued."* [10]

The day Tunstall was killed, Dr. Taylor F. Ealy, wife Mary, and their two infant children arrived in Lincoln. Their presence in Lincoln was requested by McSween, who was seeking a minister and teacher for Lincoln. They were lodged in McSween's home.[11]

Mary Ealy gave the following account of what she witnessed after her arrival:

> *"The following night Tunstall's body was brought to the house of McSween.... Among those who attended the body was Billy the Kid, Dick Brewer, and Fred Waite, men who herded the cattle of Tunstall. They were all good friends of Tunstall and were ready to take the execution of vengeance into their own hands...."*

> *"Tunstall's body was in bad shape, as he had been shot and then beaten until his forehead was battered very badly. Dr. Ealy embalmed the body, which was put in a metal coffin. As Tunstall was an Englishman, it was thought that his friends in England might wish the body sent there. Until such a time the body was to be buried at the east side of what was intended in time to be Tunstall's home."*

Susan Ellen McSween. Undated photo. Courtesy Center for Southwest Research and Special Collections, UNM.

"The funeral of Mr. Tunstall was held the next morning. As Mrs. McSween was away from home, I was asked to play two or three hymns. Beside the organ on which I played stood Billy the Kid and his cowboy friends, armed to the teeth. Billy's voice was a sweet tenor, and he sang with all his might. The service though was a fearful one, for no one knew when hostilities between the two factions would be resumed, as almost every one connected with the feud was ready to use his gun at a moment's warning." [12]

McSween wrote the following about the funeral to Tunstall's father in England:

"With my own hands I dressed his corpse and put it in the coffin. The coffin was then carried to our best room. The Rev. Mr. Ealy performed the funeral services before a large and respectable concourse of people. The organ pealed forth its sad notes; the coffin was closed and carried out by John Newcomb, R. M. Brewer, Frank & Geo. Coe and lowered into a grave in my private grave-yard, the clods of the valley rattled upon his coffin and he was covered from our sight – Not a dry eye was in the audience." [13]

McSween added in the same letter:

"Thirty of the best men in this County gathered at our house the night his corpse was brought in and remained here until last evening in the hope that parties connected with that murder could be found. They have now dispersed, but have organized themselves into bands and taken to the mountains to hunt the murders...."

"J. J. Dolan & Co. entertained fearful malice toward him and me on account of business. They could not stand to see competition. Without a doubt they planned and executed his death, and it's equally certain that business jealousy was the cause of it." [14]

Tunstall's body was never returned to England. The exact location of his grave is not known, although it is believed to be approximately where it is currently commemorated in Lincoln by a marker, at what would in 1878 have been just outside of and behind Tunstall's horse corral.

The evening Tunstall's funeral was held, an enraged crowd of 30 or more men gathered at McSween's house. They were the residents of Lincoln who were not allied with the Murphy-Dolan party. Many in the crowd wanted to take immediate revenge on the opposing party, who were holed up across the street in the Murphy-Dolan house (those sheltering in the house included Murphy, Riley, Brady, and many of the men who were in the posse that murdered Tunstall.) (Gonzales, p 83; McSween, pp 107-108.)

One action the men agreed upon was a petition asking Murphy, Dolan, and Riley to get (the hell) out of the county. Eventually the petition gathered 300 signatures:

"Gentlemen, we the undersigned residents of Lincoln County New Mexico... desire you to remove to some other County or state in order that permanent peace may be restored. On conveying you this information we merely give expression to the earnest wish of all your neighbors and fellow citizens."

Frederick Tecumseh Waite. Undated photo. Courtesy Maurice G. Fulton Papers, Special Collections, UA.

"Your reputed business connections with murderers, outlaws and cattle and horse thieves has destroyed your business connections and endangered your personal safety and makes it our imperative duty in the interest of the peace and order to ask you to leave Lincoln County." (McSween, Ex. 21, p 135-136.)

In the middle of the meeting, Riley suddenly entered McSween's house *"in a drunken condition"* and *"bareheaded and without a shirt."* [15] His motivation, to the extent it can be deduced, was apparently to mitigate some of the enmity against him.

Confronted by the angry crowd, Riley:

"...was anxious to show that he had no weapons about his person and to convince persons in the room of this fact [he] turned out his pockets. That in doing so he threw out a memorandum book and after asking the men in the house, one by one, if they wanted to kill him and receiving a reply in the negative, took his departure leaving said memorandum book on the table at the residence of deponent."

"Deponent says that he examined said book with great care. That he found a letter in it in the handwriting of said W. L. Rynerson addressed to Dolan & Riley.... That said book showed the amount of sugar [and] coffee hauled by one Stephen Stanley from the Indian Agency in said County on a particular date...."

"There was also a memorandum of cattle received by said Dolan & Riley from the notorious cattle thieves who names were given. That it also contained a list of names of persons well known in this county for their friendship for or in opposition to said Dolan & Riley. Opposite each name was a nom de plume, Catron being 'Grapes,' Godfroy 'Hampton,' Bernstein (Indian Agent clerk) 'Soapweed,' Indians 'Trees, DeLaney (A.A.Q.M. at Fort Stanton) 'Warwick,' Murphy aforesaid 'Box,' Rynerson (Dist Atty aforesaid) 'Oyster, Dowling [Dowlin] (Post Trader Fort Stanton) 'Pimp,' and McSween (this deponent) 'Diablo'– Devil &c &c." (McSween, p 113-114.)

The letter in the memorandum book was from Rynerson and addressed to *"Friends Riley and Dolan."* The letter advocated physical violence against McSween and Tunstall. It included the bizarre line:

"It must be made hot for them all the hotter the better, especially is this necessary now that it has been discovered that there is no hell." (McSween, Ex. 19, p 134.)

The reference to there being *"no hell"* was a message to Riley that his actions would not result in any Divine punishment, as there was no such thing, so he should not be constrained by that fear. Rynerson later in the letter tells Riley, *"be assured I shall help you all I can."* In other words, Rynerson, as the chief legal officer of the district, would ensure that there was no earthly punishment for any of Riley's actions. (McSween, Ex. 19, p 134.)

Fort Stanton. 1898 photo. Courtesy Archives and Special Collections, NMSU.

Justice Foiled

Knowing that Sheriff Brady would do nothing to investigate Tunstall's murder, or make arrests, Billy and Brewer went to Justice of the Peace John B. Wilson. Wilson issued the following warrants:

> *"I, John B. Wilson, Justice of the Peace in and for Precinct No. 1, Lincoln County, New Mexico, do hereby certify that on or about the 19th day of February 1878, W. Boney [Bonney] and R. M. Brewer filed in my office affidavits charging John [James] J. Dolan, J. Conovaur [Cochrane], Frank Baker, Jessie Evans, Tom Hill, George Davis, O. L. Roberts, P. Gallegos, T. Green, J. Awly [Hurley], A. H. Mills, "Dutch Charley" proper name unknown, R. W. Beckwith, William Morton, George Harman [Hindman] J. B. Mathews, and others with having murdered and killed one Jno. H. Tunstall at the said County of Lincoln, on or about the 18th day of February, 1878, that on or about the 20th day of Feby 1878, issued warrants on said affidavits for the arrest of the parties above named and directed the same to the Constable of Precinct No. One in said County to wit: Atanacio Martinez." (McSween, Ex. 13, p 127.)*

The next day, February 20, Constable Martinez deputized Billy and Waite to help him serve the warrants. The three men went to the Murphy-Dolan store, where at least 10 of the named men were. At *"the door of the said house,"* they were met by Sheriff Brady who flatly refused to honor Martinez's warrants:

"[Brady] at once covered deponent [Martinez] and Wm. Bonney and F. T. Waite with their rifles, forcibly disarmed and took prisoners this deponent and said Bonney and Waite and then demanded of them their business...."

"Deponent further says, that said William Brady and the persons with him abused deponent and cursed him, that he was held prisoner by said Brady for several hours without warrant or legal process, that subsequently he was released and allowed to return to his home, but that his arms were not returned to him. That said Wm. Bonney and F. T. Waite were held prisoners by said Wm. Brady about 30 hours and then released." (Martinez, p 93.)

What Martinez fails to mention is that Brady was backed up by a detachment of cavalry from Fort Stanton commanded by 2nd. Lt. Goodwin. On the day that Tunstall was killed, Brady sent a note to Colonel Purington, the commander of the Fort, asking for:

"... an officer and fifteen mounted men be immediately detached me to come to Lincoln – only for the preservation of the peace." (Purington, unnumbered exhibit, p 147.)

Making this request on the 18th is exceedingly suspicious. According to Widenmann, Tunstall was killed at about 5:30 p.m. Widenmann, Billy, and the others with Tunstall arrived in Lincoln at about 10 p.m.[16] Given these times, Brady must have written his note to Purington during the day, long before he learned that Tunstall had been killed (if he even did learn it that night).

After Mathew's first visit to Tunstall's ranch, he returned to Lincoln to *"obtain instructions"* from Brady. Brady told him *"to raise a posse & return & attach the property."* (Mathews, p 96).

Brady and Mathews knew that there were a number of Tunstall's employees at the ranch (Billy gives the number as eight). (Bonney, p 69.) Therefore Mathews, at Brady's direction, raised a large posse – at least 30 men. Both Brady and Mathews expected a fight, and probably welcomed it.

"When we were going to the said ranch, the deputy [Mathews] believed that we were going to have a fight so the posse was divided into two parties, one going to the front of the house & the other to the rear, until they heard from the deputy. I was with the rear party." (Dolan, p 72.)

Henry Brown, who met the posse on its way to the ranch, reported:

"I talked with Morton and Baker, since killed, near Black Water [Spring]. They said that they were going to kill parties at Tunstall's Ranch." (Brown, p 71.)

So Brady, certain the posse would get into a gunfight at Tunstall's ranch, wanted the extra protection of Fort Stanton's soldiers in Lincoln in case any survivors returned with revenge in mind. He expected that some of Tunstall men would be killed, and he had probably instructed Mathews to do so if he had a good opportunity. Supporting the argument that they planned to kill Tunstall men is the fact that Dolan was on the scene, the main

Samuel Beach Axtell, undated photo.
Courtesy Library of Congress.

instigator of the war against McSween and Tunstall, a man who had threatened both men numerous times. Dolan, rather than Mathews, was in charge, as he selected the men in the posse that chased after Tunstall:

"I do not know whether they sent for Dolan or whether he came of his own accord. He came about this time and he picked out the men to follow after Tunstall's party, to bring them back if they caught them before they reached the [Lincoln] Plaza. From this action, I thought that some of the party of Tunstall's would be killed." (Gauss, p 80.)

Why was Mathews trying to arrest Tunstall on the road? He knew Tunstall was going to Lincoln. He easily could have arrested him there. But in town his posse could not get away with murdering him – on the road they could.

Widenmann recognized that he could play Brady's troops' game too. On the same day that Brady relied on troops to avoid being arrested by Constable Martinez, Widenmann asked Col. Purington for his own squad of soldiers:

"Being informed by reliable and trustworthy men that they have good reasons to believe and do believe that Jessie Evans, Frank Baker, Tom Hill and Geo. Davis are at the house of J. J. Dolan & Co at Lincoln I would politely request you to furnish me sufficient men to surround and search said house and capture said men." (Purington, Ex. D, page 151.)

Widenmann drew upon his authority as Deputy U.S. Marshal to make this request.

Col. Purington responded to Widenmann's appeal by sending 30 men under the command of Lt. Humphreys and 2nd Lt. Goodwin. (Goodwin, p 84.) Supported by the soldiers, Widenmann went to the Murphy-Dolan store to arrest Brady and any posse members there. Brady refused to be arrested and claimed that no possemen were present. (Widenmann, p 162.)

Not deterred by Brady's words, Widenmann proceeded to search the store. No possemen were found (Goodwin, p 84; Martinez, p 93.). Riley later claimed that during the search, various items of personal property were stolen, an accusation that was vehemently denied by Widenmann. (Goodwin, p 85; McSween, p 168.)

Widenmann then went to Tunstall's store and arrested the men that Brady had stationed there when he attached the store. Longwell, who was in charge of the men, described the confrontation that resulted:

"...we saw a squad of soldiers in front of the house. The house was then surrounded by McSween's men & the soldiers. The soldiers were placed in

front of the door and McSween's men on each side of the door. Widderman [Widenmann] came along. I rapped on the window and asked him what was up. He said, you will find out d–d quick." (Longwell, p 92.)

Longwell and his men were arrested by Widenmann, but released by Justice of the Peace Wilson after a brief hearing. (Longwell, p 92.)

British Government Alerted to Tunstall's Killing

On February 26, Widenmann wrote to Sir Edward Thornton, the United Kingdom's Ambassador to the United States, to tell him that a British citizen had been murdered and that Dolan was one of the killers.[17] This, of course, got Thornton's attention. On March 9, Thornton wrote to William M. Evarts, the U.S. Secretary of State:

"My attention has been called to the murder of John H. Tunstall a British subject, which is stated to have taken place in the County of Lincoln, New Mexico eleven miles from the town of Lincoln, on the afternoon of the 18th ultimo, and to have been committed by one James J. Dolan, and others. It is also affirmed that an informal investigation of the circumstances which led to the murder will show a disgraceful state of affairs as regards not only the Territorial, but the United States officials." (Thornton, p 172.)

Thornton told Evarts that the town constable was given warrants to arrest the killers, but their arrests were blocked by the county sheriff. This allegation of corrupt officials stirred action in both the Federal and British governments.

Governor Axtell Issues a Proclamation

On the same day that Thornton wrote Evarts, March 9, New Mexico Governor Samuel B. Axtell arrived in Lincoln. His publicly stated purpose was to investigate affairs in Lincoln and *"to assist good citizens to uphold the laws and to keep the peace to enable all to act intelligently."* (McSween, Ex. 16, p 131.) Axtell was an unwavering supporter of the Murphy-Dolan party. In spite of his noble words, Axtell's only intention was to assist the Murphy-Dolan side.

The morning after his arrival, Governor Axtell met with Murphy:

"After hearing the Murphy story, the good governor was satisfied, and had neither time nor patience to hear the people's version of the difficulties. Messrs. Ellis, Shield and Widenmann offered to give him their versions and implored him to visit the people and learn for himself; this his Excellency indignantly refused to do." [18]

On his return to Santa Fe, Governor Axtell issued a proclamation which read in part:

"John B. Wilson's appointment by the County Commissioners as a Justice of the Peace was illegal and void, and all processes issued by him were void, and said Wilson has no authority whatever to act as Justice of the Peace...."

"The appointment of Robt. Widenmann as U.S. Marshall has been revoked...." (McSween, Ex. 16, p 131.)

Governor Axtell had no legal authority to nullify Wilson's office without cause. The justification he gave for his action was that Wilson's appointment as J.P. was illegal, be-

Sir Edward Thornton, undated photo.
Courtesy NARA.

cause he had been appointed by the county commissioners and not elected. However, that rationale was bogus. Section 40 of the Territorial Laws read:

"In the event that any vacancy exists now in any County office, or that it may hereafter occur in any County precinct or demarcation in any County by reason of death, resignation, or removal, or in any other manner, the County Commissioners of said County shall have the power to fill such vacancy by appointment until an election be held as now provided by law approved January 13, 1876." (Section 40, p 171.) (This section of the law was actually signed into effect by Governor Axtell.)

Wilson was appointed J.P. more than a year earlier, to replace James H. Farmer, who had resigned. (Wilson, p 171.)

Widenmann's dismissal as U.S. Deputy Marshal was also illegal. Governor Axtell gave no reason for Widenmann's removal from office.

With the dismissals of Wilson and Widenmann, Governor Axtell removed any and all legal authority opposing the Murphy-Dolan faction. It was a blatantly unlawful act with only one purpose – to prevent the arrest of the men responsible for Tunstall's murder, as the editor of the *Cimarron News and Press* pointed out:

"On what other hypothesis can this strange action of the Governor's be explained?" [19]

Death of Morton, Baker, and McCloskey

On March 7, a posse led by Brewer arrested Morton and Baker after a long horseback chase, near Aqua Negra (Black Water). The men known to be in the posse were McCloskey, Billy, Brown, Waite, Middleton, Josiah "Doc" Scurlock, Charlie Bowdre, Frank McNab, Samuel Smith, Jim French, and Martin Chavez. (McCloskey may have joined the posse after the capture.) Brewer was carrying arrest warrants for Morton and Baker issued by Wilson. (Leverson, p 175; McSween, p 111.)

The party spent the first night after the arrest at Chisum's South Spring Ranch near Roswell. When they left there on their way to Lincoln, they stopped in Roswell, where Morton mailed a registered letter to family friend Judge Hunter H. Marshal at Richmond, Virginia.

Morton had composed the letter while at Chisum's ranch. In the letter, he wrote:

"When the posse which came to arrest me and one man who was with me first saw us about one hundred yards distant we started in another direction,

when they (eleven in number) fired nearly one hundred shots at us. We ran about five miles when both of our horses fell and we made a stand, when they came up they told us if we gave up they would not harm us; after talking awhile we gave up our arms and were taken prisoners." (Leverson, pp 175-176.)

Morton wrote the letter because he feared for his life (as one of the cold-blooded killers of Tunstall, he had good reason to be afraid). He asked Marshal to investigate his death if he did not get to Lincoln safely.

How the three men met their deaths is disputed, as accounts vary. Middleton in his statement to Angel said:

"When within 25 miles of the town of Lincoln, Morton drew a revolver out of McCloskey's scabbard, they riding side by side, said McCloskey being one of the said posse, and shot said McCloskey in the head. Baker had a pistol concealed. Morton & Baker then made every effort to escape and refusing to halt were fired upon and killed about half a mile from were McCloskey was killed." (Middleton, p 137.)

A letter to the *Albuquerque Review* signed X.Y.Z, but almost certainly written by Dolan, gave this account about his long-time allies:

"The Sheriff's party, Brady with them, came back to-day after burying Billy Morton and Frank Baker. The particulars as they relate them are that after the Governor issued his Proclamation two men went express from Green Wilson and stated that he could not try them as his commission had been taken away. Brewer and party then took the 'Boys' about 60 miles to the foot of the 'Captain' and there murdered them."

"McCloskey, one of their party, objected to shooting them while tied, and said he'd testify to that effect, when one of them they say, 'Young Kid' [Billy] shot him."

"There were 9 balls in Morton's body and 1 in his head; and five in Baker." [20]

Many authors have argued that the three men were cold-bloodedly executed just as Dolan asserted, but Dolan irrefutably lied in letters to newspapers about events in which he personally participated, so his statements have little credibility.

Federal Government Takes Action

On March 13, U.S. Secretary of State Evarts, responding to Ambassador Thornton's letter, wrote to U.S. Attorney General Charles Devens, alerting him to Tunstall's killing and including Thornton's letter. Evarts asked that Devens *"cause the proper inquiries to be made into the facts of the case."* (Evarts, p 172.)

A week later, Montague R. Leverson wrote to his friend Senator Henry B. Anthony of Rhode Island about Tunstall's killing. Leverson was an Englishman who had lived in the United States since the late 1860s. He owned a ranch in Colorado. Leverson told Anthony that Lincoln is *"under the rule of a gang of thieves and associates at the head of whom are the United States officials."* Leverson referred Anthony to his letter to Marshal John Sherman, which he included. (Leverson, p 173.)

William Maxwell Evartz, undated photo.
Courtesy Library of Congress.

In his letter to Marshal John Sherman, Leverson pointed out to him that Governor Axtell's *"infamous proclamation"* violated New Mexico law and awarded Axtell executive powers he did not have:

"In case you should not have seen the proclamation of his Excellency I mailed you a copy by which you will perceive that the [governor] not only takes upon himself to decide what if his statement be true should be determined as good warrants, but actually ignores the fact of there being other Justices of the Peace elected by the people of the County." (Leverson, p 174.)

On March 27, Ambassador Thornton wrote to Secretary Devens, telling him that he was informed that Tunstall's murder:

"...was incited by the District Attorney of the Third Judicial District [Rynerson] and that the murderers are being screened or attempted to be screened by the Governor of the Territory [Axtell] and the Judge of the District [Bristol]. (Thornton, p 177.)

Thornton pointed out that by removing Wilson as J.P., Axtell had put himself *"in league"* with Tunstall's killers. (Thornton, p 178.)

On April 1, Leverson wrote to the highest U.S. authority, President Rutherford B. Hayes, arguing that Axtell needed to be removed as governor, because *"he is the mainstay of the thieves and murderers"* of Tunstall. (Leverson, p 179.)

On that same day, Leverson wrote to Secretary of the Interior Carl Schurz, telling him that U.S. soldiers have searched houses in Lincoln *"without warrant or authority of any kind and have arrested just whom they please being persons who had as much to do with the killings of the sheriff as you had."* Leverson was referring to the killing of Sheriff William Brady which happened earlier that morning. (Leverson, p 179; Gonzales, p 83; Goodwin, pp 83-84; Lust, p 149; Martinez, pp 93-94.)

Two days later, Secretary Evarts wrote to Attorney General Devens, asking that *"energetic measures may be taken to secure the arrest and conviction of the murderers."* (Evarts, p 180.) After mailing his letter, Devens got a report from Marshal Sherman that two of the murderers had been arrested, Provencio and Evans, and two killed, Baker and Morton. (Sherman, p 180.)

On April 9, Assistant Attorney General Samuel F. Phillips wrote to Secretary Evarts that on March 12 he had contacted U.S. District Attorney Thomas B. Catron about Tunstall's murder. In that letter, he <u>ordered</u> Catron to:

"...institute a thorough inquiry into the circumstances of the murder and to report promptly to me whether from the facts any steps can of should be taken by the Government in the matter." (Phillips, pp 180-181.)

Catron would not have been happy when he opened that letter. He was one of the leaders of the "Santa Fe Ring," of which Murphy, Dolan, Fritz, and Riley were charter members. The "Santa Fe Ring" was not a formal organization, and its members always denied that such a group existed, but it did. It was an informal association of the people who controlled most of Northern New Mexico politically and economically, to their mutual benefit. Now the murder of Tunstall, orchestrated by Dolan, had ensnared Catron.

Carl Christian Schurz, undated photo. Library of Congress.

As of April 9, Catron had not replied to Phillips. To be ordered to act by the Attorney General, and to not do so for almost a month, meant that Catron was seriously risking his position.

Angel Appointed Special Agent

Angel was appointed a Special Agent by Attorney General Schurz on April 15, 1878. He was given credentials by both the Departments of Justice and the Interior. His charges were to investigate: the killing of Tunstall; alleged corruption by Territorial officials, especially Governor Axtell and U.S. Attorney Catron; violence in Lincoln County; and alleged land grant frauds in Colfax County, NM.[21] (Only Angel's investigations of Tunstall's killing and Axtell and Catron's corruption are covered in this book.)

Angel left his home in New York and was in Santa Fe by May 4, 1878, when he registered in the Exchange Hotel (now the La Fonda) there.[22] He travelled by train to Trinidad, Colorado, and from there to Santa Fe by regular stage line.

On May 18, 1878, the *Las Vegas Gazette* printed a letter written May 12, signed by "A CITIZEN." It is certain that this letter was written by Angel.

"Please announce that Mr. Frank W. Angel of New York has been sent by the Departments of Justice and Interior, at Washington, to investigate the state of affairs in New Mexico."

"All persons having any complaint against any U.S. official is requested to address Mr. Angel at Fort Stanton, Lincoln Co., N.M." [23]

Political cartoon of the Santa Fe Ring published by the *Santa Fe Daily Democrat*, October 22, 1880. The Ring, represented by a three-headed snake, is holding scrolls labelled BOGUS GRANTS, LEGISLATIVE BRIBERY, BEEF CONTRACTS, CONFEDERATE RECORD, PARTY LASH, and DOCTORED ELECTION RETURNS. Those were the most common charges against the Ring. The Confederate Record reference is to Thomas B. Catron, who fought for the Confederacy during the Civil War.

The editor of the *Gazette* responded:

> *"The above communication comes directly from the city of the Holy Faith. We were entertaining an Angel unawares, because we did not know of his arrival until the reception of the above epistle. However, if he does not get his wings shot off, or take his departure prematurely for the New Jerusalem, all of which he is liable to do if he fools around Lincoln county, we hope he will investigate fully and freely all officials whose conduct seems to require it."* [24]

The *Las Vegas Gazette* was a strong supporter of the Santa Fe Ring. Angel would have to get used to many sarcastic and derogatory comments from the "Ring" newspapers of the Territory.

Two days after mailing his letter to the *Gazette*, on May 14, Angel began taking sworn statements from people who were involved in or knew about the events surrounding Tunstall's death. Angel was also asking about evidence of corruption by Territorial officials. On that day, a Tuesday, Angel took statements from Lawrence G. Murphy, James J. Longwell, and Pantaleon Gallegos.

Between May 14 and July 1, Angel took an additional 37 statements. On June 25, Colonel George A. Purington, commander of Fort Stanton, voluntarily submitted a statement to Angel. He included with his statement, as exhibits, statements by George W. Peppin, Houston Lust, and William Dowlin. Purington's purpose in submitted a statement was to combat disparaging assertions made against him by McSween and others. (McSween, p 113; Robinson, p 153.)

On June 8, the *Las Vegas Gazette* published an article praising Angel and his investigative efforts:

> "*Mr. Angel is said to be a very fair minded man, well qualified to find out and judge between proper and improper actions. He seeks information from every place he can get it and will, no doubt, unhesitatingly condemn, or justify, official acts, as the case may warrant....*"

> "*Evidence, in cases of that kind, is often difficult to find, and every citizen who has knowledge of facts, does no more than his duty in making them known to Mr. Angel.*" [25]

The editor of the *Gazette* went on to criticize and make fun of the editor of the *Cimarron News and Press*, a non-Ring publication:

> "*That fellow has knowledge; he is possessed of information; he is fully rounded out to bursting with damning facts.... Let Mr. Angel call him and pump his dry as a town-pump; wring him like a dish-rag, and squeeze him like a lemon, in a squeezer, and he will get richness. He can tell all about the ring influence, in Lincoln county....*" [26]

After it became clear that Angel was finding damning facts against those "in league" with the murderers of Tunstall, and on the corruption of members of the Santa Fe Ring, the Ring newspapers became progressively more critical of him. Some examples:

> "*He went to bed in April last a common unvested Angel; he woke to find himself clothed upon with powers too numerous to mention. The President rummaged around among some old wardrobes at the White House and vested him as a Court.... The Department of Justice clothed him in ermine, and the Department of the Interior vested him with shirts !Ecce homo!*"

> "*But his little vessel is not yet full. He has the confidence of at least one of the editors of the [Mesilla Valley] Independent, of a sleeve button lawyer in Santa Fe, of two butchers, and of four pimps at large. Can a mere man hold any more and not burst?*" [27]

> "*[Angel's] pretensions are too vast to be thoroughly understood by the ordinary mind.*" [28]

> "*...the people of New Mexico are just beginning to arrive at the conclusion that Judge Angel is a weakling, if not a fraud.... An egotist and a man who is over anxious to convince the public of his own importance.... Such a man is invariably more anxious to manufacture personal capital than to arrive at a fair determination.*" [29]

Angel Gives Interrogatories to Governor Axtell

On August 11, Angel, in a personal visit to the Governor's mansion in Santa Fe, gave Governor Axtell 31 interrogatories (questions). They began with questions regarding his personal and official behavior following Tunstall's murder. A good example is Interrogatory 2, *"Under what law by what authority, and under whose advice did you issue your proclamation of March 9, 1878?"* (Interrogatories, p 46.) They ended with questions regarding Axtell's connection to certain events in Colfax County.

On August 17, the interrogatories became public knowledge.[30] The Ring papers were incensed by Angel's arrogance in presuming to question Governor Axtell, and especially in posing questions that implied that he was corrupt. The *Mesilla News* wrote:

> *"This, without question, is the most important pub. func. [public functionary] who has ever visited New Mexico. The President of the Untied States vested him in April last with extraordinary powers; afterwards, date not stated, the Department of War and the Department of the Interior each severally vested him as aforesaid. He is an 'Inspector of inspectors, and Judge of judges.' He seeks out corruption with an impartial nose, and goes through the Governor, the Chief Justice, General of the Army and the U. S. Attorney with the same ease and grace with which he tosses off a gin cocktail or balances his partner in a Mexican baile [dance]."* [31]

The *Grant County Herald* wrote:

> *"We have read the history of the Spanish Inquisition; we are well informed as to the methods used in gathering evidence against the persecuted Huguenots; the secret and disreputable spying system employed by Napoleon Third is a matter of recent history; but the following list of questions addressed to the Governor of this Territory by an investigator presumably authorized by one or two Departments at Washington, caps the climax.* [32] (The interrogatories followed this comment.)

One of the few non-Ring newspapers in the Territory wrote:

> *"Mr. Angel, in 31 sharp interrogatories propounded to Gov. Axtell, adroitly encompasses the Alpha and Omega of the existing troubles in that county [Lincoln], and slightly seasoned with a few questions relating to other matters."*

> *"Mr. Angel's surest way to arrive at a knowledge of the Governor's action in the prémisses was to ascertain the facts from the Governor himself. This he attempted to do by submitting a number of questions to the Governor and politely requesting him to answer the same. These questions the Governor complains were coached in offensive language, and some of them he regards as an insult which he resents and repels."* [33]

Axtell's interrogatories and his published responses are given in Chapter 2.

Angel Submits His Report

Angel left Santa Fe on August 14, 1878, for his home in New York City. He arrived in New York on August 24. A few days after his return, Angel was summoned to Washington D. C. to meet with Secretary Schurz. As Angel did not have his written report on his investigations ready, Schurz requested and received a verbal report. That verbal report led directly to the firing of Governor Axtell, as described in the next section.[34]

On October 3, 1878, Angel submitted to Attorney General Devens a list of 12 formal charges against Governor Axtell (see Chapter 3). The same day, he submitted his written report on the killing of John Henry Tunstall (see Chapter 4).

On October 29, Angel was appointed Assistant District Attorney for the Eastern District (New York), doubtlessly a reward for his service to the Federal Government.[35] Angel continued to serve as Assistant District Attorney until February 4, 1886, when he resigned and entered private practice.[36] On January 10, 1879, Devens forwarded Angel's written report to the Secretary Schurz. (Devens, p 188.)

Governor Axtell Fired

On August 20, 1878, the *New York Times* noted:

> *"A delegation of Iowa statesmen, accompanied by the Secretary of War, visited the President to-day to urge the name of Gen. True for the Governorship of New Mexico, in the event of the removal of Gov. Axtell. There is no doubt that strong pressure is being brought to bear upon the President to remove Gov. Axtel... it is understood that the recent disorders in New Mexico are attributed to his maladministration of affairs."* [37]

This report shows the powerful effect Thornton and Leverson's letters – and the newspaper accounts coming out of New Mexico – were having on President Hayes' cabinet officials.

On August 12, the day after Governor Axtell received Angel's interrogatories, Axtell wrote Southern Pacific Railroad lobbyist and long-time friend Collis P. Huntington:

> *"There is a man here by name of Frank Warner Angel... [who] is especially instructed to find out all he can against me. This man it is said acts under another man by name of Chase who is a sort of spy or detective in the service of Department of Justice."* (There was no Chase.)

> *"My impression is that Angel is intending to send in an adverse report on my case. He will not charge corruption or willful misconduct in office, but lack of ability and partisan feeling in managing Lincoln Co troubles.... What I want is to modify his report before Chase files it in the Interior Dept. This Evarts can have done, as these men are his men."* [38]

From the tone of the interrogatories, it was clear that Angel was probing for corruption. Thus, Axtell was falsely characterizing the nature of Angel's investigation to his correspondent. Nor does Axtell mention that Angel has already met with him and given him a long list of questions to answer.

President Rutherford B. Hayes, 1878
photo. Courtesy Rutherford B. Hayes
Presidential Library & Museums.

Governor Axtell in the letter also asks that Huntington use his influence to get Secretary of State Evarts to modify Axtell's eventual report. <u>This is in itself corruption</u>.

On August 31, Secretary Schurz wrote to President Hayes, noting he had just met with Angel:

"After listening to Mr. Angells [sic] verbal report, it became clear to my mind that we ought to make a change in the Governorship of N.M., the sooner the better...." [39]

Secretary Schurz recommended that Axtell be replaced by Lew Wallace:

"... as Genl. Wallace has indicated his willingness to serve, we ought to have him on the spot as speedily as possible. It is also desirable that Genl. Wallace should come here before going to his post, in order to receive all the information Mr. Angells [sic] can give him, so as to be well posted and to avoid mistakes in the beginning." [40]

Wallace was an attorney and a Mexican-American and Civil War veteran. In the Civil War he attained the rank of brigadier general.

On September 3, 1878, Secretary Schurz met with President Hayes in the White House. After the meeting, Schurz announced to the press that Governor Axtell was *"suspended"* – a charitable word for "fired." [41]

On receiving word of his appointment, Wallace immediately travelled to Washington D. C. There he met separately with the President and with Angel. At their meeting, Angel gave Wallace a hand-written notebook in which he had recorded his opinions on various persons in New Mexico. [42] Most of his evaluations were uncomplimentary. Some examples from his notebook:

"Axtell, S. B. – Santa Fe – Conceited – egotistical, easily flattered – Tool unwittingly of the Ring – goes off 'half-cocked'"

"Barrier, Adolf P. – Las Vegas – Dept. Sheriff – favors McSween party – has acted for the right so far"

"Chisom [sic], John S. – Pecos – backbone of the McSween party – sharp – be careful with him"

"Dolan, J. J. – Lincoln – Leader in Lincoln Co. trouble – Murphy party – brave, sharp – determined fellow – Badly mixed up with the Ring &c"

"Elkins, S. B. – 'Silver tongued' further comment unnecessary"

"Liverson [Leverson], M. R. – Now on his ranch, Larkspur Colo. – knows 6 times more than he can prove & 6 times more than anyone else – He can be of service to you – USE HIM – Don't commit yourself – STRONG – McSween man 'THE GREAT AMERICAN LETTER, NEWSPAPER, & C WRITER'"

"Murphy, L. G. – Santa Fe – mixed up in Lincoln Co. – now a drunkard – no reliability – He believes himself a martyr and McSween the devil – Handle him with gloves"

"Peppin, G. W. – Present Sheriff – Lincoln Co. – weak – Murphy man – partisan not reliable"

"Widenman [Widenmann], R. A. – Now at Mesilla – Great friend of Mc-Sween – given to boasting, veracity doubtful when he speaks of himself – well connected in the east & well educated" [43]

On September 19, after learning of his removal, Governor Axtell wrote to Huntington, saying:

"I do not know whether or not it is possible to undo any of Angel's evil work. I know him to be a dirty slanderous liar and I am not willing to allow his accusations to pass uncontradicted."

"...there is not a charge against me nor a stain upon my office and record even this scrub Angel dares not say that there is."

"Do you think it right that I should step down and out with a smile and a bow? I'll see them damned first and then I would. They did not even have the grace to wait thirty – no not ten days to receive my answers, but threw me overboard without a chance even to reply to his dirty insinuations!" [44]

Axtell was told to stay in office and continue to act as governor until his replacement Wallace arrived, which Wallace did on September 30. The next morning Wallace handed Axtell his formal notice of removal from office:

"I transmit herewith an order from the President for the suspension of Mr. Samuel B. Axtell from his office as Governor of the Territory of New Mexico, together with a designation for yourself to perform the duties of said suspended officer, subject to all provisions of law applicable thereto."

"You will deliver said order of suspension to Governor Axtell upon your arrival at the capitol of New Mexico, and when you enter upon the duties of your office you will at once repost the fact to this Department." [45]

The Ring faction was vociferously unhappy with Axtell's removal. The *Las Vegas Daily Gazette* wrote:

"We infer from the action of the president directly after the return of Mr. Frank Warner Angell [sic] to the capital that the quarrel between him and Gov. Axtell had more to do with the latter's removal than any misdemeanors in office. Mr. Angell is a satrap of Carl Shurz [sic] sent out on the European plan, with a wave of the hand like a Bismarck, and instructed that if any one presumes to differ with you, refer them to me. Angell got mad, went off huffy, reported Axtell, and Shurz [sic] at once recommended removal." [46]

Thomas Benton Catron, circa 1900. Courtesy C. M. Bell Studio Collection, Library of Congress.

The *Santa Fe New Mexican* wrote:

"There probably never was less partisan politics or demagoguism in a territorial administration than that of Governor S. B. Axtell.... the most respectable and intelligent portion of this people have come to and still do regard Gov. Axtell as the purest and best executive ever appointed over them. Hence, we, with them, and the people generally, learn with profound regret of his suspension or removal." [47]

Despite his dismissal for his dreadful performance as governor, Axtell was appointed the Chief Justice of the New Mexico Territorial Supreme Court four years later by President Chester A. Arthur. [48] (Vice-president Arthur was made president by the assassination of President James A. Garfield on September 19, 1881.)

U.S District Attorney Catron Fired

On August 19, 1878, Catron wrote Attorney General Devens:

"Mr. Frank Warner Angel who has been here for some time, about one week since furnished me with some affidavits of parties which reflect somewhat upon me in my official character. I requested of him sixty days in which to answer them and furnish other affidavits. He declined but allowed me thirty days. The affidavits he has furnished except in a very few instances do not give me names, places, dates nor particulars, so that I am absolutely compelled to prove a negative. To do this I am compelled to travel over several counties and find all the persons who would know of such facts, at least a sufficient number to establish the folly of the charges." (Catron, p 181)

Catron asserted that he could disprove all of Angel's allegations against him, but he would need 60 days to do so.

Devens' chief clerk, in response to Catron's request for more time, wrote, *"you have had ample opportunity to answer charges and no extension of time can be granted."* (Wing, p 182.)

Catron then appealed to Stephen B. Elkins, Territorial New Mexico's Congressional Representative, and the acknowledged leader of the Santa Fe Ring, to appeal to Devens on his behalf. Elkins asked that Devens grant Catron 15 more days to respond. (Elkins, p 182.) Devens replied to Elkins:

"I do not feel that Mr. Catron should require a longer time than he was given to reply with sufficient distinctness to all that has been inquired of him. Especially since he appears to have considered the matter of answering not of sufficient importance as to take precedence of his private matters, I cannot think that he now considers further time essential." (Devens, p 185.)

On September 18, Elkins wrote Devens saying that Catron's evidence of his innocence was being mailed, but it could be delayed. Elkins then asked if Devens would meet with him personally so he could verbally present Catron's case. (Elkins, p 185.) Elkins was refused.

On October 10, Catron submitted his resignation:

"In accordance with a purpose long entertained I hereby tender my resignation as United States Attorney for New Mexico to take effect November 10, 1878." (Catron, p 186.)

On the same day that Catron resigned, Elkins wrote Devens that Catron's resignation fell on the day the Third District Court term opened. Elkins informed Devens that Catron was willing to continue to serve until his replacement was appointed. (Elkins, pp 186-187.) Devens agreed, and Catron served until December 16, 1878, when his replacement, Sidney M. Barnes, was confirmed by the U.S. Senate. (Devens, pp 189-190.) [49]

Main Street, Lincoln, New Mexico, looking West. Visible on the left is the fence fronting the Bonito Inn (Dolan House). In the distance in the center is the Courthouse (Murphy-Dolan Store). On the right is the Tunstall store. Undated photo.

Chapter 2 | Governor Axtell's Interrogatories

Here are the 31 interrogatories that Frank Warner Angel gave to Governor Axtell to answer on August 11, 1878.

Interrogatories

1. What official action have you taken to quiet the troubles in Lincoln County? Please give full particulars; attach copies of all proclamations.

2. Under what law by what authority, and under whose advice did you issue your proclamation of March 9, 1878?

3. Did you consult with and listen to both sides of the Lincoln County troubles?

4. Did any citizen or citizens come to you and desire to be heard as to the existing troubles at that time in Lincoln County? Did you or did you not refuse to hear them?

5. Did you not act simply on the reports brought you by what is called the "Murphy party," without giving what is called the 'McSween party" a chance to be heard?

6. Were you not at that time just before then, or now indebted to either L. G. Murphy, J. J. Dolan or [John H.] Riley in the sum of two thousand dollars, or thereabouts, for money loaned to you?

7. Have you paid them or either of them said sum? How did you pay them? When did you pay them?

8. By or under whose advice was Sheriff Copeland removed and Sheriff Peppin appointed?

9. Who recommended to you the appointment of Peppin as Sheriff?

10. Did you not know, or were you not informed that at the time he was a strong partisan of what is called the "Murphy party?"

11. When was Peppin appointed and when did he qualify?

12. Has he given bonds as tax collector? If yea, when?

13. Have you not received, during the last four months, letters from Thomas B. Catron, in which he claims he is interested (as contractor or otherwise) in Government contracts? If yea, please attach copies of the same to your answer.

14. Have you not acted under and by the advice of Hon. T. B. Catron, U.S. District Attorney, in the issuing of your proclamations as to the Lincoln County troubles, knowing that said Catron had large interests at stake in said County?

15. Have the proclamations issued by you as to the Lincoln County troubles had the effect of quieting or increasing those troubles?

16. Do you not know that Sheriff Peppin was accompanied to Lincoln by John Kinney and quite a number of his followers, and that said John Kinney and his followers have the reputation of being bad men, outlaws with indictments standing against them?

That the Sheriff had called upon these outlaws as a posse? And do you not know or believe that they accompanied said Peppin to Lincoln for the sole purpose of assisting said Peppin in carrying out and enforcing the law?

17. Do you not consider it is an anomaly for noted outlaws to be called upon to enforce law and order?

18. If you shall answer that Sheriff Peppin has not given his bond as collector, then please state why he has not been removed, and in what way his case differs from Sheriff Copeland?

19. Do you know that Sheriff Copeland was to blame for not giving his bond as collector?

20. Did you not know at the time you issued your proclamation removing Sheriff Copeland that the proper officials had not fixed upon the amount of his bond as collector, and that it was impossible for said Copeland to give his bonds as collector until the amount of taxes to be collected by him had been ascertained?

21. Please give your reasons for removing Sheriff Copeland, and the sources of your information on which you based your reasons, giving names of persons, dates and papers?

22. Was Copeland a partisan? Give source of your knowledge.

23. Is and was not Peppin a partisan? Give source of your knowledge.

24. Did Copeland enforce warrants impartially? Give source of your knowledge?

25. Has Peppin enforced warrants impartially? Give source of your knowledge?

26. Do you know that by your proclamation of March 9, 1878, you assumed the powers of the judiciary, and made person who were and had enforced the warrants Justice Wilson outlaws?

27. Was not there a political scheme to divide Colfax County, from another County, out of said County, run the Territory in the interests of certain persons, have the Territory admitted as a State, and the engineering of elections so that a certain person should be elected to the Senate?

28. If you answer yea to this question then please state if the defeat of this plan was not the cause of the legislation as to Colfax County, and in trying to defeat said plan did not the troubles in Colfax County arise?

29. Do you know the reputation for honesty of J. F. [José Francisco] Chavez?

30. Did you not know at the time of his appointment by you as District Attorney that he was a bad man and had falsified the election returns? Were you not informed of these facts?

31. On whose recommendation did you appoint him? [1]

Governor Axtell's Reply

Three days after giving Governor Axtell his interrogatories, Angel left Santa Fe for New York. He did not wait for Axtell to reply.[2]

Before leaving Santa Fe, Angel gave an interview to the *Rocky Mountain Sentinel*, in which he spoke about the allegations against Governor Axtell and why he had given the Governor interrogatories to answer. On August 19, the *Sentinel* gave Axtell space in the newspaper to reply to Angel's charges.[3] Unfortunately, no copies of these issues are known to exist. However, Axtell's reply in the *Sentinel* was reprinted in the August 31, 1878, issue of the *Mesilla News*. Here is Axtell's reply to Angel as reproduced by the *Mesilla News*:

"Axtell's Defense"
"Santa Fe, Aug 19, 1878"

"Editors 'Sentinel'"

"In your published interviews with F. W. Angel, Esq., in reply to your question 'What, if any, charges have been made against Gov. Axtell?' he [Angel] replies that there is an affidavit of Frank Springer in relation to Colfax troubles, and also reports in Lincoln County that the Gov. had acted in their troubles in a strictly 'partisan manner.' Again he [Angel] says, 'I have given the Gov. a chance to refute these allegations and requested his answer to quite a number of questions,' while it appears to me that it was his duty, under his instructions, as he stated them to you [the Sentinel], to investigate these reports, yet as he does not choose to do so, but throws the burden upon me, and forces me upon the witness stand in my own case."

"I will, to the best of my ability, briefly reply to his allegations. They are in the form of questions. Before proceeding, however, permit me to enter a protest against this whole proceeding."

"I am Gov. of this Territory by virtue of the Organic Act which created the office. That Act is our Charter, or Constitution. That Act created the office of Gov. and fixes the term and defines the duties. While it is true that the Gov. is appointed by the President, by and with the advice and consent of the Senate of the U.S., he is not a Federal but a Territorial officer. He is a part of the Legislature, and assists in making as well as in executing the laws."

"The office is one of considerable importance, and calls for a constant exercise of sound judgment and discretion. His Legislative power, his appointing and pardoning powers are all very important trusts. In executing these trusts for the good of all the citizens of the Ter. there must be allowed to his office much scope for his direction, and so long as he acts to the best of his judgment, he must be sustained. Corrupt misconduct in office must be shown, and not mere error in judgment, before he can properly be impeached or removed."

"I speak for the office and not for myself. I magnify the office in the interests of good government, not in the interests of the incumbent. Who is probably the best judge of what laws I ought to approve in this Territory – Mr. F. W. Angel, Attorney at Law, 62 Liberty St., N.Y., or myself? Again, if the President of the U.S. desired to question me as to my private affairs, or public or official acts, why not permit me to come to Washington and ask me face to face?"

"Mr. Angel puts the Gov. of New Mex. on the witness stand and cross examines him with all the sharpness of a criminal lawyer, and if the Gov. does not answer, reports him, I presume, for contumacy; or, in his own words to... [unreadable] preserve the public peace. (See Message to 23d Session, page 8; title: 'Bad White Men.')"

"My second act was to forward to the President immediately, upon hearing of the death of Tunstall and the disturbances which followed, a letter of Sheriff Brady's addressed to U.S. Dist. Att. T. B. Catron, Esq., and officially referred by him to me, and also to state to the President the condition of affairs and to request that U.S. troops might be directed to assist the civil officers of the Ter. in serving legal process, and in maintaining the public peace."

"This letter and this statement and request I forwarded by telegraph, and immediately started for Lincoln. When I arrived at Fort Stanton, on the fourth day after leaving Santa Fe, I was informed by Col. Purington commanding post, that my request had been granted, and that he had orders to assist the civil authorities. He also informed me that there appeared to [unreadable] certain writs issued out of the Dist. Court."

"A Deputy Sheriff of San Miguel Co. [Barrier] had McSween in charge and declined to deliver him to Brady. Wilson, Justice of the Peace, had issued warrants against the Sheriff and his deputies; and a deputy U.S. Marshal for Lincoln Co. [Widenmann] claimed the right to direct the movement of the troops."

"Under these circumstances Col. Purington asked my advice as to whom he should render assistance. I told him that Widerman's [sic] appointment as Deputy Marshal had been revoked. As Wilson had been appointed Justice of the Peace by the Co. Commissioners, and that the appointment was good for nothing – that a J.P. must be elected, could not be appointed, that it was so established by our Ter. Constitution, the Organic Act."

"Col. Purington went with me to Widerman's office and saw him, and he admitted that his appointment had been revoked. We also went to the office of Wilson, J.P. and informed him what was the law in his case. He said he would not act as Judge any more, and bundled up his papers and retreated in good order into his bar room. I did not remove him from office – he was not in office."

"Col. Purington asked me to put these facts in writing for the information of the people – I did so. This is my Proclamation of March 9th 1878. (McSween, Ex. 16, p 131). If it makes anybody an outlaw the fault is in the facts, not in me. Up to this time no man had been killed except Tunstall. I conversed with all the citizens I could meet, I advised them to seek peace and pursue it, to be in earnest

to uphold the law. I told them, that I would use my best exertions to have every man who was present when Tunstall was killed, and who took part whatever against him, indicted and tried, and as they claimed to justify as officers resisted in the discharge of duty, they must make this claim good on their trial and in open court. I told them Judge Bristol would be with them in about three weeks, and would organize a Grand Jury, and investigate all the facts."

"There were four men said to be in the Sheriff's party spoken of by what is called the McSween party as outlaws [Evans, Baker, Hill, and Davis], said to be very bad men, the same men whom I refer to in my Message. It was feared by the McSween men that Sheriff Brady would not be active in their arrest. I talked with Col. Purington about this, and told him I would give him a request in writing to arrest these four men, and to keep them in his guard house till the Court should sit. We did not think it best to inform any one of this for fear it might thwart our purpose. Col. Purington, I presume, still has this paper and I cheerfully refer to him for the correctness of these statements."

"Nearly all my information as to Lincoln Co. troubles has been obtained from him and other officers at Fort Stanton. I have also some information from Col. Dudley after he took command. I have never corresponded with either side, nor to the best of my judgment, have I been biased or prejudiced for or against either one."

"The path of duty was so plain to my feet that I must walk in it. That was, to sustain the lawful authorities, and to aid them to execute the laws. Neither in Lincoln, nor in Colfax, have I ever been willing to accept any compromise with mobs or "regulators." I have not the least doubt that had the McSween party accepted my views, and followed my advice, that no blood would have been shed after the death of Tunstall. Nor have I any doubt that what that homicide would have been thoroughly enquired into by the District Court, and all fully parties justly punished."

"My advice, however, was not followed; but a vigilance committee or band of regulators was organized to resist the Sheriff, and over-ride and violate the law. Murder followed murder with sickening rapidity. Finally Brady with one of his Deputies was shot down in the open day in the public street. After his death the Co. Commissioners as they had a right to do, appointed John N. Copeland Sheriff."

"I am asked in questions 22 and 24, if Copeland was a partisan, and if he enforced warrants impartially, and I am commanded to give the sources of my knowledge. Col. Dudley informed me by letter that Copeland was daily in company with noted desperadoes for whom he had warrants, and that he failed, and refused to arrest them, and Angel himself on his first return from Lincoln, and again first before leaving for New York, told me that Copeland did not serve warrants impartially."

"Copeland also was called to give a bond as collector of Taxes, and the law makes it my duty in such cases to remove him, and to appoint a Sheriff. (See acts 22nd Session Legislative Assembly, page 51, Sec. & and 8.) This I did and *appointed Geo. W. Peppin. He was highly recommended to me by Col. W. L. Rynerson, the Dist. Att. for the 3d. District which included Lincoln Co."*

"He is a married man; a resident and property holder in the town of Lincoln; is industrious and strictly sober, and came to the Ter. as a soldier with the California Volunteers; he has given both his bonds and both have been properly approved, and a copy of his bond as Collector of Taxes is on file with the Auditor of the Territory. It would have put Mr. Angel to very little trouble to have ascertained these facts. Peppin was a Deputy of Brady's, and was with that brave officer and good citizen when he was murdered, and if by "partisan" is meant that Peppin is red hot against those murderers, and means to ride day and night and to see all possible means to bring them to justice, then I pray God that he and all good men may grow more "partisan" every day till his good work is accomplished."

"I have been informed by Col. Dudley and others that Peppin has been vigilant, active and courageous. I know his life is in danger, but should he live to read this, I want to thank him for accepting this dangerous appointment, and for the brave and prudent manner in which he has executed its arduous duties. I call attention to my proclamation appointing Peppin Sheriff, wherein I forbid all men and bodies of men to act as a Sheriff's posse."

"Second – I command all men and bodies of men, now under arms and traveling about the county, to disarm and return to their homes and their usual pursuits, and so long as the present Sheriff has authority to call upon U.S. troops for assistance, not to act as a Sheriff's posse. And, in conclusion, I urge upon all good citizens to submit to the law, remembering that violence begets violence, and that they who take the sword shall perish by the sword."

"S. B. Axtell"
"Governor of New Mexico"

"If John Kinney acted with Peppin at that time it was against my express orders. Afterwards when the troops were withdrawn from the Sheriff, and he was left to his own resources, I cannot blame him, if when attacked, he took into his service all who offered. I am informed that Kinney and his band have returned to Mesilla, and I believe if Sheriff Peppin is sustained he will rid Lincoln County of all thieves, assassins and desperadoes."

"As to what effect my Proclamations have had, I am unable to state; I can see nothing in them which is calculated to do hurt, I annex copies of them to this answer, and will leave it to men of riper judgment to determine this difficult question. I am frank to say, that I would have rather have a few troops than a cord of Proclamations."

"As to the question of my indebtedness to Murphy, Riley, or Dolan, while I consider the question impertinent, yet out of respect to the Depts. which send Angel on this singular mission, I will state that I am not indebted to either of these gentlemen at present, nor have been for nearly two years. In May 1876 I borrowed $1,800 of Mr. Riley, and paid the same in November of the same year,

in legal money of the United States, over the counter of the First National Bank, at Santa Fe."

"The questions relating to Hon. T. B. Catron are also easily disposed of. I have received no letters from him, nor have I acted under his advice, in my official matters. Mr. Catron is a good lawyer and an honorable man, and I am proud to have him for my friend, but, when I have needed legal advice to guide my official acts, I have gone to my own Atty. Gen. and I am of opinion that I have had two as good ones as to be found in any Territory in the Untied States, Hon. Wm. Breeden for about three years, and on his resignation, Hon. Henry L. Waldo, late Chief Justice of this Ter."

"The next questions relate to Colfax Co., and like all others inspired by the Cimarron Ring are very amusing. I know nothing whatever about any political scheme to divide Colfax Co.; run the Ter. in the interest of certain persons, bring it in as a State, and make a certain person Senator; nor am I able even to imagine how the division of a Co. could do all or any of these things. Colfax. Co. embraces a section of country of about 120x80 miles in extent, and is larger than the state of Conn. There are but two Co. on our northern line which is 330 miles long. I think it would be for the interest of the Ter. to have at least four Co. now, by and by more, but this question was not agitated as far as I know, nor as far as the Cimarron Ring swear, till my visit to Colfax with Senator [Stephen W.] Dorsey, in July 1877 while their troubles and the legislature of which they complain took place nearly ten years before; how could the defeat of this plan have caused the trouble of ten years previous?"

"This talk about a certain person being made Senator is childish. I resent what is said about Col. Francisco Chavez as it applies both to him and to myself. I met Col. Chavez in Washington when were then both members of Congress. I think he has been elected Delegate three times from this Ter.; he is a member of one of the very best families here; he is a member of the Bar in good standing, and I have never heard his honesty questioned, nor have I ever heard that he had falsified election returns."

"I have heard Democrats complain that Valencia Co., where Col Chavez lives, sent up some awful Republican majorities, but I never head any one say that he had falsified the returns. Angel's charge that I would appoint a bad man to office, a man who had falsified election returns with a full knowledge of the facts, is an insult which I resent and repel. I am asked on whose recommendation I appointed Col. Chavez. I answer a majority of the Territorial Senators recommended him, but I really appointed him on my own knowledge of the man. I enclose you both my Proclamations in regard to Lincoln Co. affairs, and also a copy of my Message."

"Respectfully, etc."
"S. B. Axtell"
"Governor of New Mexico" [4]

Notes on Governor Axtell's Reply

Early in his lengthy reply, Governor Axtell refers to his "Message." This was a reference to Axtell's State of the Territory address to the New Mexico Legislature on January 7, 1878. Excerpts of that speech were published in the *Las Vegas Gazette*, but it does not include a section entitled "Bad White Men," and the full text of his speech is apparently lost.[5]

Governor Axtell's Message was not well received by the non-Ring faction of the Territory. The *Albuquerque Review* editor commented:

> "'There is no foundation whatever in fact for this assertion that there is at Santa Fe a ring or combination of men who desire to plunder the Territory' [quoting Axtell in his Message]. O Sapient Samuel! O Axtell Astute! How did thou reach such 'lame and impotent conclusion' 'Good Easy man.' How have they hoodwinked thee! ...his Innocency not only certifies that there is no combination of men at Santa Fe which has plundered the Territory, but in the effusive simplicity of his un-obfuscated heart, he alleges that no one has even the desire to do so."[6]

Governor Axtell's reply to Angel contains several glaring lies. He writes that when he was asked by Colonel Purington *"as to whom he should render assistance,"* he replied:

> *"...Widerman's [sic] appointment as Deputy Marshal had been revoked. As Wilson had been appointed Justice of the Peace by the Co. Commissioners, and that the appointment was good for nothing – that a J.P. must be elected, could not be appointed, that it was so established by our Ter. Constitution, the Organic Act."*

Axtell asserts as a fact that Widenmann's marshal office was revoked before it was *"revoked"* by his proclamation, which was only issued after his conversation with Purington. Even if it is accepted that Axtell's had the legal power as chief executive of New Mexico to remove Widenmann for no cause (which he did not), it still requires a formal legal act, not a self-serving remark in a discussion.

Axtell continues, as he did in his proclamation, to assert that a Justice of the Peace must be elected, even though he knew differently, that Territorial law permitted County Commissioners to fill vacant offices. (Section, p 171.) Axtell had himself signed this law into effect.

He adds:

> *"Col. Purington went with me to Widerman's office and saw him, and he admitted that his appointment had been revoked. We also went to the office of Wilson, J.P. and informed him what was the law in his case. He said he would not act as Judge any more, and bundled up his papers and retreated in good order into his bar room. I did not remove him from office – he was not in office."*

This appears to be another lie. Col. Purington in his statement says nothing about the two of them visiting Widermann and Wilson (Purington, p 146), and both men continued to operate in their offices after Axtell left Lincoln. McSween, in a letter written to the

Cimarron News and Press about events in Lincoln, stated that Axtell's *"stay in Lincoln did not extend three hours."* [7]

Axtell says that he *"conversed with all the citizens I could meet."* This is contradicted by both McSween and the *Cimarron News and Press.* (McSween, pp 110-111.) McSween says:

> *"D. P. Shield, I. Ellis and R. A. Widenmann informed me that the Governor positively refused to hear any thing from the people about the troubles. That when they asked him to visit the people and give them an opportunity to be heard he replied that he was posted as well as he wanted to be and that he did not want to hear any more from them."* (McSween, pp 110-111.)

The Lincoln County Grand Jury that met April 18, 1878, made the same point, after hearing sworn testimony on the subject:

> *"Had his Exc. S. B. Axtel [Axtell] when here ascertained from the people the cause of our troubles, as he was requested, valuable lives would have been spared our community; especially do we condemn that portion of his proclamation relating to J. B. Wilson as Justice of the Peace. Mr. Wilson acted in good faith as such J. P. over a year."* [8]

Axtell was willing to say whatever he thought necessary to make his actions look appropriate and justifiable. His attitude is well expressed in this line from his letter to his friend Huntington disputing Angel's allegations:

> *"You can rely perfectly upon what I say...."* [9]

A last point – Axtell says that on learning of the *"disturbances"* in Lincoln, *"he immediately started for Lincoln."* He says it took him four days to get there. The distance from Santa Fe to Lincoln is about 200 miles. Taking four days to get to Lincoln was travelling slowly, even for 1878. He clearly was in no great rush to get to Lincoln.

Chapter 3 | Angel's Charges Against Governor Axtell

On October 3, 1878, Angel submitted to Interior Secretary Schurz a list of 12 charges he had collected against Governor Axtell through investigations, interviews and witness statements. These are the charges that Angel tasked himself with formally investigating. Following the list of charges, Angel added his conclusion as to whether he considered a charge sustained or not sustained.

Angel found 10 of the 12 charges sustained – charges 1, 2, 4, 5, 6, 7, 8, 9, 11, and 12 – and two charges unsustained – 3 and 10.

Ten out of 12 charges sustained is of itself devastating – but the content of the sustained charges are even more devastating – especially charge 11 in which he quotes a letter written by Axtell in which Axtell plans the murder of political enemies!

When President Hayes removed Axtell as governor on September 3, 1878, he did not have this written report. But after hearing Angel's verbal report on Axtell, President Hayes did not consider formal, written charges necessary to make his decision.

Charges Against Axtell

Interior Department

In the matter of the investigation of the charges against S. B. Axtel [sic], Governor of New Mexico

To the Honorable C. Schurz, Secretary of the Interior:

In compliance with your request made at the time I made my first report herein, I herewith make my supplemental and final report as to the charges against said S. B. Axtell. Since making said report I have found no reason for changing the same, but on the contrary believe as I did then that the best interests of New Mexico demanded the removal of S. B. Axtell as Governor.

A brief resume of the facts laid before you at that time will be necessary to make this report complete.

Under your instructions I visited New Mexico for the purpose of ascertaining if there was any truth in the repeated complaints made to the Department as to fraud, incompetency, and corruption of United States officials. I determined to see with my own eyes and hear with my own ears. I traveled over most of the Territory. I visited almost every important town and talked with the principal citizens thereof.

I was met by every opposition possible by the United States civil officials and every obstacle thrown in my way by them to prevent a full and complete examination with one exception and administration of affairs in the Territory and from facts coming under my observation and affidavits of the people the following charges in substance were made against the Governor of said Territory.

First. That the Governor had taken strictly partisan action as to the troubles in Lincoln County.

Second. That he refused to listen to the complaints of the people of that County.

Third. That he had been paid the sum of two thousand dollars to influence his action.

Fourth. That he arbitrarily removed Territorial officials thereby outlawing citizens, and usurping the functions of the judiciary.

Fifth. That he removed officials and in their place appointed strong partisans.

Sixth. That all action taken by him has increased rather than quieted the troubles in Lincoln County.

Seventh. That he appointed officials to office and kept them there who were supported by the worst out-laws and murderers that the Territory could produce.

Eighth. That he knowingly appointed bad men to office.

Ninth. That he was a tool of designing men [and was] weak and arbitrary in exercising the functions of his office.

Tenth. That he was a Mormon and desired to turn the Territory into a Mormon settlement.

Eleventh. That he conspired to murder innocent and law abiding citizens because they opposed his wishes and were exerting this influence against him.

Twelfth. That he arbitrarily refused to restore the courts to Colfax County and refused to listen to the petitions of the people of that County for the restoration thereof.

Angel's Conclusions

The Governor at first refused to be investigated preferring to ignore the complaints against him on the ground that the Department of the Interior had no power to investigate him. He has not even answered the charges by a sworn statement. I received just before making my first report, a newspaper article which was not even signed by him in reply to the charges against him. [Angel is referring to the *Rocky Mountain Sentinel* article discussed in Chapter 2.]

By much care and patience I have investigated the above charges impartially, seeking to obtain the truth and punish the guilty.

Many things came to my notice and observations and of which no affidavits could be obtained. Many suspicious circumstances existed which convinced me beyond a peradventure that Gov. Axtell was an improper person for the place. He is a man of strong prejudices, impulsive, conceited, and easily flattered. All these make a man easily influenced, a complete tool in the hands of designing men.

As to the charges one and two, I found Lincoln County convulsing by an internal war. I inquired the cause. Source one was responsible for the blood shed in that County. I found two parties in the field, one headed by Murphy, Dolan and Riley, the other led by McSween – both had done many things contrary to law – both were violating the law.

McSween I firmly believe acted conscientiously – Murphy, Dolan, & Riley for revenge and personal gain. The Governor came, heard the Murphy, Dolan, & Riley side, refused to hear the people who were with McSween or the residents of the County and acted strictly in advancing the Murphy, Dolan, and Riley party.

Murder and unlawful acts followed instead of peace and quiet which could have been accomplished if the Governor had acted as he should have done and listened patiently to both sides. The opportunity presented itself to him to have quieted and stopped the trouble in Lincoln Co. By his partisan action he allowed it to pass and the continuations of the troubles that exist today in Lincoln County are chargeable to him. He was a partisan either through corruption or weakness and charges first and second have been sustained.

Charge Third. The facts are that in May 1876, Gov. Axtell borrowed of Mr. Riley $1800 and it is alleged that the same was paid in November. I do not believe that Gov. Axtell received this money to directly influence his action. It was some time before the troubles actually commenced in Lincoln Co. – although they were brewing at that time. The only influence this transaction could have on the action of Gov. Axtell was in as much as Riley had befriended him to return the compliment, and certainly his official action lays him open to serious suspicion that his friendship for Murphy, Dolan, and Riley was stronger than his duty to the people and the government he represents.

Charge Fourth. I find that this charge has been freely sustained by his proclamation of March 9, 1878. He usurped the functions of the judiciary and in fact removed J. B. Wilson, a Justice of the Peace, and thereby made certain persons who were in good faith enforcing the warrants issued by said Wilson outlaws. What right had he to do this? He did not veto the bill under which Wilson was appointed and suffered him to act some months before he arbitrarily removed him.

Charge Fifth. John Copeland after the murder of Sheriff Brady was appointed Sheriff. He was an honest, conscientious man, perhaps he was not the strongest man in character that ever existed, but I am yet to hear of any arbitrary act on his part, any murder, robbery, arson in which he has been a party or of his being supported while in office by a band of notorious outlaws and nonresidents. He was on the contrary surrounded by and had the confidence of a majority of the residents of the county – one of the County Commissioners his bondsman. By the laws of the territory, the Sheriff is ex-officio Tax Collector. The bonds as collector have to be fixed by the County Commissioners after they have ascertained the amount of taxes to be collected. Copeland had nothing to do with this – and owing to the troubled state of affairs in the county, the County Commissioners could not find the amount of taxes to be collected.

The Governor immediately seized the opportunity to aid Murphy, Dolan, & Riley. He this time acts strictly within the letter of the law, and would that I could say the interest of the law and non-partisan[ism]. He removes Copeland and appoints G. W. Peppin, one of the leaders of the Murphy, Dolan, and Riley party – who comes from Mesilla accompanied by John Kinney and his murderous outfit of outlaws, as a body guard to assist him in enforcing law and order. Again we have an unusual number of murders, robbers, and accompanied with arson, and after Kinney and his party have accomplished their mission of murdering McSween and robbing and stealing all they can, they retire on their laurels and return from whence they came, and Sheriff Peppin without the confidence of the people or even himself retreats to Fort Stanton, at which place he is under the care and protection of the soldiers. [Angel is referring to the five-day war in Lincoln which ended with the burning down of McSween's house and the killing of McSween, Harvey Morris, Vincente Romero, Francisco Zamora, and Robert Beckwith.]

I find that Gov. Axtell acted in the interests of the Murphy, Dolan, & Riley party and was strictly partisan and that the charge is sustained.

Charge Sixth. I report that this charge has been sustained as already set forth.

Charge Seventh. I report that this charge has been sustained as appears by facts set forth under Charge Fifth.

Charge Eighth. Under this charge is the appointment of Col. Chavez and Peppin. It was rumored that Col. Chaves had falsified the election returns and as a reward he was nominated and appointed Territorial District Attorney. There is however no evidence of this fact and I accordingly report that as to this part of the charge the same is not sustained. But that as to Peppin, the charge is sustained. The Governor replies that he appointed Peppin under recommendation of W. L. Rynerson. Rynerson is undoubtedly a good lawyer and a gentleman, but he is never the less a strong partisan and his record in the Lincoln County troubles show that he has used his office for oppressive purposes. The Governor must have known this, therefore with knowledge of Peppin's character he acted again strictly partisan and appointed an improper man.

Charge Ninth. I find has been sustained as appears from facts set forth herein.

Charge Tenth. As to this charge there are no substantial facts to show that he is a Mormon. I therefore report that the source is not sustainable. [Axtell was appointed governor of Utah in 1874, but removed after only one year in office due to extensive criticism that he unfairly favored the Mormons of the state. This led to the false, but persistent rumor that he was a Mormon himself.]

Charge Eleventh. On considering this charge we must go back in the unwritten history of New Mexico to the time when Colfax County by the arbitrary and unlawful acts of certain officials, became too hot for them, and they had to leave the County for the County's good. The plan was devised and carried out to join Colfax County to Taos County for judicial purposes and a bill was rushed through the Legislature and signed, at once accomplishing this design.

Immediately the people at Cimarron telegraphed Gov. Axtell "Requesting him to withhold his signature until a delegation from Colfax could wait upon him." The reply came back "Bill signed, S. B. Axtell." If there was trouble in Colfax County which could not be quieted then there was a justification in having this bill – it would have then been an excellent measure. But the facts show that when this bill was passed the troubles in Colfax Co. had been quieted and stopped and that there was more lawlessness in other parts of the Territory than in Colfax.

No benefit resulted from the change – but on the contrary it was a gross injury and injustice to the people of Colfax County. The two counties are separated by a range of high mountains, the lowest pass 9000 feet in altitude, which when the court is in session are difficult and dangerous to cross. It required a journey over these mountains of 54 miles to reach court. The juries were entirely taken from Taos County, manipulated by Pedro Sanches, a ringite, and prejudiced by outside influence. There never could be a fair trial in criminal proceedings and all most all civil business was suspended. It was a great expense to Colfax Co. for witnesses and fee[s].

It is [not[surprising that opposition to the arbitrary Governor arose and with opposition came vindictiveness and revenge on the part of the opposed.

The Governor was visited at Santa Fe said he was heartily in favor of the bill and spoke with extreme bitterness about the people of Colfax County – and refused to go to Colfax Co. and investigate the facts for himself saying "He was fully advised about matters in that County and didn't need further information."

After this at a public meeting at Cimarron an invitation in courteous language was addressed to the Governor inviting him to visit Colfax County and make a thorough investigation for himself. This invitation was signed by ten or twelve prominent citizens. To this the Governor makes no reply or acknowledgement.

At this stage Ben Stevens, territorial District Attorney and appointee of the Governor appears.

He circulates the report that he is going to try and have the Governor visit Colfax, leaves Cimarron, goes to Fort Union, and returns in a few days with a company of soldiers and exhibits a telegram from the Governor which reads as follows: "Do not let it be known that I will be in Cimarron on Saturday's coach. Body guard all right," and said it was proof that the Governor was coming to visit the County and would expect to meet those who had signed the invitation and that they must be on hand on the arrival of the coach to meet him. He requested that the matter be kept quiet as the Governor did not want a crowd, but only wanted to meet those who had invited him.

The facts subsequently show that the Governor did not intend to visit Colfax Co. and that the action of Stevens was in furtherance of a plot as will appear by the following letter:

"Dear Ben [Stevens]"

"The second telegram delivered to you at Fort Union directed to Cimarron was intended to leak but the operator here says he cannot raise the Cimarron office. If I was expected, our friends would probably be on hand, as the guard is only a Government escort. I do not think your definite business is expected. Wade informed [Colonel Edward] Hatch that he has been ready all the time to assist you, but could not find that you wanted to do it. "

"Hatch says their opinion is that you weakened and do not want to arrest the man. Have your men placed to arrest him and to kill all the men who resist you or stand with those who do resist you. Our man signed the invitation with others who were at the meeting, for me to visit Colfax – Porter, Morley, Springer, et. al. Now, if they expect me Saturday, they will be on hand. Send me letters by messenger, and do not hesitate at extreme measures. Your honor is at stake now, and a failure is fatal."

"If others resist or attempt murder, bring them also. Hatch is excited and wishes to put all the blame on the civil officers. I am more anxious on your account than for any other reason. I clearly see that we have no friends in Colfax, and I have suspected all along that some of our pretended friends here were traitors."

"Yours, &c."
"S. B. Axtell"

Was there ever a cooler devised plot with a Governor as sponsor? The Governor admits the letter in toto [total]. <u>"That it sounds like me."</u> And then subsequently attempts to explain away part of its terrible features.

He makes no attempt as to the telegram. Nor why he wished it to "leak." But by a down right falsehood he attempts to assemble certain persons who are obnoxious to him so that in the event, of the resistance to be arrested, of a person by the name of [Clay] Allison as excuse would be offered, <u>"to kill all the men who resist or stand with those who resist you."</u>

He does not explain this – he cannot – Stevens and the soldiers were sent by Governor Axtell ostensibly to arrest a person by the name of Allison – but reading the foregoing telegram and letter I do not believe that it was the real object, for Allison was afterwards arrested and at once set at liberty and Governor Axtell subsequently made an appointment and traveled with said Allison in a friendly way in the stage coach.

Any man capable of framing and trying to enforce such a letter of instructions as the one set forth in this report is not fit to be entrusted with any power whatever. I therefore report that this charge has been sustained.

<u>Charge Twelfth</u>. On February 1876, a bill was passed through the Legislature providing that the Courts should be removed from Cimarron, Colfax County, to Taos, Taos County, and that after two terms the Governor might at his option restore the Courts to Colfax County. For the reasons set forth under Charge Eleventh, I find that under this, charge is sustained.

<u>In conclusion,</u> I respectfully submit that whether through ignorance or corrupt motive the actions of said Axtell has been to keep many parts of the Territory of New Mexico in a state of turmoil and confusion, when intelligent and non-partisan action on his part might have avoided much of the difficulty, and that the removal of Governor Axtell viewed with the evidence and his reply received before my first report, was an absolute necessity, and it becomes still more evident that such was the right course on receiving his subsequent replies.

It is seldom that history states more corruption, fraud, mismanagement, plots, and murders than New Mexico has been the theatre under the administration of Governor Axtell.

I transmit herewith the testimony herein.

All of which is respectfully submitted.

Washington
October 3, 1878
Frank Warner Angel
Department of Interior [1]

Chapter 4 | Witness Statements

Introduction

The Angel Report report follows. The Report consists of 40 sworn witness statements, two with attached exhibits, those of Alexander A. McSween and George A. Purington. The statements are listed here by last name in alphabetical order for easy reference. Angel seems to have followed no logical principle in his ordering of the statements. His table of contents lists the statements in alphabetical order, but they are not arranged that way in his submission.[1]

For William "Buck" Morton's brief account in his letter to H. H. Marshal of the killing of Tunstall, see pages 175-176. For Jesse Evans' brief account, see page 158.

Department of Justice

In the matter of the cause and circumstances of the death of John H. Tunstall a British subject to the honorable Charles Devens, Attorney General

In compliance with your instructions to make careful inquiry into the cause and circumstances of the death of John H. Tunstall, a British subject, and whether the death of said Tunstall was brought about through the lawless and corrupt conduct of United States officials in the Territory of New Mexico, and to report thereon.

I have the honor to submit the following report in relation to the premises.

FIRST: As to the cause of the death of John H. Tunstall.

Mr. John H. Tunstall by his straight forward and honest business transactions with the people of Lincoln County, New Mexico, had almost overthrown a certain faction of said county who were plundering the people thereof.

He had been instrumental in the arrest of certain notorious horse thieves. He had exposed embezzlement of Territorial officers. He had incurred the anger of persons who had control of the County, and who used that control for private gain. He had introduced honesty and square dealings in his business, and to the enmity of these persons, can be attributed the only cause of his death.

SECOND: As to the circumstances of his death.

An attachment had been obtained against the property of one Alexander A. McSween. It was claimed that said Tunstall was McSween's partner.

The Sheriff in order to attach certain property, viz stock and horses, alleged to belong to McSween and Tunstall, sent his deputy to Tunstall's ranch to attach the same. When said deputy visited said ranch and was informed that he could attach the stock and leave a person with it until the Courts could adjudicate to whom the stock belonged, he left without attaching said property and immediately assembled a large posse among whom were the most desperate out-laws of the Territory.

They again started for Tunstall's ranch. In the mean-time, Mr. Tunstall had been informed of the action of the Sheriff, and believing that the real purpose was to murder and not attach, left his ranch, taking with him all the horses and started for Lincoln, the County seat.

Directly after Tunstall had left his ranch, the Deputy Sheriff and said posse arrived there, and finding that Tunstall had left with the horses, deputized W. Morton, who selected eighteen men and started out ostensibly to capture the horses. After riding about thirty miles, they came up to Tunstall and his party with the horses, and commenced firing on them. Immediately Tunstall and his party left the horses and attempted to escape, were pursued and Tunstall was killed some hundred yards or more from the horses.

Who shot Tunstall will never be known. But there is no doubt that Wm. S. Morton, Jesse Evans and Hill were the only persons present and saw the shooting, and that two of these persons murdered him. For Tunstall was shot in two places – in the head and breast. Of these persons, Morton and Hill were afterwards killed, and the only survivor is Jesse Evans, a notorious out-law, murderer and horse-thief. Of these persons, Evans and Hill had been arrested at the instigation of Tunstall.

They were at enmity with Tunstall, and enmity with them meant murder.

There was no object for following after Tunstall, except to murder him, for they had the horses which they desired to attach before they commenced to pursue him and his party. These facts, together with the bitter feelings existing against Tunstall, by certain persons to whom he had become obnoxious, and the deputy allowing these notorious out-laws to accompany him, lead me to the conclusion that John H. Tunstall was murdered in cold blood, and was not shot in attempting to resist an officer of the law.

THIRD: Was the death of John H. Tunstall brought about by the lawless and corrupt action of United States officials?

After diligent inquiry and examination of a great number of witnesses, I report that the death of John H. Tunstall was not brought about through the lawless and corrupt conduct of United States officials in the Territory of New Mexico.

All of which is respectfully submitted.
Frank Warner Angel (signed)
Special Agent

Department of Justice

In the matter of the Lincoln County troubles to the honorable Charles Devens Attorney General

The history of Lincoln County has been one of blood shed from the day of its organization. These troubles have existed for years with occasional out breaks, each one being more severe than the other. L. G. Murphy & Co. had the monopoly of all business in the County, controlled government contracts, and used their power to oppress and grind out all they could from the farmers, and force those who were opposed to them to leave the County.

This has resulted in the formulation of two parties, one led by Murphy & Co., and the other by McSween (now dead). Both have done many things contrary to law, both violated the law. McSween, I firmly believe acted conscientiously, Murphy & Co. for private gain and revenge.

Bands of desperate characters who are ever found on the frontier, particularly along the Texas border, who have no interest in Lincoln County, men who live by plunder, and who only flourish where they can evade the law, have naturally gravitated to one or the other of these parties, and are now in their pay, being hired for so much a day to fight their battles.

Gov. Axtell appoints Peppin, a leader of the Murphy & Co. faction, as Sheriff. He comes to Lincoln accompanied by John Kinney and his notorious band of out-laws and murderers as a body guard to assist him in upholding law and order. McSween then collects around himself an equally distinguished body. The County becomes the Elysium [in classical Greek mythology the final resting place of the souls] for out-laws and murderers.

A battle is fought – for five days it rages – more desperate action than was seen on these unfortunate days, by both sides, is rarely witnessed. Both parties desire revenge, and they are now reorganizing, and collecting more desperate characters (if it were possible), than they previously had. Before I left Santa Fe, it was reported that there were two hundred armed men in the field.

Men are shot down "on sight" because they belong to one or the other party, and the residents of the County have been forced to take one side or the other either from inclination or necessity. One day Murphy & Co. and his party of out-laws control the County – the next day McSween and his "out-fit" would be the masters.

When these men were not engaged in battle, and when the County seemingly was at peace, they were employed to steal cattle, either from the farmers or the Indians – a ready market and no questions asked, was found in the persons who held government contracts. If the people protested, they were persecuted and driven out the County. This state of affairs would be carried to such an extent, that it would end in a fight and a war similar to the one now being waged in that County.

During these years the law-abiding citizens, or those who would be if they could, have been reduced to poverty by professional thieves, who have made the county their camping ground without the least fear of molestation. The laws cannot be enforced, for the reason that if the Murphy party are in power, then the law is all Murphy – and if the McSween party are in power, then the law is all McSween.

The leaders of these parties have created a storm that they cannot control, and it has reached such proportions that the whole Territory cannot put it down. Lands go uncultivated; ranches are abandoned, merchants have closed their stores, citizens have left the homes they have occupied for years, business has ceased, and lawlessness and murder are the order of the day. These out-laws who prowl the County with the avowed purpose of murder, who have no interests in the County or wrongs of their own to redress, no matter on which side they belong, should be hunted down, and made to answer for their crimes.

The Territory has no militia, and the County being in the hands of these armed out-laws, the laws and mandates of the Courts cannot be enforced or respected, nor lives or property protected, It is impossible for even the Courts to be held.

I would respectfully refer to my report to the Interior Department on the charges against Governor Axtell as to the additional causes for the existing troubles in Lincoln County [see Chapter 3].

I would most respectfully recommend that such assistance be given the Governor of New Mexico that the laws may be enforced and respected, and life and property protected.

All of which is respectfully submitted.
WASHINGTON, OCTOBER 7th, 1878
Frank Warner Angel (signed)
Special Agent

Daniel M. Appel - July 1, 1878

Daniel M. Appel being duly sworn says that he is Assistant Surgeon U.S. Army and have been and are now stationed at Fort Stanton New Mexico.

That on or about the 21st day of February 1878 I made a post mortem examination of John H. Tunstall. I found that there were two wounds in his body, one in the shoulder passing through and fracturing the right clavicle near its center coming out immediately over the superior border of the right scapula passing through in its course the right sub-clavicle artery. This wound would have caused his death in a few minutes and would have been likely to have thrown him from his horse.

It would not have produced immediate insensibility. The other wound entered the head about an inch to the right of the medial line almost on a line with the occipital protuberance and passed out immediately above the border of the right orbit. There was a fracture of the skull extending around the whole circumference from the entrance to the exit of the ball, and a transverse fracture across the middle portion of the base of the skull extending from the line of fracture on one side to that of the other. In my opinion, the skull both on account of its being very thin and from evidence of venereal disease was very likely to be extensively fractured from such a wound and the fracture in this case resulted entirely from said wound. A wound of this kind would cause instantaneous death passing as it did through the most vital portion of the brain.

There were no marks of violence or bruises on the body except the two above wounds – nor was the body or skull mutilated. The cap of the skull was not fractured.

It is my opinion that both of the wounds could be made at one and same time – and if made at the same time were made by different persons from different directions and were both most likely made while Tunstall was on horse back in as much as the direction of the wounds were slightly upward.

There being no powder marks on the body to indicate that the wounds were made at a short distance – and the further fact that the edges of the wounds of exit were not very ragged, I am of the opinion that they were both made by rifles. Powder marks would be shown on the body if the gun or pistol was fired within about six feet of the body.

D. M. Appel
Asst. Surgeon U.S.A.

Read, subscribed & sworn to before me this 1st day of July 1878
Frank Warner Angel

Special Agt
Depts Justice & Interior

William Baker - June 13, 1878

County of Lincoln

William Baker being duly sworn says he is private in Company H 9 Cavalry. That I with other soldiers were put in charge of McSween, Widenmann, Robinson, Shields [Shield] & Washington, and we were instructed by Col. Purington to protect them in every way. That if the Peppin party tried to take them away to shoot them (Peppin party) down and to keep the said prisoners safe.

Sworn to before me this 13 day of June 1878
William Baker (by his X mark)
M. A. Upson
Notary Public

Adolph P. Barrier - June 11, 1878

Territory of New Mexico
County of San Miguel

Before the undersigned clerk of [the] Probate Court within and for the County & Territory aforesaid personally came Adolph P. Barrier who being duly sworn according to law, deposeth and saith that I am, and have been, for nearly three years, a resident of the County & Territory aforesaid. That on the 4th day of January 1878, I was sworn in as Deputy Sheriff and had placed in my charge Alexander A. McSween of Lincoln County N.M. who had been arrested at Las Vegas, by the Sheriff of San Miguel County upon a warrant issued by Warren Bristol, Associate Justice of the Supreme Court, a Judge of the 3rd Judicial Dist. of New Mexico, upon a charge of having Embezzled Ten Thousand Dollars belonging to the Estate of Emil Fritz, dead. Immediately after being sworn in, I together with Antonio Campos, another deputy, started with said McSween to Mesilla N.M. where Judge Bristol resides.

When we reached Lincoln we learned through the *Mesilla Valley Independent* that Judge Bristol was absent from home. We remained at Lincoln a few days. Immediately after learning that the Judge had returned home, I started with said McSween in company with J. H. Tunstall, J. B. Wilson, and D. P. Shield (the said Antonio Campos Deputy having returned to Las Vegas from Lincoln Co.).

We arrived at Mesilla on the 28th day of January 1878 [February 1 is the correct date]. The examination of said McSween was at the residence of said Judge Bristol. I was present during the entire examination and had McSween in my charge. The examination commenced on the 2nd day of Feb. and closed on the 4th. William L. Rynerson, the District Attorney, while said examination was in progress, frequently used insulting language towards said McSween, while he was a prisoner which I regarded as unbecoming in an officer.

At the suggestion of Judge Bristol, the examination was continued to District Court on account of the absence of Juan B. Patron, Florencio Gonzales, two witnesses whom McSween wished subpoenaed. The conduct of Judge Bristol during said examination convinced me that he was very much prejudiced against McSween. After the examination was continued & the amount of bail fixed, the Judge delivered a lecture to McSween, which was very unbecoming and showed himself to be a bitter partisan. He ordered that the bond should be approved by W. L. Rynerson Dist Atty.

On the 5th day of February, the Judge delivered to me an instrument of writing by which I was required to take said McSween to Lincoln and deliver him to the sheriff of said County. On the morning of the 6th of Feb. I started from Mesilla with Mssrs. Tunstall, Wilson & Shield & McSween for Lincoln. We camped that night at San Augustine [Shedd's Ranch].

Shortly after our arrival there, Frank Baker, Jesse Evans, and Long known as outlaws and desperadoes arrived. Baker came to where we were camped and inquired if James J. Dolan was coming out from Las Cruces or Mesilla, said that Dolan was to meet him there that night on business, that he thought that D. would be there. About the middle of the night, Dolan, Charles Fritz & James Longwell arrived there.

The next morning, Dolan & Evans came to our camp both well armed. Dolan wished to fight Tunstall, drew his gun on T. three times. Tunstall said he was not a fighting man, did not get his living that way. Dolan, as he left the camp, said, "Damn you, I'll get you yet you damned coward," or words to that effect as near as I can recollect.

On that afternoon Dolan & party passed us. On the front seat of Dolan's carriage were Frank Baker, Charles Fritz, Dolan & Jesse Evans on the back seat, Longwell & Long on horseback. We camped that night near Whitewater, and in the morning after eating our breakfast, a man came to our camp [and] said he was going to Lincoln, showed us a letter addressed to Riley, a member of the firm of J. J. Dolan & Co. After passing Tularosa, Frank Baker, Tom Hill, another desperado, Long, & the man with the letter to Riley came up with us. They said Evans had gone up ahead with Dolan to the Indian Agency.

At the agency, we learned that Dolan, Evans & the man with the letter to Riley had left the agency on the evening of the 8th for Lincoln. We arrived at Lincoln. On the evening of the 10th of Feb. we found the Sheriff of Lincoln in charge of Mr. Tunstall's store. Also learned that men had laid in wait between Dolwingl's [Dowlin's] Mill & Fort Stanton to kill McSween & Tunstall.

Having noticed the conduct of Dolan at Mesilla, his conduct on the road, and the character of his associates, and knowledge the influence he had with the sheriff and the information then rec'd, I was satisfied that if McSween was turned over to said Sheriff he would be murdered. I then felt it was my duty to remain with him and protect him until his bond could be made. A bond was made in which the sureties justified for more than four times the amount required by the Judge, and sent to Mesilla for the approval of Rynerson the Dist Atty.

After the bond had been forwarded, Mr. Tunstall was killed by the Sheriff's posse as appeared from the evidence at the Coroner's inquest. In a few days after Tunstall's death, I learned that Dolan had gone to Mesilla to obtain a warrant from Judge Bristol to take McSween from my custody and also to have me arrested for failing to turn McSween over to Sheriff Brady.

The [McSween] bond was returned disapproved by Rynerson. In a few days we rec'd reliable information about midnight that Riley (Dolan's partner) had rec'd a letter from Dolan, directing him to have the Military ready to assist Brady in arresting McSween & myself, and that he should have Baker, Evans & Co. ready to do their part, as soon as the Military left, but that he should be careful and not let the Military know [what] they were about.

This we learned about midnight about the last of February. In consequence of said information, I left town that night with McSween to protect & guard him, camping out most of the time until the 29th of March 1878, when learning of the losses in my business, in consequence of my absence from home, I felt it my duty to return here, and intended to return to the Lincoln Court and to make return of the warrant and report all the facts to the District Judge.

Having heard the evidence against McSween, as well as for him, and from what I learned while he was in my custody in regard to his anxiety for a thorough investigation of the charges made against him, I was satisfied that he would not leave or attempt to evade the law, that my action in regard to said McSween was only for the purpose of preserving his life, and not for any pecuniary or personal consideration. That I have no interest in the difficulties & troubles existing in Lincoln County, other than as a citizen of the Territory, & that Justice should be meted out every citizen, without fear, favor, or affection.

Affiant further states that on the 24th day of January, while on the road to Mesilla, about 15 miles north of the Mescalero Apache Indian Agency, we met S. Stanley with a load of goods, supposed to be coffee, sugar, & other articles. Upon inquiring of him as to what he had, he in the Jocular Manner said Hooppoles. [A hooppole is a straight sapling of hickory used to make the hoops of barrels. The usage here means a necesessay or needed thing.]

A. P. Barrier

Sworn to and subscribed before me this 11th day of June A D 1878 and I further certify that said deponent is a credible and reliable witness whose statements are entitled to credit and belief.
Felipe Baca
Clerk of the Probate Court

Robert W. Beckwith - June 17, 1878

Robert W. Beckwith being duly sworn says he was one of the posse of the Sheriff that went from the Pecos [River]. I heard Morton, Evans & Hill say that they saw Tunstall coming towards them and that Morton commanded him to halt & commenced reading the warrant to him. That Tunstall commenced to fire at them & fired two shots one just passing over the neck of Morton's horse, that thereupon they (Evans, Hill & Morton) fired at Tunstall & Tunstall was shot. I was at the horses about the time of the shooting of Tunstall. There were quite a number of shots fired in quick session at least ten shots.

I did not hear any threats used against Tunstall.

R. W. Beckwith
Subscribed and sworn before me this 17 day of June 1878

Frank Warner Angel
Special Agt
Depts Justice & Interior

William H. Bonney, alias Billy the Kid - June 8, 1878

Territory of New Mexico
County of Lincoln

William H. Bonney being duly sworn, deposes and says that he is a resident of said County.

That on the 11th day of February A.D. 1878 he in company with Robt. A. Widenmann and Fred T. Waite went to the ranch of J. H. Tunstall on the Rio Feliz. That he and said Fred T. Waite at the time intended to go to the Rio Penasco to take up a ranch for the purpose of farming.

That the cattle on the ranch of said J. H. Tunstall were throughout the County of Lincoln known to be the property of said Tunstall; that on the 13th of February A.D. 1878 one J. B. Mathews claiming to be a Deputy Sheriff came to the ranch of said J. H. Tunstall in company with Jesse Evans, Frank Baker, Tom Hill and Rivers [Jack Long] (known outlaws who had been confined in the Lincoln County jail and had succeeded in making their escape), John Hurley, George Heinman [Hindman], Roberts and an Indian and Ponceaso [Ponciacho], the latter said to be the murderer of Benito Cruz, for the arrest of the murderers of whom (Benito Cruz) the Governor of the Territory offers a reward of $500.

Before the arrival of said J. B. Mathews, Deputy Sheriff, and his posse, having been informed that said Deputy Sheriff and posse were going to round up all the cattle and drive them off and kill the persons at the ranch, the persons at the ranch cut portholes into the walls of the house and filled sacks with earth, so that they, the persons at the ranch, should they be attacked or their murder attempted, could defend themselves. This course being thought necessary as the sheriff's posse was composed of thieves and murderers, outlaws and desperate characters, none of whom had any interest at stake in the County nor being residents of said County.

That said Mathews when within about 50 yards of the house was called to stop and advance alone and state his business. That said Mathews after arriving at the ranch said that he had come to attach the cattle and property of A. A. McSween. That said Mathews was informed that A. A. McSween had no cattle or property there, but that if he had, he said Mathews could take it. That said Mathews said he thought some of the cattle belonging to R. M. Brewer, whose cattle were also at the ranch of J. H. Tunstall, belonged to A. A. McSween. That said Mathews was told he, Mathews, could round up the cattle and that he, Brewer, would help him.

That said Mathews said that he would go back to Lincoln to get new instructions and if he came back to the ranch he would come back with one man. That said Mathews and his posse were then invited by R. M. Brewer to come to the house and get something to eat.

Deponist [deponent] further says that Robert A. Widenmann told R. N. Brewer and the others at the ranch that he was going to arrest Frank Baker, Jesse Evans, and Tom Hill, said Widenmann having warrants for them. That said Widenmann was told by Brewer and the others at the ranch that the arrest could not be made because if it was made, they, all the persons at the ranch, would be killed and murdered by J. J. Dolan & Co. and their party. That said Evans advanced upon said Widenmann and said Evans swinging his gun and catching it cocked and pointed directly at said Widenmann. That said Jessie Evans asked said Widenmann whether he, Widenmann, was hunting for him, Evans, to which Widenmann answered that if he was looking for him, he Evans would find it out.

Evans also asked Widenmann whether he had a warrant for him; Widenmann answered that that was his (Widenmann's) business. Evans told Widenmann that if he ever came to arrest him (Evans), he, Evans would pick Widenmann as the first man to shoot at, to which Widenmann answered that that was all right, that two could play at that game. That during the talking, Frank Baker stood near said Widenmann, swinging his pistol on his finger, catching it full cocked pointed at said Widenmann.

The persons at the ranch were R. M. Brewer, John Middleton, G. Gauss, McCarty [an unrecognized reference], R. A. Widenmann, Henry Brown, F. T. Waite, Wm. McCloskey, and this deponist.

J. B. Mathews, after eating, started for Lincoln with John Hurley and Ponceano [Ponciacho], the rest of the party or posse saying they were going to the Rio Penasco.

Deponist started for Lincoln with Robt. A. Widenmann and F. T. Waite and arrived at Lincoln the same evening and again left Lincoln on the next day, February the 14th, in company with the above named persons, having heard that said Mathews was going back to the ranch of said J. H. Tunstall with a large party of men to take the cattle and deponist and Widenmann and Waite arrived at said ranch the same day.

Deponist states that on the road to Lincoln he heard said Mathews ask said Widenmann whether any resistance would be ordered if he, Mathews returned to take the cattle, to which said Widenmann answered that no resistance would be offered if the cattle were left at the ranch, but if an attempt was made to drive the cattle to the Indian Agency and kill them for beef as he, said Mathews had been heard to say would be done, he said Widenmann would do all in his power to prevent this.

Deponist further says that on the night of the 17th of February A.D. 1878 J. H. Tunstall arrived at the ranch and informed all the persons there, that reliable information had reached him that J. B. Mathews was gathering a large party of outlaws and desperadoes as a posse and that said posse was coming to the ranch, the Mexicans in the party to gather up the cattle and the balance of the posse to kill the persons at the ranch.

It was therefore decided that all persons at the ranch, excepting G. Gauss, were to leave and Wm. McCloskey was that night sent to the Rio Penasco to inform the posse, who were camped there that they could come over and round up the cattle, count them and leave a man there to take care of them, and that Mr. Tunstall would also leave a man there to help round up and count the cattle and help to take care of them, and said McCloskey was also ordered to go to Martin Martz who had left Tunstall's ranch when deponist, Widenmann and Waite returned to the town of Lincoln on the 13th of February, and ask him said Martin to come to the ranch of said Tunstall and aid the sheriff's posse in rounding up and counting the cattle and to stay at the ranch and take care of the cattle.

Deponist left the ranch of said Tunstall in company with J. H. Tunstall, R. M. Brewer, John Middleton and F. T. Waite, said Tunstall, Widenmann, Brewer, Middleton and deponist driving the loose horses, Waite driving the wagon. Said Waite took the road for Lincoln with the wagon. The rest of the party taking the trail with the horses. Deponist says that all the horses which he and party were driving, excepting 3, had been released by Sheriff Brady at Lincoln. That one of these 3 horses belonged to R. M. Brewer, and another was traded by Brewer to Tunstall for one of the released horses.

Deponist further says, that when he and party had traveled to within about 30 miles from the Rio Ruidoso he and John Middleton were riding in the rear of the balance of the party and just upon reaching the brow of a hill they saw a large party of men coming towards them from the rear at full speed and he and Middleton at once rode forward to inform the rest of the party of the fact. Deponist had not more than barely reached Brewer and Widenmann who were some 200 or 300 yards to the left of the trail when the attacking party cleared the brow of the hill and commenced firing at him, Widenmann and Brewer.

Deponist, Widenmann and Brewer rode over a hill towards another which was covered with large rocks and trees and in order to defend ourselves and make a stand. But the attacking party, undoubtedly seeing Tunstall, left off pursuing deponist and the two with him and turned back to the cañon [canyon] in which the trail was.

Shortly afterwards we hear two or three separate and distinct shots and the remark was then made by Middleton that they, the attacking party, must have killed Tunstall. Middleton had in the meantime joined deponist and Widenmann and Brewer.

Deponist then made the best of his way to Lincoln in company with Robt. A. Widenmann, Brewer, Waite and Middleton, stopping at the Rio Ruidoso [John Newcomb's ranch] in order to get men to look for the body of Tunstall.

Deponist further says that neither he nor any of the party fired off either rifle or pistol and that neither he nor the parties with him fired a shot.

William H. Bonney
Sworn and subscribed to before me this eighth day of June A.D. 1878
John B. Wilson
Justice of the Peace

Henry N. Brown - June 13, 1878

The Territory Of New Mexico
County of Lincoln

Personally appeared Henry Brown who having been duly sworn according to law deposeth and saith he is well acquainted with L. G. Murphy, J. J. Dolan & J. H. Riley, known here as "the house," and have been so for years. That he has worked for them and that they have failed to pay him according to agreement.

I was acquainted with Tunstall in his lifetime. On the 18th of February, A.D. 1878, a few miles from the cattle ranch of said Tunstall, on the Rio Feliz, I saw J. B. Mathews and posse. In that posse with said Mathews I recognized J. J. Dolan, Pantaleon Gallegos, W. Morton, Frank Baker, Jessie Evans, Tom Hill, R. W. Beckwith, Sam Perry, Chas. Marshall, Tom Cochran [Cochrane], A. H. Mills, Tom Moore, Frank Rivers [Jack Long], Geo. Hindman, Bill Williams alias A. L. ["Buckshot"] Roberts, Tom Green & John Hurley.

I talked with Morton and Baker, since killed, near Black Water [Agua Negro]. They said that they were going to kill parties at Tunstall's Ranch; Tunstall and party had left said ranch before this. I traveled a mile with Tunstall and party. They were going, as they informed me, to the town of Lincoln. By Tunstall's party I mean Tunstall, Widenmann, Middleton, Bony [Bonney] and Brewer.

Mathews' posse appeared to be very much excited. Tunstall informed me that he took his men away from the ranch for fear they would be murdered by Mathews & posse, as he had learned that they intended to do so.

I worked with said "House" about sixteen months. I could not help myself, I had to take what they gave me. During that period of time I have often heard the "House" say that they would have Alex. A. McSween killed. In December 1877, speaking of a check of J. J. Dolan & Co. that Tunstall refused to cash, I heard J. J. Dolan say that when the time came and he got ready, he would kill Tunstall.

They hated Tunstall because he was opposed to them in business.

H. Brown (by his X mark)
Witness B. N. Ellis
Subscribed and sworn to before me this 13th day of June 1878
John B. Wilson
Justice of the Peace

Thomas Cochrane, alias Thomas Corcoran - June 17, 1878

County of Dona Ana:

Thomas Cochrane being duly sworn according to law says he was one of the posse that went from the Pecos and who followed after Tunstall's horses. I did not see the shooting of Tunstall. There was at least ten or a dozen shots fired at the time. Morton told me that Tunstall had fired two shots at him & that he, Hill & Evans, fired back & killed him and his horse. I heard nothing about either Morton, Hill or Evans having fired off two loads from Tunstall's pistol. I heard nothing about any one firing at a mark. I never heard Baker, Evans or Hill use any threats against Tunstall. I do not know whether the horses were captured before or after the shooting of Tunstall.

Thomas Cochrane (by his X mark)
Read, subscribed and sworn to before me this 17 day of June 1878
Frank Warner Angel
Special Agent
Depts Justice & Interior

James J. Dolan - June 25, 1878

County of Lincoln

James J. Dolan being duly sworn says he resides at Lincoln and has resided there about four years – and have resided at Fort Stanton for about seven years. I am a merchant and contractor and one of the firm of James J. Dolan & Co. of Lincoln.

The cause of the present troubles in Lincoln County arises out of one A. A. McSween trying to defraud Emil Fritz estate out of a life insurance policy for $10000, or rather the proceeds of said policy.

The existing troubles have not existed before this attempt of A. A. McSween. I know of no other cause at the time of the above attempt which would cause the present trouble in Lincoln County and I believe that this is the only cause of the present trouble.

This was what started the troubles. They (McSween, Tunstall, & John S. Chisum & their employees) afterwards formed a combination to ruin deponent & his partner in business, spread the reports that our checks had been protested, sent untrue reports to commercial agencies at Denver & St. Louis as to our commercial standing stating that we were not worthy of credit. I thereupon, in order to counteract the reports circulated by them as to our checks going to protest, went to Santa Fe and obtained a sworn statement from the Acting Cashier of the 1st National Bank of Santa Fe, with whom we had always deposited our money, swearing that our checks had never up to that time been protested, and returned to Lincoln & showed it to Mr. McSween & he read it. I desire to add the name of Ellis Sons to the combinations of persons against us. W. Dowlin informed Howison (as I am informed by J. H. Riley), traveling Agent of Dodd, Brown & Co., with whom we were dealing, that we were broken up & to be careful of us. He (Howison) informed Riley afterwards that he had applied to one T. B. Catron of Santa Fe who informed him that we were perfectly good and would endorse our notes for ten thousand dollars.

Catron was endorser for us at that time to the amount of about $6000. This occurred about last June – and before we had given a chattel mortgage on our property here to said Catron. Mr. Catron since then has endorsed and advanced to us more than $20000. We gave the chattel mortgage to Catron voluntarily & with out his asking for it.

I was not with Deputy Mathews the first time he went to Tunstall's ranch on the Feliz, but was with the sheriff's posse as one of them the second time that Deputy Mathews went to make the attachment. I joined the posse on the Rio Penasco at Paul's – coming from Lincoln. Deputy Mathews personally summoned me. From Paul's we went to the Rio Feliz.

On our way to the Rio Feliz we met Henry Brown, he did not speak to me nor I to him except to pass the compliments of the day, viz bidding him good day &c. McCloskey came to Paul's [ranch] while the posse were there. He did not speak to me nor I to him.

When we arrived at Tunstall's ranch on the Feliz and while we were there we found Martin (Dutch Martin) and Gauss. When we were going to the said ranch, the deputy believed that we were going to have a fight so the posse was divided into two parties, one going to the front of the house & the other to the rear, until they heard from the deputy. I was with the rear party. We could see the other party come to the house & hearing no shots we also came to the house and found cattle on the ranch. Gauss informed us that the horses and party had left about two hours ago for either Lincoln or Brewer's ranch.

Deputy Mathews then divided his posse, swore in W. S. Morton as deputy & sent him & part of the posse after the horses. Deputy Mathews selected the men that were to go with Morton. He called each man by name that was to go with Morton. He kept the list of the names of the persons he sent, or rather he had a list of the persons who composed the whole posse & he put a check opposite the name of the person he sent with Morton. I was not one of the men that was either selected or went with Morton. I remained in camp near the house on the Feliz until the return of Morton after the death of Tunstall.

I was about the first person Morton spoke to on his return. He said that Tunstall had resisted and fired two shots at him (Morton). Tunstall was called to throw up his hands & he would not be hurt, but that Tunstall fired two shots at him and that he thereupon returned the fire, shooting him in the breast. He said he was sorry for it & had rather had it been any other person of the party (meaning Tunstall's party). He said nothing about any one being with him at the time of shooting – or that any more shots had been fired at Tunstall. This was all he told me.

I brought the attachment papers against McSween's property at the suit of Charles Fritz & Emile [Emilie] Scholand from Mesilla & delivered it to Sheriff Brady. I left Mesilla on the 5th of February 1878. At San Augustine [Shedd's Ranch] on my way, I heard that McSween, Tunstall, Barrier, Shields [Shield] & Wilson were there. I went to their camp the next morning. I went to see Tunstall. I heard about a letter he had <u>written</u> to the *[Mesilla Valey] Independent*. It was untruthful & as to his attempt to injure us and these facts made me very angry. I was armed. I talked to Mr. Tunstall in a very severe manner. He acted in a very childish manner & I tried in every way to see if he was a man. He made no resistance although he was armed.

I did not drop my carbine on him, I threw it over my shoulder with the butt towards him. I told him that I was ready to give him any satisfaction he wanted. I made no threats against him. I never said that when you write to the *Independent* say I am with the "boys" or any words to that effect. I did not say I won't shoot you now but I will get you soon nor any words to that effect, any any [sic] ascertains to the contrary by anyone are absolutely false & untrue. I went there to take no advantage of him – my gun was neither loaded or cocked nor did I sneak up to him.

I wanted him to stop his lying statements about me or stand accountable for his ascertains to me personally. That was the only object I had in going to see him. Jessie Evans was standing at the corner of the stable near McSween's party camp. He evidently saw that I was excited and followed after me. He did not follow me by my request either directly or indirectly. I had no appointment or engagement with either Baker, Evans or Rivers [Long] to meet me at San Augustine or any where on the road, and any ascertains made by them is absolutely false and untrue.

The way Evans came to be riding with me in the ambulance from San Augustine was as follows. Evans could not ride in a saddle on account of his being wounded. I am not positive whether I asked him or he me, at any rate I allowed him out of charity to ride with me in the ambulance. Baker & Rivers [Long] followed behind us horseback. I must confess that I was afraid that I would be killed on the road and I did not object to their following after us for that reason. At White Water I left Fritz, Longwell, Rivers & Evans & went on to Tularosa on horseback, insisting on going alone but not with standing Baker rode with me as far as Tularosa, where he left me and I went on alone to the Indian Agency [at Blazer's Mill] where I obtained conveyance and reached Lincoln.

I never made use of any expression either directly or indirectly that I wished he (Tunstall) was killed or out of the way – on the contrary I have treated him kindly up to the time this trouble commenced.

I did write a letter to Chas Fritz, knowing that he was in the habit of getting intoxicated, not to make any settlement with McSween before first consulting his lawyers. I never threatened him either directly or indirectly as to the same. I did this out of friendship to Fritz & his sister [Emilie Scholand], and for the further fact, in as much as the matter was in the hands of the court, if a settlement was made by Fritz, it might prejudice us in court in matters arising out of the same transactions that we had had with McSween.

I did not know that Evans, Baker, Hill & Rivers were trying to escape from the jail at Lincoln. I neither aided them or assisted them in any way to escape and any ascertains to the contrary are absolutely false and untrue.

In relation to the Fritz estate, the papers are in the exclusive charge of Judge [Simon B.] Newcomb at Mesilla & W. T. Thornton at Santa Fe, and they have all the papers in relation thereto. I could give no detailed statement for this reason. I could say that deponent & his partners have paid about $30000 of the indebtedness of the old firm of L. G. Murphy & Co., composed of L. G. Murphy & E. Fritz, deceased. I was book-keeper for the said firm of L. G. Murphy & Co. & examined them about the time of the death of said Fritz and at that time said firm was insolvent.

Deponent further says that as to the alleged $23000 found by the commissioners, A. A. McSween, J. B. Patron and F. G. Christie, that amount was found by reason of said commissioners taking the good & bad debts into account & making no deduction for bad debts and refusing to allow said Murphy credit for about $57000 which he said Murphy had paid individually on account of said estate.

About the 1st of December 1877 I had a conversation with A. A. McSween as to the Fritz estate and the money collected on the policy. I told him that I was desirous of having the estate matter settled up & requested him to call a special session of the Probate Court if it was possible & he said it was, & that he would.

He however kept putting it off from time to time until I saw Judge Gonzales the Probate Judge who called a special session of the court for I think the 10th of December 1877. On that day I attended. Mr. Fritz the Administrator, Sheriff Brady, D. P. Shields [Shield], F. G. Christie & R. Gutierrez were present. McSween was sent for & he came & said he was ready to pay over the money if Mrs. Scholand the co-administratrix with Chas. Fritz was present. I & others informed him that the parties were very much troubled about the situation & wanted the money and requested him in order to quiet every one to deposit the money with the court subject to the order of the court. This he refused to do.

The result was that the court adjourned till 1st Monday in January 1878 at which time Mrs. Scholand was to be present, she being notified by the clerk of the court & the money paid over. McSween was to be present and turn over the money – he made no objection nor did he say that he was going away or could not be present.

That before the meeting of the court said McSween left for St. Louis as every one believed never to come back. That I went to Mesilla & communicated the facts to Mrs. Scholand and whereupon McSween was arrested at Las Vegas and brought back to Mesilla on the charge of embezzlement.

The only interest I had in this money was to have the court decide to whom it belonged, whether it belonged to us or whether the estate should keep it.

Deponent further says that his interest in said money arose out of the fact that L. G. Murphy & Co. had a claim against the estate. There has never been any suit or legal proceedings had in said claim – and I am informed that Charles Fritz refused to recognize it. This was the only claim I had against the estate. I desire to say that as to legal proceedings having been instituted, I testify only as to my own knowledge. I do not know whether L. G. Murphy ever instructed any proceedings on said claim or not. The amount of our claim I think amounted to about $57000.

Deponent further says that the way that he came to go to Mesilla was that directly after meeting McSween on or about the 10th of December 1877 before the Probate Judge as mentioned herein before, he became suspicious of McSween and believed that he never intended to pay the said insurance money over.

That the only object deponent had in going to Mesilla was to obtain legal advice and have counsel represent him before the Probate Judge at Lincoln on the 3d Monday of January 1878. That while at Mesilla word was brought to deponent from Lincoln by James J. Longwill [Longwell] that McSween had left for St. Louis as afore mentioned with the intention of never returning. That deponent did not go expressly from Lincoln to Mesilla to communicate with Mrs. Scholand, but to obtain counsel as mentioned afore-said. I do not remember whether I called on her before I received the information of McSween's leaving, or whether I called on her after I had received the information.

Jas. J. Dolan
Read, subscribed and sworn to before me this 25th day of June 1878
Frank Warner Angel
Special Agent
Departments of Justice & Interior

Thomas F. Frederick - June 13, 1878

County of Lincoln

Thomas F. Frederick being duly sworn says he is a Sergeant in Company H 9th Cavalry. That he had heard read the foregoing affidavit of Sergeant Lust [page 148] & that the same is true to the best of deponent's information and that so far as the same state the circumstances of the search by Deputy Sheriff Peppin of the McSween's house after the arrest of said McSween, and the statements made at that time by Col. Purington to Peppin & McSween and the conversations had, and words used, the same is true to deponent's knowledge.

Thomas F. Frederick
Sergt Co. H 9 Cav
Sworn to before me this 13 day of June 1878
M. A. Upson
Notary Public

Pantaleón Gallegos - May 14, 1878

Territory of New Mexico
County of Santa Fe

Pantaleon Gallegos being duly sworn says that he was with the sheriff's posse at the time of the death of Tunstall.

I went to Tunstall's ranch with the posse. We there made a levy on some cattle, but found no horses.

Deputy Mathews and Mr. Dorlan [Dolan], A. H. Mills, Thomas Moore, Andrew Roberts, E. H. Wakefield, Pablo Pino Y Pino, Juan Andres Silva, Felipe Mes, Pablo Pino Y Pino's son, I do not now recall any others were left with the cattle and Wm. S. Morton, your deponent, Geo. Hindman, John Hurley, Tom Cochrane, R. W. Beckwith, Geo. W. Kitt, Thomas Green, Ramon Montoya, Juan Segovia, Wallace Olinger, Charles Krelling [Kruling] ("Dutch Charley"), and Charles Marshall – Frank Baker & Jessie Evans following behind – started off for Tunstall who had gone off with the horses, as we were informed by Martin & Gauss, who were in charge of the cattle at the time of the levy.

We rode about thirty miles before we came up to Tunstall and his party with the horses. Morton was ahead and the rest of us were riding behind as near as possible. There was only a trail through the mountains and it would not permit of our riding close together.

Billy Morton and I first saw a man ahead riding a grey horse [Billy], who upon seeing us called out to the men driving the horses ahead of him. It was too far to distinguish what he said. Thereupon Tunstall and his men left the horses [and] run and scattered. Morton and John Hurley followed after them. Myself, Robert Beckwith, "Kitt," and Thomas Green went after the horses. I do not now remember sufficiently to name any other persons that were with either me or Morton.

The next thing that occurred was my hearing shots fired in quick succession. I did not see the shooting, because it took place in the bushes. It was all over in a moment. There might have been others with me or Morton. There was so much excitement at the time that I cannot tell exactly who was with me or who was with Morton.

Afterwards Morton returned and said that a man had been shot and killed. I asked who. He said Tunstall. I asked how it occurred. He said I rode after Tunstall calling to him to halt and waiving at him the attachment. Suddenly Tunstall wheeled his horse around and came towards me (Morton) on a jog trot with his hand on his revolver. I (Morton) asked him to halt, again, as I (Morton) desired to serve a writ and to throw up his hands and he would not be hurt. In place of which he Tunstall pulled out his "six shooter" and fired at me (Morton), whereupon I (Morton) and those with me returned the fire.

The rest of Tunstall's party were not near him at the time [he was] shot. Tunstall was shot about one hundred yards off the trail, just upon the top of the hill. Morton was going North west at the time of the shooting. That about the time that Tunstall fell, his (Tunstall's) horse fell too.

All this was told me by Morton. Hurley at the same time, told me and the rest of our party the same story, and the above was told deponent immediately after the shooting – not over five or ten minutes thereafter.

Deponent further says that he desires to explain how Baker and Evans appears to have been part of our posse. At the Rio Penasco we met Baker & Evans for the first time and afterwards at Rio Feliz [at] a cow camp of Tunstall's. I heard Billy Morton tell them that he did not want them along and that they could not go with the posse. Then Jesse said, we are not going with you, we are here for our own business, we are after our horses which had been loaned to "Kid Antrim" (Wm. H. Antrim). They tell us that they have been taken away by Tunstall with the other horses – they continued to follow behind us although told not to and were not part of our posse.

Deponent further says that at Tunstall's ranch I saw said boys before the doors of the house and port holes cut between the logs. The said bags looked new and the port holes looked as though they had been recently cut.

We had been informed that Tunstall intended to resist and fight. We never received word to my knowledge that Tunstall did not intend to resist and fight. We expected that there would be resistance and Tunstall was killed while trying to run his horses off so that they could not be levied upon & and was shot after he had attempted the life of the person trying to serve the writ, as deponent is informed by said Morton and verily believes.

Pantaleón Gallegos
Subscribed & sworn before me this 14th day of April [May] 1878
W. W. Griffin
U.S. Commissioner

County of Lincoln

Pantaleon Gallegos being duly sworn says he desired to correct the above affidavit so far as the same states or conveys the idea that John Hurley was present at the immediate time of the shooting.

Deponent does not know whether he was there or not. He was part of the posse & Morton did not tell that Hurley was present with him at the immediate shooting of Tunstall.

Pantaleón Gallegos
Read, subscribed & sworn to before me this 26th day of June 1878
Frank Warner Angel
Special Agent
Departments of Justice & Interior

John C. Galvin - June 17, 1878

Territory of New Mexico
Dona An County

Personally appeared before me John Galvin who being duly sworn deposes and says, that on the 1st day of April 1878 I was one of Deputy Sheriff Geo. W. Peppin's posse, who arrested R. A. Widenman [Widenmann], A. A. McSween, D. P. Shields [sic], Geo. S. Robinson & Geo. Washington. That Deputy Sheriff Peppin arrested all these parties at Lincoln, Lincoln Co. New Mexico. I was present all the time that Col. Purington was at Lincoln at this time. At the time of the search of McSween's house, I heard Col. Purington say to Peppin and to all persons present, he said it so that all could hear, that whatever Peppin did, he (Peppin) did on his own responsibility. There was no doors or locks broken in the search, nor was there any property taken or disturbed except some arms and ammunition.

I did not hear Col. Purington use any language unbecoming a gentleman and officer, nor did he insult any one or use insulting language to any one. I did hear an Englishman named Levison [Leverson] harangue the soldiers telling them that they would get into trouble &c.

Deponent further says that the afore mentioned persons refused to surrender themselves unless they had the protection of Col. Purington and his soldiers. I heard Col. Purington request Deputy Sheriff Peppin to allow him to take them to the Fort. Col. Purington agreeing to be responsible for their appearance before the Court.

Deponent further says that R. W. Widenman [Widenmann] was not arrested by the order of Col. Purington nor was any of the afore mentioned persons.

John Galvin
Sworn to and subscribed before me this 17th day of June 1878.
G. W. Smith
2d Lt 9 Cav
I certify that Para 1031 RAR 1863 has been complied with.
Geo. A. Purington
Captain 9th Cavalry

Godfrey Gauss - June 6, 1878

Territory of New Mexico
County of Lincoln

Godfrey Gauss being duly sworn says that he has been in the employ of J. H. Tunstall & now is working for his estate. I was at the cattle ranch of Tunstall when the sheriff's posse came to it for the first time.

The posse was composed of Billy Mathews, George Hindman, John Hurley, Jessie Evans, Frank Baker, Jack Long alias "Rivers," George Davis & O. L. ["Buckshot"] Roberts. There was at the Ranch with me, R. A. Widenmann, R. M. Brewer, John Middleton, William Boney [Bonney], F. T. Waite, & McCloskey.

As the posse approached, Mr. Widenmann went out and called on them to stop and for Mathews to come over alone, which he did and commenced reading a paper & said he came to attach McSween's property.

It was reported by Alex Rudder that the posse was agoing to kill us, and that is the reason why we did not want them to come up and I believed this because Evans, Baker, Hill & Davis, who were notorious thieves and murderers, were with them.

I remember that Martin Martz was with me also at the ranch & left when the posse did.

We replied that they might attach any cattle here that belonged to McSween, but that there was none here.

Mathews then replied that I shall have to go to Lincoln for further instructions if that was the case. I then gave them something to eat. Mathews told us that when he returned he would bring back only one man. They then left.

While they were there, Evans asked and wanted to know if Widenmann was going to arrest him. Widenmann said that is my business.

Widenmann told Dick (meaning Brewer) in my hearing that he had warrants against them and that he wanted to arrest them, but Dick said not to do it, for if he did we would all surely be killed. Widenmann did not arrest them.

Alex Rudder was sent over by Brewer to the Penasco to get a load of corn and when he returned he said he had been taken prisoner by the Sheriff's posse on the Penasco and that they told him that they were waiting for reinforcements from the Pecos and that as soon as they arrived they were coming to "round us up." Afterwards they let him go and he told us that if we remained we would be killed.

On the 17 of February 1878 Mr. Tunstall came to the Ranch. He told Widenmann that there must be no blood shed. We must not remain. Let them attach what cattle they please. We will leave Gauss here. He is an old man and they won't touch him.

On the next morning after breakfast, Mr. Tunstall, Widenmann, Brewer, Henry Brown, Waite, Middleton, & Bonney, there was no one left but me, started with all the horses six or eight in number for Lincoln.

On the night of 17th Mr. Tunstall sent McCloskey over to the Penasco to get Martin Mertz to come over to the ranch to help turn over the cattle to the Sheriff's posse. The Sheriff had been informed by Martin that the levy was made against his (Tunstall's) consent, but there would be no resistance.

On the 18th of February Billy Mathews came up to the ranch and asked where was Brewer & the rest of the party? I told them they had all left this morning. There was a large party with him (Mathews). I should judge at least 30. I gave them something to eat, or rather they helped themselves to what they wanted.

Mathews then said to me why did not someone remain to turn over the property? I said that Mertz would be here to do that. They commenced to shoeing their horses out of Tunstall's property. Three or four horses were shod. Mathews said if only Jimmy (meaning Dolan) was here – I have a notion to send after them and bring them back.

I do not know whether they sent for Dolan or whether he came of his own accord. He came about this time and he picked out the men to follow after Tunstall's party, to bring them back if they caught them before they reached the [Lincoln] Plaza. From this action, I thought that some of the party of Tunstall's would be killed. I heard, I think it was Morton, cry out, "Hurry up boys, my knife is sharp and I feel like scalping some one." They were all excited and seemed as though they were agoing to kill some one.

The party that remained went into camp about 300 hundred from the house. I cannot tell who was there. I did see Mathews & Mills. I did not see Dolan. Dolan did not sleep in the house that night, I am sure of it, there were two or three who slept in the house. I only know one of them, Charley Wolf who slept in the house.

P. Gallegos started to make a list of the posse and started to put down the parties who were with them and had started to write Davis's name when Mathews stopped him and said don't put them "boys" down at all, meaning Baker, Evans, Hill & Davis.

Some of the posse who remained rounded up the cattle – and the rest of the afore mentioned party started after Tunstall & his party.

I heard no one object to Baker, Evans, Hill & Davis going with the party.

I am positive that Mathews and Dolan picked out the men. They would say, "you go" "you go" and so on, pointing out each person and these persons commenced to examine their arms & horses. I saw Baker, Evans, Hill & Davis at this time getting ready with the rest of the party. I heard no one make any objections to their going. I was in the shanty cooking. They might have objected to their going. I did not hear them. I was in and out of the house, the door was open all the time and the party were coming in and out of the house shouting a great deal.

During the night the party who went after Tunstall returned and the next morning I heard that Tunstall had been killed. Baker told me, he gave me no particulars.

I know L. G. Murphy. He has treated me very badly. I hired his brewery for a year. I wrote him that I wanted it in writing. He wrote me that as long as I held to my bargain he would to his. I thereon commenced the business of brewing and had been there about two months and at that time I had 400 gallons of beer ready when Murphy sent Dolan & Mathews with arms and told me that I must leave, claiming that he had sold the brewery.

I was forced to leave and sell him my beer at forty cents a gallon. It was worth then seventy five cents per gallon. I could not take the beer away because I had nothing to put it in, and that he well knew that I could not take it away. And told me to come down & settle, my account was made out & then they owed me $160 and they not having the money, the next day thereafter they made me another statement in which they owed me only about $28. I do not think that they had sold the brewery, and I believe that it still belongs to them.

This is only a sample of the way they did business through out the county – and they would fix up their account to suit themselves.

When I went to any one for advice, they always told me you can't do any thing against that Murphy gang. That as long as any one sticks to the Murphy crowd, they were all right, but as soon as they left that gang then to look out.

G. Gauss
Read, subscribed and sworn to before me this 6th day of June 1878
Frank Warner Angel
Spe Agt.
Depts Justice & Interior

Florencio Gonzales - June 8, 1878

The Territory of New Mexico
County of Lincoln

Personally appeared before me the undersigned authority Florencio Gonsales [Gonzales], who, having been duly sworn according to law, deposes and saith: I have resided in the County of Lincoln since A.D. 1863. I am Probate Judge of said County and have filled that position since [the] 1875 election: I am well acquainted with L. G. Murphy, J. J. Dolan & J. H. Riley and have been so for the time they have done business in said County.

In 1867 I settled upon and improved a piece of Public Land, unsurveyed, about eight miles from the town of Lincoln, in said County and after remaining thereon and improving it for three years, I was obliged through law of said Murphy to abandon it in favor of said Murphy. Murphy's power in the County was absolute. It was almost impossible for any one who did not do his bidding and aid him in his corruption to live in said County, as he and those allied with him in business had absolute sway, and those who did not do as they bid, were kept so poor that they could not do anything, and if they undertook to oppose L. G. Murphy & Co., they were either killed or run out of the County.

Untold suffering has been endured by the people of this County at the hands of this firm, they being the only or principal merchants in the County. The people were obliged to submit, obliged to patronize them, obliged to buy goods of them at exorbitant prices and terms on their produce at Fort Stanton at prices to suit said L. G. Murphy & Co., who had a monopoly of contracts, military & Indians.

That for the past few years the power of said L .G. Murphy & Co. was visibly declining. Strangers were settling in the County and the oppression of L. G. Murphy & Co. had become so heedful opposed that the people for the past two or three years began to show a disposition to withstand the tyranny of L. G. Murphy & Co.

That in 1873 what is known here as the Horrell war broke out and was maintained by and with the connivance of said L. G. Murphy & Co. and Sheriff Brady deceased, such war being considered a war between Mexicans and Americans owing to the attitude of said L. G. Murphy & Co. and Sheriff Brady aforesaid, they having taken a collusive stand against the Mexicans and in favor of said Horrells, who has killed some Mexicans whilst seeking to serve the orders of Courts as Constables.

That after the shedding of much blood, said Horrells left this County and said L. G. Murphy & Co. repeated their reward by buying a large number of cattle at low figures from said Horrells and otherwise taking possession of Government land occupied by said Horrells.

That from this time last mentioned their power, influence and authority began to decline and culminated in the murder of John H. Tunstall, late of said County.

That as a sample of the oppression of said L. G. Murphy & Co., I cite the fact that if a farmer undertook to keep his corn from them unless he got a fair price for it, they would send to other Counties for corn paying a higher price then that asked in this County for the purpose of teaching a lesson to parties disposed to throw off their yoke, and that in this way deponent virtually lost about 800 fanegas (140 lbs each) in one season.

That on or about the month of November, 1876, John H. Tunstall came to the town of Lincoln and shortly afterwards located there and began substantial improvements by acquiring land for [a] stock ranch, purchasing stock, building, opening a store &c, to the great benefit of said County and people generally.

That said Mr. Tunstall had the reputation of being a man of means who could command all the capital he would require. That from what I know of Murphy, Dolan & Riley, their past and present history and their way of doing business, and their determination to put opposition or competition down, that their power of extorting from farmers might continue, and what I know of Mr. Tunstall and his ways of doing business with the people, I have no doubt that the murder of John H. Tunstall was premeditated and designed by L. G. Murphy, J. J. Dolan and J. H. Riley, commonly known as "The House" and carried out by their tools.

Among many other things which induces me to this conviction, I will mention that the posse who murdered him and the deputy who was in charge of them were the employees of said "House", men of low reputations and without any interests in this County.

That after the murder of said John H. Tunstall, to wit, on the 19th of Feby 1878, I, in company with John Newcomb, Patricio Trujillo, Lazar Gallegos and Roman Barragon [Barregon], went in search of the body of said John H. Tunstall, having been previously informed that he was murdered by sheriff Brady's posse on the 18th Feby, 1878, and found the same about ten miles from the town of San Patricio in the said County of Lincoln.

We found said John H. Tunstall dead, laying closely by the side of his horse. The corpse had evidently been carried by some persons and laid in the position in which we found it. A blanket was found under the corpse and one over it. Tunstall's overcoat was placed under his head and his hat placed under the head of his dear horse. By the apparent naturalness of the scene, we were forced to the conclusion that the murderers of Mr. Tunstall, his dear horse and himself in the position indicated considering the whole affair a burlesque.

It has been claimed that Mr. Tunstall fired upon the posse and had some horses they wished to attach and that he fired two shots at them out of a Colts Improved Revolver. We found his revolver quite close to the scabbard on the corpse. It must have been placed there by some one after Tunstall's death. We found two chambers empty, but there were no hulls or catridge [cartridge] shells in the empty chambers – the other four chambers had catridge [cartridges] in them.

On examination [of Tunstall's body] we found the skull broken. We found that a rifle or carbine bullet had entered his breast and a pistol bullet entered the back of his head coming out in the forehead.

The corpse of Mr. Tunstall was found over 100 yards off the trail on which the horses traveled – in advance of those said to have been driven by Mr. Tunstall, showing clearly by fresh horse tracks which were seen by us distinctly and plainly that the horses the posse claim to have been trying to recover from Mr. Tunstall must have been quite a distance behind Mr. Tunstall and must have been passed by the posse before they could get Mr. Tunstall.

By John Newcomb aforesaid, the corpse of Mr. Tunstall was taken to the town of Lincoln agreeable to the instructions of Alex. A. McSween, so am informed and believe. I subsequently saw the dead body of said Mr. Tunstall at the house occupied by said Alex. A. McSween in said town of Lincoln and saw said corpse whilst a post mortem examination thereof was made by Drs. Ealy and Appel and the same embalmed.

I attended the burial of said J. H. Tunstall in said town of Lincoln on the 23rd day of Feby, 1878. On the last mentioned day, after said burial, a meeting of citizens of said County was held at the town of Lincoln to prevent the shedding of blood if possible. That I, with John Newcomb aforesaid and Isaac Ellis, merchant, and Jose Montaño, merchant of said town, was one of a committee, composed as aforesaid, to wit upon the late Sheriff Brady and ascertain from him why he had taken as prisoners, without warrant, complaint or authority of law, the constable Atanacio Martinez and his posse W. Bonny [Bonney] & Fred T. Waite who went to the house of said Murphy, Dolan & Riley to arrest the alleged murderers of said Tunstall where said Brady was with several of [the] alleged murderers of said Tunstall and prevented them from arresting such murderers. Brady replied in substance that he kept them prisoners because he had the power.

Said Committee offered to give him bonds in double the value of the property attached by said Sheriff as that of said Alex. A. McSween. That such property would be forthcoming to answer the degree of the Court that issued the writ of attachment, and for that purpose requested him to appraise and set a value upon such property that such bond would be approved by said Sheriff and if he failed to so approve he could do as he pleased with the property.

Said Sheriff refused to take bond as aforesaid. In the month of March, 1878, I was informed by Sheriff Brady, and issued by him, that no matter how many alias warrants he had against McSween aforesaid he would not undertake to serve them. I believe that the only thing that saved the life of said McSween was that he was not delivered into the custody of said Sheriff Brady, notwithstanding any guarantees by said Brady as it was notorious and known of all men who cared to inform themselves, that said Brady was a tool for "the House."

Deponent further says, that in the month of July 1876 he was invited to attend a meeting to organize a Vigilance Committee for the purpose of putting down horse stealing and that he declined to do so. That he afterwards learned and now believe that that steps was [sic] taken by "The House" aforesaid for the ostensible purpose of putting down horse stealing, but really for the murder of citizens obnoxious to them in business.

That said "House" for years have had the reputation of surrounding themselves with bad characters for the purpose of carrying out their schemes. That they have the reputation of receiving stolen cattle to fill their Government contracts. That during the month February, A.D. 1878, I and Stephen Stanley pass [passed] through the town of San Patricio in said County, that I asked said Stanley what he had in his wagon, whereupon he informed me that it was loaded with coffee taken by him from the Indian Agency at Blazer's Mill for Murphy, Dolan & Riley at Lincoln. It was. That so far as I think the present troubles are the result of the treatment of the people of this Co. by said "House."

During the month of April 1878, I had a conversation with Alexander H. Mills who was of the posse who murdered Tunstall. He informed me during that conversation that he told J. J. Dolan that the murder of Tunstall was a bad thing and would cause the people to raise up against "The House." Said A. H. Mills states that he was not present at the murder of Tunstall being then on the Feliz, but that those who were informed him that when Tunstall saw the posse, he appeared to be excited and act as if he would fall off his horse though riding a good horse. That Morton, deceased, informed him, the said Mills, that he with [a] portion of posse called to Tunstall to come up to them and that Tunstall sang out "yes yes!" That he walked up to them and that some one then fired at him, the ball taking effect in Tunstall's breast. That as he fell some one shot him in the head and then broke his skull, and then killed his horse lying both as deponent elsewhere describes. That then they took Tunstall's pistol and fired two shots out of it and threw it away, and that then some one placed it as found by deponent.

Florencio Gonzales
Sworn to and subscribed before me this 8th day of June, 1878
John B. Wilson
Justice of the Peace
Precinct No. 1, Lincoln Co. N.M.

Millard F. Goodwin - First Statement - Purington Exhibit E - June 24, 1878

County of Lincoln
Territory of New Mexico

Personally appeared before me the undersigned authority, M. F. Goodwin 2nd Lieut Ninth Cavalry who being duly sworn according to law deposes as follows. That on or about the 20th day of February 1878 he with Lieut B. S. Humphries [Humphreys] 9th Cavalry with 30 enlisted men was ordered to report to Deputy U.S. Marshall R. A. Widenmann as a posse to arrest Jessie Evans, Frank Baker, Hill, Davis and others.

Deputy Marshall Widenmann told deponent that these men were in the house occupied by the firm of Dolan & Riley, said house was searched without finding the above named persons and the store and bank of A. A. McSween was searched with same result. From all information received, the men had not been there. In searching both places, Citizens came in with the soldiers and served civil writs on the occupants of the buildings and arrested them. Deponent spoke to said Widenmann and told him he did not think it right to use the troops for the purpose of allowing these people to serve their writs. Widenmann said he was sorry for it and regretted that it had occurred.

While deponent was still present with the troops, writs were attempted to be served on the sheriff of the County, Sheriff Brady, and others. Said writs were resisted and the constable who attempted to serve them told the deponent that he did not wish to serve them, but was told by Antrim "Kid" and others at McSween's house if he did not serve them, they would kill him.

Said Widenmann asked deponent if he would not leave the town and allow the two parties to fight it out, the sheriffs party on one side and Widenmann and the men at McSween's house on the other, which deponent refused to do. Then said Widenmann asked deponent if an attempt was made to arrest the sheriff and others in Dolan & Riley's house if he would interfere, saying he would burn down the house if necessary. Deponent told him he most certainly would not interfere with any civil authorities, but that he considered it would be a mob and that blood would be shed and under the circumstances he would be obliged to post troops between the two parties, which he did.

Deponent firmly believes that the only purpose the troops were asked for and used by Deputy Marshall Widenmann was to obtain entrance in the house of Dolan & Riley and the store of McSween [then] in possession of the sheriff – Brady. Mr. John H. Riley reported to me, deponent, that articles of jewelry were stolen from the bureau in his bedroom by either some of the Deputy Marshal's posse or other citizens who were in the building serving writs.

Deponent further states that the facts stated in this affidavit were reported by him officially to the Commanding officer of Fort Stanton N.M., Capt Geo. A. Purington 9th Cavy and that Lieut B. S. Humphries [Humphreys] who was second in command to deponent can be called on to corroborate this statement.

M. F. [Goodwin] (signed)
2d Lieut 9th Cav
Sworn to and subscribed before me this 24 day of June 1878
Thos. Blair (signed)
Capt 15th Infy
Judge Advocate Gen. C.M.
I certify that Par 1031 R.A.R. has been complied with
Geo. A. Purington
Capt. 9th Cavy
A True Copy
G. W. Smith
2d Lt 9 Cav

Millard F. Goodwin - Second Statement - June 24, 1878

Personally appeared before me the undersigned authority, M. F. Goodwin 2nd Lieut. 9th Cavalry who being duly sworn according to law deposes as follows. That on or about May 6, 1878, he was ordered to report to Sheriff Jno. Copeland of Lincoln Co. N.M. with Lt. Smith 9th Cavalry and twenty-five men as a posse to arrest several parties at San Patricio N.M. Arriving at San Patricio the people were found but owing to the failure of the Sheriff to perform his duty and make the arrests, he was obliged to notify said Sheriff that if he did not arrest the parties inside of five minutes he would return with his posse to Fort Stanton N. M.

The arrests were made except in the case of A. A. McSween. The said sheriff did not think it necessary to arrest him. The deponent then told the sheriff that he had shown the deponent a writ for said McSween, and he the Sheriff would not be doing his duty if he arrested the others & not McSween, who was then arrested. Deponent then spoke to McSween and asked him what had become of Antrim, Bowdray [Bowdre], Middleton, and others (accused of murder). McSween said he had not seen them. Deponent told him he had seen them, deponent having been informed that he had been with them and paid for their dinners at Dow's Store, San Patricio. McSween then accused deponent of grossly insulting him. This about 11:30 P.M. May 6.

When starting to return to Fort Stanton, McSween told deponent that he was afraid of being killed on the road. Deponent assured him that all the posse would defend him. Deponent told the sheriff he did not think it would be best to go beyond Fritz's Ranche, 18 miles from Ft Stanton that night. The Sheriff was of the same opinion. The night was dark that the road could only be seen a few paces ahead and the driver of the wagon in which McSween was sitting, and the Sheriff lying in the bottom, did.

The deponent does not know by whose orders [sic] pass Fritz's Ranche.

As soon as it was discovered, the deponent told the driver to turn around and go back to the Ranche. The Sheriff told the driver that he would be responsible for the persons, to keep on. Owing to the fact that it was a dark night and McSween having told the deponent that he was afraid of being killed on the road, the deponent could not allow him to proceed, as he felt he was responsible for the safety of both Sheriff and prisoner.

Sheriff told deponent next morning that what he did was exactly right. Sheriff was newly appointed and did not know his duty, and in deponent's opinion did not have the necessary intelligence to carry it out, if he had known what it was.

Deponent considers he would have been highly culpable to ride the road on a dark night knowing there were armed bands of men in the Country and the road he was traveling being well adapted to waylay and ambush a party, and then being no necessity for traveling by night.

Deponent further says that no insult of any kinds was was offered to said McSween, in his presence or hearing, nor would he have permitted it.

M. F.
2d Lieut 9th Cavalry
Sworn to and signature acknowledged before me this 24th day of June 1878.
Thos. Blair
Captain 15th Infantry
Judge Advocate Gen C M

Albert H. Howe - May 22, 1878

Territory of New Mexico
County of Lincoln

Albert H. Howe being duly sworn says he resides in the aforesaid Territory and County.

That some time ago he had a conversation with Geo. B. Kitt as to the death of Tunstall. That said Kitt told deponent that he was with the sheriff's posse at the time of the killing of Tunstall and was a member of said posse. That he went to Tunstall's ranch on the Rio Feliz. When the levy on the property there was first attempted, that at first Tunstall said he had no objection to their making a levy, that thereupon one Widerman [Widenmann] who was with Tunstall interfered and said that if we wished to make a levy we would have to fight for it.

That we not feeling strong enough returned to Lincoln and obtained a large posse and returned to Tunstall's ranch and found the cattle there but that Tunstall had left with his party and all the horses. That they started after them to obtain the horses.

That he did not see the shooting but was informed how Tunstall was killed by the boys. That Tunstall was some distance off from the road, and when he found that he had been deserted by his party. He turned and rode towards Hill & Morton. That when he came in sight of them, he seemed very much surprised and hesitated. That Hill called to him to come up and that he would not be hurt at the same time both Hill & Morton threw up their guns, resting the stocks on their knees. That after Tunstall came nearer, Morton fired and shot Tunstall through the breast and then Hill fired & shot Tunstall through the head. Someone else fired and wounded or killed Tunstall's horse at the time Tunstall was shot through the head by Hill. That two barrels of Tunstall's revolver were emptied after he was killed. That Tunstall fired no shots and that Tunstall was killed in cold blood.

That deponent knows said Hill and considered him a desperate man who would kill a man on sight that he had any dispute with or spite against.

Deponent further says that he knows or had heard that Tunstall had some horses stolen & was instrumental in having Hill arrested for the same. That Tunstall used to curse Hill & tell him he ought to be hung. This occurred while Hill was in jail and I believe that Hill had a spite against Tunstall.

Albert H. Howe
Subscribed and sworn to before me this 22 day of May 1878
Morris Bernstein
Notary Public

John Hurley - June 25, 1878

Territory of New Mexico
County of Lincoln

John Hurley being duly sworn says he resides at Lincoln. I have resided in Lincoln County about six years.

I was with Deputy Sheriff Mathews the first time he went to Tunstall's ranch to levy on property of McSween's at the suit of C. Fritz & Co. There were present with us as posse Deputy Mathews, myself, Geo. Hindman and ["Buckshot'] Roberts, and I think Saboya [Segovia], a Mexican.

We saw at the ranch of Tunstall, Widenmann, McComick, Brewer, McCloskey, Henry Brown, W. H. Antrim alias "Kid," Waite, Gauss, "Dutch Martin," Middleton. I do not now recall any more. There were twelve or thirteen there.

As we were riding up they all came out & Widenmann called out to us to stop. And desired to know who was in charge of the party and on being informed Deputy Mathews, he called him up.

After awhile Widenmann said that if we desired to round up the cattle in order to attach them that we had better try it. Mr. Mathews then informed him that if they would not let him attach the cattle, that he would have to return & get more men. Widenmann said there were no cattle there of McSween's but if we wanted them he had better try and round them up.

I did not hear Mathews say that he would go to the [Lincoln] Plaza and get instructions and when he returned he would return with one man. Nor did I hear any one offer to allow or permit us to attach any cattle. I was not present but saw Widenmann & Mathews talking. They asked us to take breakfast which we refused but we returned to the [Lincoln] Plaza.

When we first came to the ranch, Widenmann invited Baker, Evans, Hill & Rivers [Long] to come & get something to eat & that the rest of us should stay back. They accepted the invitation.

When we left Lincoln to go to the ranch, there was only myself, Mathews & the Mexican. We went first to the [Indian] Agency & was joined by Geo. Hindman & Roberts. This was about the 8, 9, or 10th of February 1878. We knew that they were at the Agency before we went there. From the Agency we went to the Penasco as far as Paul's [ranch]. Between the Agency & Elk Springs, Evans & Hill came up to our party and traveled after us saying that they had horses at Tunstall's camp on the Feliz and were going after them. We all stayed at Paul's one night and the same evening Baker & Rivers came to Paul's and joined Evans & Hill.

We did not know that Baker, Evans, Rivers & Hill were anywhere in the neighborhood when we left Lincoln. We did not go the way we did to meet them, they were not part of the posse. The next day we all started for Tunstall's Camp on the Feliz. I had always thought it was the McSween camp. Baker, Evans, Hill & Rivers accompanied us on the trail to the Feliz.

We left Baker, Evans, Hill & Rivers at the [Tunstall] Ranch the first time we were there. When we left it they were shoeing their horses. We made no engagement to meet them nor did we know where they were going.

We reached Lincoln the same night we left the Feliz and started back the next day with a larger posse to the Ruidoso at Ham Mills' Ranch. Next night we camped at Turkey Springs, and the next night we camped at Paul's. We were joined here by a party from the Pecos. Baker, Evans, Hill & Rivers were at Paul's when we reach[ed] there or came there after we arrived there.

We stayed at Paul's till the following Monday morning when we all started for the Feliz to attach the property. We reached the ranch the same day and found that the horses had all been taken away and Gauss said he did not know where they had gone. Mathews sent a part of the posse after the horses. I was one of the persons that went.

We rode about 30 miles when we saw some men ahead of us. I was about the centre of the party. We followed up and after the horses we were after. I did not follow after the men, but looked after the horses. Just before I got up to the horses, I heard some shots. How many I cannot tell. I was not present when Tunstall was shot. I did see him shot. Nor did I see any one shoot at him. It was scrub timber & a person could not see.

If any one says I was with the [sic] any person at the immediate time of shooting Tunstall, they are mistaken. I did not see his body nor did I go to look at it. I helped attend to the horses & helped take them back to camp.

I do not know of any more direct route from the Agency to the Feliz than that we took.

Read, subscribed and sworn to before me this 25th day of June 1878
John Hurley
Frank Warner Angel
Special Agent
Departments Justice & Interior

Charles Kruling, alias "Dutch Charley" - June 5, 1878

Territory of New Mexico
County of Lincoln

Charles Kruling being duly sworn says that I reside in Lincoln County. I am called Dutch Charley.

Just before the death of Tunstall, I was on the way to Lincoln from the Pecos to transact business of my own. I was not coming up to join either party.

I met at Paul's [ranch] on the Penasco J. J. Dolan, Billy Mathews, Ham Mills, E. Wakefield and quite a number others, four Mexicans, in all 18 men. Billy Mathews asked me to accompany them to attach McSween's property at the Rio Feliz.

That they had been there before but had not attached the property. He summons me to go. I got there in the evening (at Paul's). The next morning we left Paul's for the Feliz and met Henry Brown on the road who told us that Tunstall and Brewer had left for Lincoln with the horses. Jessie Evans, Frank Baker, Tom Hill, Davis followed our party and caught up with us at the Feliz.

I heard Mathews tell Morton that he did not want Evans, Baker, Hill & Davis with the posse. Morton agreed not to let them come. I heard Dolan tell Morton at the Feliz just before starting to be very careful and do nothing, but what was lawful. This was at the Feliz where we had arrived at about 9 in the morning.

Gauss was there. Martin came after we left as I am informed. There were only cattle there. We left at [the] Feliz Dolan, Mathews, Wakefield, Davis, Roberts, six Mexicans, Woltz. I do not recall now anyone else. The rest of us followed on after the horses. Baker, Evans, and Hill did not leave with us but followed after the party. I saw Baker, Evans & Hill for the first time after we had left the Feliz at a place distant about 20 miles from the Feliz and from this place they rode with the party.

Baker's horse was used up and he rode behind. No one was riding Dolan's horse. Dolan I think wore a dark suit of clothes. I do not know what kind of a shirt he wore. He wore a dark felt hat. I am sure he did not leave the Feliz with us or join us afterwards.

About six miles after Baker, Evans & Hill joined, we heard a report from the front of our party that "here they are."

The next thing I saw was two men about 500 yards away, one was riding a grey horse [Billy]. The part of our party that was ahead of us rode ahead about 500 yards and then turned off the trail following Tunstall's party (we could not see any of the horses that Tunstall's party was driving off). Supposing that they had the horses, the rest of us in the rear then struck off the trail in the same direction so as to meet the rest of the party.

When we got up to our party, Billy Morton told us that Tunstall was killed. He said he rode up to Tunstall and called on him to surrender holding the papers in his left hand, and that Tunstall pulled his pistol out and fired twice at him, one shot going over his mare's neck, and that he Morton then fired & shot Tunstall. Evans, Hill, & Green came out of the bushes with Morton after the shooting of Tunstall.

Most of our party then went to the place where Tunstall was lying. I found Tunstall lying on his back some blood coming out of his forehead and one foot against or sort of under the saddle, his left foot. The horse was kicking being wounded in the breast. Hindman then said let us lay him out. I do not recollect who shot the horse. I picked up Tunstall's pistol after we had laid him out & found two shots out of it.

I, George Hindman, Sam Perry, Wallace Olinger laid him out. We than got the horses together six or seven and started back to the Feliz, one horse dying on the way. We reached there about 12 at night. I saw Dolan in bed there when we arrived.

At the time of the killing of Tunstall, I was in the rear about 200 yards with Wallace Olinger, Tom Corcoran [Cochrane], Johnny Hurley.

Dolan could not have been with the party after we left the Feliz with out my seeing him.

I do not know whether they fired a shot out of Tunstall's pistol to kill the horse or not.

Tunstall was not touched either before or after I had assisted in laying him out by any one in our party.

Evans was present when Morton was telling us of the killing of Tunstall. He did not say any thing about it nor did Hill or Green. In going back to the Feliz, Baker, Evans & Hill rode a good deal with Morton.

McCloskey rode with us from the Penasco to the Feliz and about seven or eight miles after we had left the Feliz after Tunstall when he left us.

C. Kruling
Read, subscribed and sworn to before me this 5th day of June 1878
Frank Warner Angel
Special Agent
Depts Justice & Interior

James J. Longwell - May 14, 1878

Territory of New Mexico
County of Santa Fe

James J. Longwell being duly sworn says that he is the person who was deputized by the late sheriff Brady of Lincoln County for the purpose of guarding and protecting the goods & chattels attached under and by virtue of a writ of attachment issued out of the 3d District Court in favor of Fritz & Scholand against A. A. McSween and which goods were in a house at Lincoln, Lincoln County, known as the Tunstall store house, and consisted of a general stock of merchandise and bank property, safe, fixtures &c.

I knew J. H. Tunstall. He came into the store while we were making the inventory with a man named Widderman [Widenmann] and made threats against the sheriff telling the sheriff that he was taking his Tunstall's property for McSween's debts. That he would make all of the party suffer for it hereafter and that they had better look out. Both Tunstall and Widdermann [Widenmann] were armed with revolvers, and two of Tunstall's party called "Kid" &"Waite" came up to the door with them and stood there with Winchester rifles and pistols and acted in a threatening manner.

I was in possession of the goods from the 11th day of February until the 23d. Frequently during this time these men with the exception of Tunstall came around the store armed and threatened myself and my assistants with violence, as did quite a number of the other adherents of Tunstall and McSween, viz Bowdre, Scurlock, Middleton, George Washington, Robinson, Ygnacio Gonzales, Jesus Rodriges, Kid Antrim & others. They would call us d–d sons of bitches & tell us to turn loose (that is to fire upon them as to give them a chance to return the fire). That they were ready for the ball to open and tried in every way to provoke a quarrel with deponent and his men.

On one occasion Tunstall told me that I ought to be ashamed to be found in such an outfit taking his property. I told him that if the property was his, that he could take it to the courts and recover. He said d–d the the court. I then told him that if the court here did not do him justice that he could appeal it to the supreme court or go the the [sic] United States Court at Santa Fe. He said God-d–n that ring [meaning the "Santa Fe Ring"]. It is the worst G-d d–d outfit of them all. On one occasion Tunstall called me a damned thief and at the same time placed his hands on his pistol in a threatening manner.

This was the last conversation I had with him. The day prior to his death or the second day prior thereto he was out of town all day. He returned the evening before he was killed just about dark. I do not know at what time he left town that night, but I have heard that he was at his ranch after the horses the morning of the day upon which he was killed, this was 30 or 40 miles distant. I never saw him alive after the time of his return the evening previous and now [know] nothing of the manner of his death except hearsay.

I talked with a man named Middleton who was a friend of Tunstall and was with him at helping him at the time of his death. He Middleton told me that he was present when Tunstall was killed and that Tunstall fired two shots at the sheriff's posse before they shot him. On the day he was killed & before it was known that he was killed or had been shot, a large number of armed men collected at the house of A. A. McSween & were there when they heard of his death, but I do not know for certain that Tunstall had been to see them the day prior to his death and requested them to come to that place. A. A. McSween's house was the headquarters of the McSween or Tunstall party.

Tunstall was killed on the 18th of February. I think some days after his death the McSween party prevented our cook from bringing us our food. "Kid" and "Waite" stopped him in the street or ordered him to go back. I was standing in the door at the time and saw it. The cooks name was Sam Worthy [Wortley]. The "Kid" & "Waite" were armed and "Kid" threw his gun down on the door of the house I was in and told a man named Steve Stanly [Stanley] to get out of the road, and hallowed to me and my men to turn loose you sons of _____, we will give you a game.

I only had five men with me in the house. They at the time had about forty men and A. A. McSween, Widenmann [Widenmann] & Shields [Shield] were of the party. We closed the doors & windows expecting a fight on the next day. I think from this or a few days afterwards being the 23d of February, while I was still in possession of the goods, we saw a squad of soldiers in front of the house. The house was then surrounded by McSween's men & the soldiers. The soldiers were placed in front of the door and McSween's men on each side of the door. Widderman [Widenmann] came along. I rapped on the window and asked him what was up. He said, you will find out d–d quick.

Lieutenant then came up and I rapped on the window and he recognized me before I could speak & he said there is Longwill [Longwell], I am not afraid to talk to him. I sat my gun down and unlocked the door and walked out and asked what was the matter. He said the Deputy U.S. Marshal was there with a warrant to arrest Jessie Evans and he had brought the soldiers to help him search the house. I told him I had no objections to the soldiers looking through any part of the house they wanted to. They looked through the house but did not find Evans. Evans had not been in the house while I was there. I then went back [inside].

Lieut called me out and said he wanted to talk to me & we went out of and around the corner of the house. Someone then spoke and said you had better look out they are disarming your men. I went back when the McSween party threw two or three guns down on me [and] ordered me to give up my arms. I asked them what they wanted to arrest me for? They said that they had a warrant for me issued by Green [John B.] Wilson & they said they had one for every one of my men. They arrested and disarmed us all & took us to jail & they then took possession of the store & the attached goods and kept it as long as I remained in Lincoln, which was until the 4th of May.

We had an examination before Squire Wilson & not one of the party who were in possession of the store with me were bound over. We were turned loose, but the goods in the store were retained. I believe they would have killed us all had not Col. Purington discovered their game and been present at the trial with the soldiers.

The attachment has never been vacated to my knowledge. It has never been enforced for the reason that the Courts were powerless to do so. The only witnesses produced against us before Square Wilson were Sam Corbet, Widderman [Widenmann] & a soldier, I do not remember his name. I received an order from Sheriff Brady to send some hay for the soldier's horses. I weighed out one hundred and twenty pounds and delivered it to a corporal, who brought the order. The order was in writing & was delivered to Squire Wilson at the examination of deponent. The order was signed by Brady with the exception of one hundred & twenty pounds, no other hay was taken to my knowledge. The order was signed by Brady.

I was informed by George Hindman, who was with the Deputy Sheriff's posse, that Morton who was at that time in command of the posse came up to Tunstall, who was driving the horses, and waived the attachment and called upon him to halt & Tunstall & his men ran & scattered & then Tunstall turned back & fired. He did not inform me who fired first, he did not say how many shots were fired at Tunstall. He said that Tunstall & his horse were killed at about one time.

I was present and heard Tunstall testify that McSween was his partner. This was at Mesilla before Judge Bristol.

The object of my arrest & the persons with me was to oust us and put McSween's men in possession and that Squire Wilson knew that, that was the object of the arrest of deponent & his men, and during the examination before him, [Wilson] frequently consulted with McSween. Deponent further states that he has always been a law abiding citizen and obeyed the laws of the land.

Jas. J. Longwell
Subscribed & sworn before me this 14th day of May 1878
W. W. Griffin
U.S. Commissioner

Atanacio Martinez - First Statement - Not Dated

Territory of New Mexico
County of Lincoln

Attanacio [Atanacio] Martinez being duly sworn deposes and says that he is a resident of Lincoln County Territory of New Mexico. That he is a mason by trade. That he is the regular constable for and in Precinct No 1 County and Territory of aforesaid. That on or about the 21st day of February A.D. 1878 [the correct date is February 20] warrants for the arrest of J. J. Dolan, J. B. Mathews, Jesse Evans, Frank Baker, Tom Hill, George Hinman [Hindman], John Hurley, Pantaleón Gallegos and others charged with the murder of J. H. Tunstall were placed in his hands for execution.

That being informed that said persons named in said warrant were at the house of J. J. Dolan & Co. in Lincoln, he summoned Wm. Bonney and Fred T. Waite, in the name of the Territory of New Mexico, as a posse, to aid him in serving said warrant. That in company with said Bonney and Waite he proceeded to the house of J. J. Dolan & Co. and, at the door of said house, was met by William Brady deceased, then sheriff of Lincoln County, who with others for whose arrest this deponent had warrants, at once covered deponent and Wm. Bonney and F. T. Waite with their rifles, forcibly disarmed and took prisoners this deponent and said Bonney and Waite and then demanded of them their business.

Deponent produced the warrant above mentioned and commenced reading it, when said William Brady, the then sheriff of Lincoln County, as soon as the heard the purpose of said warrant, told deponent that he, deponent, could not arrest any persons in the house of J. J. Dolan & Co. That the persons then in said house, were his, Brady's posse, and as such could not be arrested. That he, Brady, did not recognize J. B. Wilson, who had issued said warrants as justice of the peace.

Deponent further says, that said William Brady and the persons with him abused deponent and cursed him, that he was held prisoner by said Brady for several hours without warrant or legal process, that subsequently he was released and allowed to return to his home, but that his arms were not returned to him. That said Wm. Bonney and F. T. Waite were held prisoners by said Wm. Brady about 30 hours and then released.

Deponent further says that after the District Court had adjourned here, he, this deponent, went to the house of J. J. Dolan & Co. and while standing near said house he saw John H. Riley and W. L. Rynerson, District Attorney, in earnest conversation. That this deponent got as near as he could to said Riley and Rynerson and heard said Rynerson say to said Riley, that he, said Riley should not give up, but stick to them, meaning the opposite party. That he, said Rynerson, would aid him, Riley, whenever he could and would send him 20 men. Said Rynerson also told Riley to stick to the fight and give it to the sons of bitches [written and deleted] guns of the opposite party. That this alone would win the fight.

Deponent further says, that he is well acquainted with L. G. Murphy, J. J. Dolan and John H. Riley and that he verily and truly believes that said Murphy, Dolan and Riley have been and are the cause of all the troubles in Lincoln County, that they, said Murphy, Dolan and Riley, have through their system of oppression and persecution, ground down the people of this county to the utmost poverty. That it is currently reported throughout this County, that said Murphy, Dolan and Riley would not and could not brook opposition or competition in business and that they would either drive from the County or have killed any person who thus opposed or entered into competition with them.

That he, this deponent believes this to be the cause of the murder of J. H. Tunstall, who was an honorable and honest man through his manner of conducting his business, an enormous benefit to the County.

Atanacio Martinez

Sworn and subscribed to before me a Justice of the Peace for and in Lincoln County, Territory of New Mexico

John B. Wilson
Justice of the Peace

Atanacio Martinez - Second Statement - Not Dated

Territory of New Mexico
County of Lincoln

Attanacio [Atanacio] Martinez who being duly sworn according to law deposeth and saith. That on the morning of the 21st of February A.D. 1878 about 11 o'cl [o'clock] Robert A. Widenmann, Deputy U. S. Marshal surrounded the house of J. J. Dolan & Co. with U.S. Soldiers preparatory to searching it and the store of J. H. Tunstall, deceased, for the purpose of arresting Jesse Evans and others against and for whom he had warrants. That the said Martinez informed the said Widenmann that he desired to search said house in company with the said Widenmann for persons for whose arrest he, the said Martinez, had warrants in his possession. That Widenmann informed him, Martinez, that the said Widenmann would not allow this. That he the said Martinez could not enter either house until they had been searched and the soldiers withdrawn from them by the said Widenmann and that what he, the said Martinez, after the said Widenmann had withdrawn, he would do on his own responsibility. That he the said Martinez searched the house of J. J. Dolan and Co. and arrested J. H. Riley and searched the store of J. H. Tunstall and there arrested sundry persons after said Widenmann had searched and and [sic] with the troops withdrawn from said house.

That one of the persons arrested in the store of J. H. Tunstall delivered to him the said Martinez the keys of the store of J. H. Tunstall and that the keys were never again demanded by the Sheriff or any of his deputies.

Sworn and subscribed to before me the ___ day of April A.D. 1878
Notary Public

Jacob B. Mathews - June 26, 1878

Territory of New Mexico
County of Lincoln

Jacob B. Mathews being duly sworn says I reside in Lincoln & have resided in Lincoln County about four years.

Q. Were you one of the sheriff's posse that attached McSween's property at the suit of Charles Fritz & etc?
A. I was deputy sheriff under Sheriff Brady. I helped attach the store property at Lincoln & went twice to the Feliz to attach property.

Q. What property did you help attach at Lincoln?
A. The store & goods in it.

Q. Were you one of the posse that went to Tunstall's ranch on the Feliz the first time to attach property?
A. Yes sir, I was the deputy sheriff.

Q. Who composed your posse?
A. John Hurley, Manuel Segovia, Andrew Roberts, George W. Hindman. These were all.

Q. Who went with you from Lincoln?
A. Hurley & Segovia.

Q. Where did Roberts & Hindman join you?
A. At Dolan & Riley's store South Fork, Indian Agency.

Q. How did you know they were there?
A. Because both had been working for Dolan & Riley at the agency.

Q. When did you leave Lincoln for the agency?
A. I think the 9th of February 1878.

Q. Did you meet any one else at the agency who accompanied you?
A. No sir.

Q. Were Baker, Evans, Hill & Rivers [Long] a part of your posse or were they with you or accompany you to the Feliz?
A. They were not part of the posse. Evans & Rivers I think met us at the agency. They did not leave with us, but caught up to us about five miles from the agency this side. Baker & Hill came to us at the Penasco. They did not meet us at our request either directly or indirectly. We did not know they were there. They said that they were going to the Feliz after some horses.

From the Penasco we went to the Feliz at Tunstall's Ranch. We saw there Widenmann, Brewer, "Dutch Martin," Henry Brown, Antrim alias "Kid" alias "Bonney," McCloskey, McComick, Gauss, Waite & Middleton. I believe that these are all that I can now remember. There were twelve or thirteen there.

I had considerable talk with Widenmann & Brewer as to attaching the property. Brewer was willing that I should attach leaving the question to the courts as to the title to the same. But Widenmann positively refused to allow me to attach the cattle. I told Brewer privately that if he would allow me to attach the cattle I would come to the ranch with only one man. I never told this to Widenmann and after Widenmanns refusal to allow me to attach we left for Lincoln to obtain instructions.

I was instructed by Sheriff Brady when I returned to Lincoln to raise a posse & return & attach the property. When I was at the ranch the first time I saw some 15 horses. I sent Telesfore Lopez to the Pecos to raise a posse. No one went with him to my knowledge. I did not send anyone with him. I nor Sheriff Brady did not send any one with him. Nor did I know any one went with him. I raised a part of the force here and went to Ham Mills' [Ranch] there at night. Next morning we went to Turkey Springs and stayed the next night there. The next day we went on to Paul's Ranch and reached there in the afternoon of Saturday.

At this place, Evans & Hill came to our camp. They were not sent for by me or requested to come there. Nor did I expect them there. They came of their own free will. On Sunday Baker & Rivers came to the camp. They were around this camp. None of these men were part of the posse, but on the contrary were ordered away by me. We were met here by the party from the Pecos.

On Monday we started for the Feliz, Tunstall's ranch. We had been informed by "Dutch Martin" that if it was not for Widenmann there would be no trouble as Brewer would make no resistance but that he was afraid that there would be resistance. We went to the ranch carefully, one party in front of the house & the other from the rear. Myself & Roberts being the party in front. We found that there was no one there except Gauss & I think "Dutch Martin." The party had left with the horses.

I then deputized Morton & selected a party to go with him after the horses and they left. I having instructed them to over take the horses and bring them back and in case there was any resistance to arrest the men & bring them back too. If he did not over take them before they reached the [Lincoln] plaza, if he found they were going to Lincoln, then to follow them in and have Sheriff Brady attach the horses.

He returned at about 2 A.M. of the next day & reported to me that he caught up with the horses about 30 miles away and that Tunstall resisted & fired at him & that he returned the fire & Tunstall was killed. That the resistance was made by Tunstall while he was reading the attachment to him, and that he notified Tunstall that if he would throw up his hands he would not be hurt, instead of which Tunstall fired at him. That he fired back killing Tunstall.

Q. Did Baker, Evans, Hill & Rivers get their horses the first time they went to the Feliz with or after the posse?

A. I do not think they did. I left them there when I left & can not say why they did not get the horses they claimed they had there.

Q. Did they get them the second time?

A. No sir, they claimed two of the horses & I refused to give them up referring them to Sheriff Brady.

Q. The first time you went there, did they demand the horses of Widenmann or any one of his party?

A. Not to my knowledge. They seemed very friendly with Widenmann & his party. Took breakfast there. We were afterwards invited but declined. Evans & his party remained behind shoeing their horses.

Q. Were the Baker party riding different horses the second time they met you?

A. I think Baker was.

Q. Did you see any horses the second time you went to the ranch or any time among the horses of the ranch that Baker or his party rode the first time you met them?

A. No I did not. There were none among the horses attached. I do not know what horses Tunstall's party were riding on & rode away with.

Q. Please give the names of every man that composed the posse the second time you went to attach?

A. Myself, John Hurley, Manuel Segovia, Geo. W. Hindman, Andrew Roberts, Pantaleón Gallegos, James J. Dolan, A. H. Mills, J. W. Olinger, Thomas Moore, R. W. Beckwith, Ramon Montoya, Felipe Mes, E. H. Wakefield, Wm. S. Morton, Charles Woltz, Charles Kruling, Charles Marshall, Pablo Pino Y Pino, Thomas Green, Thos. Cochrane, George Kitt, Samuel Perry.

Q. Please give the names of every man that composed the party that went after the horses?

A. John Hurley, Manuel Segovia, George W. Hindman, Pantaleón Gallegos, J. W. Olinger, R. W. Beckwith, Ramon Montoya, W. S. Morton, Thos. Green, Thos. Cochrane, Chas. Kruling, Geo. Kitt, Charles Marshall, & Sam Perry.

J. B. Mathews
Read, subscribed & sworn before me this 26th day of June 1878
Frank Warner Angel
Special Agent
Departments of Justice & Interior

Alexander A. McSween - June 6, 1878

Territory of New Mexico
County of Lincoln

Alexander A. McSween being duly sworn says. I have resided in Lincoln County since the 3d day of March 1875 and since that time I am conversant with the state of affairs that has existed in that County and I am acquainted with the people in that County. I am a lawyer by profession and have been and now am engaged in the practice of my profession.

I have given the subject of what has caused the trouble in Lincoln County considerable attention and study, and have inquired and talked with a great number of persons as to the causes which has produced this state of affairs which as resulted in the death of John H. Tunstall and as to the general lawlessness that exists in said County.

From this examination and inquiry of the matter I am informed that Lawrence G. Murphy and Emil Fritz doing business under the style of L. G. Murphy & Co. had the monopoly for the sale of merchandise in this County, and used their power to oppress and grind out all they could from the farmers and force those who were opposed to them to leave the County. For instance the farmers would buy merchandise of them at exorbitant prices and were compelled to turn in their produce in payment thereof at prices that suited L. G. Murphy & Co., and if a farmer refused so to do, they were subjected to litigation and the whole judicial machinery was used immediately to accomplish that object. The result of these proceedings were that L. G. Murphy & Co. were absolute monarchs of Lincoln County and ruled their subjects (the farmers & others) with an oppressive iron heal.

This state of affairs has existed for some time, at least ten years, and was carried out either by L. G. Murphy & Co. or their successors.

The said L. G. Murphy & Co. in carrying out their schemes would drive out a settler who had opposed them or who would not follow their beck and call, and without a particle of right title or claim take possession of such person's real estate and claim that it belonged to them, and then rent it to some other person who was led to believe that it belonged to them. And if such person should afterwards find out that they had no right title or interest in the property, and refused to pay them for the rental thereof, a system of persecution would be instituted which resulted in either the opposing party giving in or leaving the County.

This rule of Murphy & Co. and their successors continued until the matter was precipitated by the event of the killing of John H. Tunstall – and that in order to support this monarchy it is reported that L. G. Murphy & Co. and their successors have latterly surrounded themselves, and were employing the most desperate characters in this County. And affairs were carried by such a high hand after deponent came to this county and Murphy desiring to regain lost power and obtain control over the people desired and wished to organize a Vigilance Committee ostensibly to put down horse stealing but really, as after facts show, to kill persons who were opposed to him, and among other persons to be disposed of he named to me, that he was going to have this Vigilance Committee kill Hon. J. B. Patron, Stephen Stanley and Richard M. Brewer, since deceased, and he informed me that in as much as I appeared to support them I would have to leave the County.

Deponent further says that he discountenanced in every way this measure and used his influence to prevent this state of affairs, wishing rather that the courts be resorted to, and that the people would stand by and see the laws enforced. These facts and the further fact that the people were determined to throw off the burden of Murphy & Co. and the fact that Murphy & Co. found that the power to influence Courts, juries and even to kill persons was being lost, rendered [them] more desperate and compelled them to resort to more desperate measures which culminated in the death of John H. Tunstall.

Deponent has heard L. G. Murphy assert that he controlled not only the Courts and juries, but that he could cause the death of any person who opposed him. Deponent verily believes that so far as the Courts are concerned that they were made unknowingly the tools in his hands to work out his schemes and revenge.

The foregoing facts I believe are the primitive cause of the troubles in Lincoln County at the present time. The direct and immediate cause or the event that precipitated the matter was the death of John H. Tunstall which occurred as herein stated.

In November 1876 John H. Tunstall came to this county for the purpose as he said of going into the stock raising business, & took steps to secure four thousand acres of land for that purpose and invested about $25000 in his business of stock raising and in merchandise for a store which he opened at Lincoln.

At this time the firm of J. J. Dolan & Co. composed of J. J. Dolan and John H. Riley seemed to be friends of his, and knowing that he had considerable money to invest, they tried to have him as far away from Lincoln as they could and also to get his money away so that he would be financially crippled and for that purpose tried to have him purchase L. G. Murphy's ranch at Fairview about 35 miles from Lincoln and knowing that I was a friend of Tunstall, they tried to induce me to use my influence with Tunstall to have him buy it and promised me if I would induce Tunstall to buy it, that they would give me $5000. I informed Tunstall of this offer and told him that they had no good title to the land and Tunstall refused to buy – this was the beginning of the enmity of Murphy, Dolan & Riley against Tunstall.

During the month of August 1877 horses were stolen from Tunstall and myself by Jessie Evans and Tom Hill, the said Evans & Hill afterwards admitted to me, Mr. Tunstall, Harwood, & others that they had taken the horses. They were afterwards arrested at Beckwith's on the Seven Rivers by Sheriff Brady and lodged in jail at Lincoln under an indictment for stealing said horses. That on or about the __ [16] day of November 1877 I was informed by J. B. Patron that Evans, Baker, Hill, and Davis had filed off their shackles and cut the logs in their cell and were ready to make their escape. I told him to inform Sheriff Brady who was the jailer by virtue of his office, which he did, as he (Patron) subsequently informed me, whereupon Brady, Patron & Shield went and examined the said prisoners and the jail and found Patron's statement to be true and correct. The sheriff however took no precautionary steps to better secure their confinement.

A few days afterwards Sheriff Brady came into Tunstall's store in a half intoxicated condition and indirectly accused Mr. Tunstall of giving the credit of the arrest of said outlaws to R. M. Brewer (now deceased) and had considerable talk with Mr. Tunstall, and among other things accused Mr. Tunstall of having tried to aid Baker, Evans, Hill & Davis to escape. Mr. Tunstall told him you know their shackles are filed, & there are holes cut in the logs and take no pains to secure them, and do you dare to accuse me who have aided in the arrest of these persons, who have threatened my life, with assisting them to escape.

Sheriff Brady thereupon put his hand on his revolver as though he was going to draw it and I stepped between them and placing my hand on his shoulder and said it ill becomes you as a peace officer to violate the law by shooting. Brady replied I won't shoot you now, you haven't long to run. I ain't always going to be Sheriff and then left the store. There were several present besides my self during the conversation. I now recall Atanacio Martinez & Rafael Gutierrez as being present.

A day or so after the prisoners referred above made their escape during the night. Upon hearing of the escape, J. B. Patron, J. H. Tunstall and myself went to the jail from which they had escaped and found several sacks in which rocks weighing 20 or 25 pounds were tied, augers, and files. Upon further investigation I found that no one had been left in charge of the jail that night, and that the doors had not been even locked though Brady was at Murphy's house where he made his head quarters. I am informed and verily believe that the augers and files referred to above were packed in goods bought in the store of J. J. Dolan & Co. where Murphy resided, and by one of their employees (Pantaleón Gallegos) delivered to the said prisoners.

I am also informed that they went to Brewer's ranch and took horses, saddles and guns by force belonging to Tunstall and Brewer. After their escape it was reported at Lincoln that Brewer had been killed and I went to Sheriff Brady and offered to raise twenty men to go and recapture the escaped prisoners. Brady replied, I arrested them once and I will be d–d if I am going to do it again. Hereafter I am going to look after Brady's interests, and declined the offer. Subsequently some of the prisoners, to wit ____, Davis, _____ were seen with Brady at the store of J. J. Dolan & Co. as I am informed by George Washington, and he did not arrest them or offer or try to do so.

About the 29th of September 1877, J. J. Dolan & Co. borrowed from Mr. Tunstall through me one thousand dollars. I had before this taken up a note for Mr. Richard M. Brewer held by J. J. Dolan & Co. for about $2300 in order to protect said Brewer, who had incurred the anger of said J. J. Dolan & Co. and who had determined to ruin him. About this time it was reported that J. J. Dolan & Co. were using the Territorial Tax money which Sheriff Brady had collected and not paid over to the Treasurer. In order to help them out of their financial trouble, and being anxious to find out whether there was any truth in the report, and in order to see if they were endeavoring to run the County in their own interests against the wishes of all law abiding Citizens, I inquired of them after I had agreed to furnish as aforesaid the $1000, why they did not get the tax money from Brady, and to this question Dolan said that Riley had already got it.

Subsequent facts show that that was the fact as will more freely appear by the check given by me to the sheriff, a copy of which is hereto annexed marked No 1.

About June 24, 1874, Emil Fritz died in Germany. At this time his partner L. G. Murphy was Probate Judge. No steps were taken to administrator on the estate of Fritz until about April 20, 1875, when one William Brady the late sheriff of Lincoln County was appointed Administrator by Murphy. At that time Dolan who had been clerk for L. G. Murphy & Co. and afterwards partner of L. G. Murphy, and the said L. G. Murphy admitted to me that according to the books of the firm the said Emil Fritz had an interest in the business at the time of his death to the amount of about $48000 as John Watts who had examined their books as an expert had informed them, and that they desired that Charles Fritz and Emile [Emilie] Scholand (brother and sister of the deceased) should have what ever interest Emil Fritz had in the business.

About this time I was employed by Brady [as] Administrator to make collections for the estate and instructed by him that Dolan and Murphy should receive all moneys collected. Among the assets of the estate was a life insurance policy on the life of Fritz in the Merchants Life Insurance Company of New York City for $10000. Mr. Brady, administrator, informed deponent that this policy had been placed in the hands of Levi Spiegelberg of New York City, a member of the firm of Spiegelberg Brothers of Santa Fe New Mexico, by Mr. L. G. Murphy with out consulting him (Brady).

About the month of February 1876 I went in company with Mr. Brady to Santa Fe. During our journey we became quite confidential with each other. Brady told me among other things that he was in the power of L. G. Murphy. After we got to Santa Fe he informed me that J. J. Dolan the junior partner of said Murphy had compelled him to give an order on Levi Spiegelberg, to place the money received on [the] Fritz policy to the credit of L. G. Murphy & Co. with Spiegelberg & Bros of Santa Fe New Mexico, with whom at that time said L. G. Murphy & Co. were greatly indebted for goods and merchandise.

In October 1876 Brady resigned his administratorship of the Fritz Estate and Emile [Emilie] Scholand and Charles Fritz were appointed administratrix and administrator of said Fritz Estate in his place and stead. I was then employed by them on behalf of the estate. This policy among other things was placed in my hands to be attended to. On that behalf I proceeded to St. Louis and consulted with parties as to the best course to be pursued in collecting the money, and also to obtain letters to some responsible part [party] in New York City in order to collect the money on said policy.

I received a letter of introduction to Donell [Donnell], Lawson & Co. bankers of New York City. I proceeded then to New York City – and after considerable trouble with Levi Spiegelberg who refused to recognize me or to deliver the papers in his possession belonging to the said estate, claiming among other things that he had an order from Brady the late adm. to pay the money to his firm Spiegelberg Bros of Santa Fe. After several consultations with lawyers & said Levi Spiegelberg I obtained the papers. I thereupon entered into an agreement with Donell [Donnell], Lawson & Co. under and in pursuance of a power of attorney and agreement hereto annexed marked 2. The agreement with Donell [Donnell] Lawson & Co. will appear hereafter. And returned to Lincoln.

On my return to Lincoln, I found J. H. Riley was exceedingly angry and was trying to cause trouble. During my absence he had broken into my office and destroyed some of my furniture grossly insulted my wife and vowed that he would run me out of the County.

About December 21 1876 I caused notices to be served on the administratrix and administrator of the the Fritz estate that I should apply to courts for the settlement of my account for services already rendered to the said estate. Such proceedings were there-upon had that my accounts were duly approved by the Probate Judge, copies of said notice, account, and approval are here to annexed marked Exhibit 3.

During the month of May 1877 L. G. Murphy of the late firm of L. G. Murphy & Co. petitioned the Probate Court that a commission be appointed to examine the books of said firm in order to find out if he was indebted to the estate of said Fritz or the Fritz estate was indebted to him. A copy of said petition being hereto annexed marked Exhibit 4.

That such proceedings were thereupon had, that Hon. J. B. Patron, your deponent and Morris J. Bernstein, book keeper for said J. J. Dolan & Co., who where the successors to

L. G. Murphy & Co., were appointed as such commissioners, a copy of such appointment is hereto annexed marked Exhibit 5.

Before the conclusion of the labors of said commission Mr. Bernstein resigned and his successor as book keeper with J. J. Dolan & Co., Mr. F. G. Christie was appointed.

That such proceedings were had by such commission that on or about the day of ___ 1877 the said commissioners made their report, a copy of which I attached as Exhibit 6. By this report it will appear that L. G. Murphy was indebted to said estate in the sum of $23376.10.

On or about the 1st day of August 1877 I received a letter from Donell [Donnell], Lawson & Co. dated 19 July 1877, a bill from Staw & Ruggles Attorneys, copies of which are hereto annexed marked Exhibit 7.

That thereupon and or about the 1st day of August 1877 I sent a letter to Mrs. Emilie Scholand and Charles Fritz adminstratix and administrator of said Fritz estate informing them of the fact that the policy of insurance on the life of Fritz had been collected, a copy of which letter is hereto annexed marked 8, which letter was subsequently acknowledged by them to have be received in Aug. aforesaid.

Deponent further says that on the same day that he sent the said above letter he sent a copy of the same to L. G. Murphy out of courtesy, he claiming about this time for the first time to have some claim against the estate. That hereafter and on or about the month of November 1877 I was requested to go to St. Louis on professional business, making no secret of my prospective journey. I even wrote friendly letters to my friends, among others Judge Bristol, Judge Newcomb, A. J. Fountain and J. D. Bail informing them in connection with other business of my proposed trip and of the length of time I expected to be absent which was not to exceed six months.

Deponent further says that on or about the 15th of December 1877 Charles Fritz administrator as aforesaid was in the office of deponent, then well knowing that deponent intended to go to St. Louis as aforesaid. That deponent informed said Fritz then and there that as soon as he or any other person was authorized by said Emilie Scholand to receive and receipt deponent for the money, the money would be paid. Deponent further informed said Fritz of the nature of his business to St. Louis, how long he expected to be absent and who would attend to his business during his absence.

That said Fritz thereupon expressed himself as satisfied with deponent's statements of the affairs of the estate and asked deponent to let him have $100 to which deponent did. D. P. Shield was present during said interview.

Deponent further says that he has always been ready and now is, to pay over to the administrator and administratorix of said estate the amount of money in his hands over and above the allowances made him by the Probate Court as aforesaid and his commission as per agreement already refereed to.

During January (1878) term of the Probate Court in and for said Lincoln County, said L. G. Murphy filed a claim against said estate of Fritz deceased to the amount of $76000, every dollar of which was disapproved by said Court and from which decision there has been no appeal, the proof being that said Murphy owed the said estate about $30000.

That deponent knows of his own knowledge that should he turn all the moneys in his hands over to said administrators and administratrix, without deducting his fees therefrom, he would never get a cent for his professional services to said estate, there being no other assets, the administrator and administratrix aforesaid being completely in the power of Murphy, Dolan and Riley aforesaid. That said Fritz, as deponent is informed and believes, had been threatened with summary vengeance by said Murphy, Dolan & Riley if he and the administratrix should settle with deponent upon any other terms than receiving all the money in my hands collect by me for the aforesaid estate without the deduction of my account. That it is a fact patent and notorious that said Fritz never exercises his own judgment and sense of right when said Murphy, Dolan and Riley are interested, they threatening him with ruin on the ground that he is heavily indebted to them. In this matter they (Murphy, Dolan & Riley) have threatened to run him out of the County without a shirt unless he does as they desire him to do.

I left Lincoln on the 18th of Dec. 1877 in company with my wife and John S. Chisum my client and on whose business I was then going to St. Louis [Missouri] to attend to.

On the 23 of December 1877 we arrived at Las Vegas New Mexico. On the morning of the 24 I went to the office of Louis Salebaches, a brother attorney. He informed me that he had a telegram from T. B. Catron U.S. District Attorney inquiring if I was at Las Vegas. I told him to telegraph Mr. Catron that I was, and then I determined and did want to see what he wanted of me. On the night of the 24 of December 1877 the Sheriff of San Miguel County called at my room at the hotel at Las Vegas and said he had a telegram from W. L. Rynerson Territorial District Attorney for the 3d Judicial District requesting him to arrest me for the crime of embezzlement and that the warrant would be served.

The Sheriff left me at the hotel on my parole and I waited until the warrant arrived. Whereupon I & Mr. Chisum were lodged in the jail. I requested the Sheriff to take me before Judge Bristol for examination. He refused. Whereupon I sent word to J. B. Patron to tell Sheriff Brady of Lincoln County, who were both then at Santa Fe, that I was a prisoner in jail and that I wanted him to take me down before Judge Bristol.

Not hearing from Sheriff Brady and the Sheriff of San Miguel County refusing to take me before Judge Bristol, I offered the said Sheriff of San Miguel County to give bonds in the amount of $2000 to be approved by him for my appearance before Judge Bristol within ten days, and my own expenses to answer for the charge of embezzlement of $10000 realized from the afore mentioned policy of insurance. He thereupon as I am informed and verily believe telegraphed to Santa Fe for instructions and refused to accept the said offer made by me. He subsequently in conformity to instructions received by telegraph from W. L. Rynerson proposed to me a compromise and let me go on my journey. This I refused absolutely to do preferring to return and face my accusers and stand trial.

On the 4th of January 1878 having been confined all this time in jail [11 days], I proceeded to Mesilla by way of Lincoln in charge of Deputy Sheriff A. P. Barrier. I arrived at Mesilla on or about the 1st of February and thereafter I had an examination before Judge Bristol and after the evidence against me had been introduced, and it appeared that the testimony of Hon. J. B. Patron who was in attendance at the session of the Legislature, Hon. Florencio Gonzales Probate Judge of Lincoln County and certain papers on file in his office were necessary for my case and on the suggestion of Judge Bristol and the Territorial District Attorney, I consented to a continuance until the meeting of the Grand Jury at Lincoln County April Term of the District Court of said County, whereupon bail was fixed by Judge Bristol at $8000 to be approved by the Territorial District Attorney and I was delivered to the charge of Deputy Sheriff Barrier aforesaid to be taken to Lincoln County and delivered to and held by Sheriff Brady of said County until I should give the aforesaid bail.

On or about the 5th day of February 1878 I started for Lincoln in charge of Deputy Sheriff Barrier and in company with D. P. Shield, J. P. Wilson and J. H. Tunstall. On the evening of the same day we camped at St. Augustine [Shedd's Ranch], and shortly after going into camp, Jesse Evans, Frank Baker, Long alias "Rivers," notorious outlaws came into our camp and inquired of us if we had passed J. J. Dolan on the road, where-upon D. P. Shield replied that we had not, that he understood that Mr. Dolan would not leave till tomorrow morning (the 6th). Baker said that they had found Jimmie meaning (J. J. Dolan) very punctual in their engagements with them and that Dolan had made an appointment with them to meet them here and that they believed that he would come.

Deponent further says that it was a notorious fact that this Evans, Baker, Rivers [Long] and others had determined to take J. H. Tunstall's and my life owning to our activity in having them previously arrested for horse stealers.

Deponent further says that about one or two o'clock of the morning of the 6th of February 1878 said J. J. Dolan reached San Augustine aforesaid.

About 8 or 9 o'clock of the said day while Tunstall, D. P. Shield, J. B. Wilson and this deponent were eating breakfast at their camping place at the East end of San Augustine Corral, deponent saw J. J. Dolan with gun in hand and another man descending [from] a house occupied by Mr. Shedd, said house being situated about 70 or 80 yards due South of where deponent, Tunstall, Wilson, Shield and Barrier were camped. Said J. J. Dolan and the person accompanying him appeared to be going in a Westerly direction, thus hiding themselves from us by the South East corner of said corral.

In a few minutes said J. J. Dolan and Jesse Evans came around the South east corner of said corral and Mr. Dolan drew his Winchester carbine on Mr. Tunstall and asked him if he was ready to fight and settle their difficulties. Mr. Tunstall asked him if he asked him to fight a duel. Mr. Dolan replied, "You d—d coward. I want you to fight and settle our difficulties." Dolan drew his gun cocked on Mr. Tunstall three times. Mr. Barrier placed himself between or in line with Dolan & Evans and saved as I believe the lives of Tunstall and myself. When Mr. Dolan was leaving he used these words, "You won't fight this morning, you d—d coward but I'll get you soon."

After he had gone off about 20 yards he turned around and said to Tunstall, "When you write the 'Independent' again, say that I am with 'The Boys.'" The term "The Boys" being used in Lincoln and neighborhood to denote notorious thieves and murderers such as Evans, Baker, Hill and Davis and the reason he mentioned the [Mesilla Valley] "Independent" was because Tunstall had written said newspaper published at Mesilla New Mexico a letter dated January 18, 1878, which letter was published in said newspaper in its issue of the 26th of January 1878 charging Wm. Brady Sheriff as aforesaid with having allowed said J. J. Dolan & Co. to use the Territorial Funds collected by said

Brady as Ex officio collector of said Lincoln County and the Governor of said Territory in his message to the Legislature having reported that said Brady was in default in the payments of the money collected by him (said Brady).

A copy of which letter to the *Independent* is hereto annexed marked Ex 9. Reference being also had to the afore mentioned check Exhibit No 1.

Deponent further says that said letter elicited a reply from said J. J. Dolan, which was published in said Independent on or about the 2nd of February 1878, a copy of which is hereto annexed and marked Ex 10.

Deponent further says that after the occurrence of the attempted killing of Tunstall and myself related above we started for Lincoln. After traveling about 20 miles we were passed on the road by said J. J. Dolan, Evans, Baker, Hill and Long alias "Rivers." Evans and Baker rode with Mr. Dolan in his ambulance. It was known to Mr. Dolan at this time that all of these men were highwaymen and escaped prisoners.

On or about the 7th we saw Baker, Hill and Long alias "Rivers" at the Mescalero Indian Agency [at Blazer's Mill]. At this place they appeared to be quite familiar with Maj. Godfroy the agent. Godfroy told Mr. Tunstall then and there that he bought a horse from Hill aforesaid that was at Mr. Tunstall's cattle ranch and requested Mr. Tunstall to give him an order for him, dictated to the man in charge at the ranch. This Mr. Tunstall did. The way the horse came to be at Tunstall's ranch was this, as told me by Mr. Tunstall. The man that went in pursuit of the horses stolen from Tunstall and myself found the horse referred last above among the others. He knew the horse to have once having been my property and the man holding them at the time having no other than that derived from Evans, Hill and Baker, the said horse was taken among with the others.

Upon the arrival of this man (who had captured the horses) I informed them that I had sold the said horse and thought that it had been stolen from the person I had sold it to, by Evans, Hill and Baker aforesaid, that I had no claim to him neither did Mr. Tunstall, no one having put in a claim for him.

The order was given to Godfroy for him as heretofore mentioned.

Deponent further says that when he arrived at the Town of Lincoln he was informed that a courier had preceded me from Mesilla with a writ of attachment. That Riley, Dolan and Murphy and Sheriff Brady were in ecstasy over deponent's prospective confinement in the County jail and I was informed that Sheriff Brady was making the occasion a subject of merriment by making contracts to grind corn in the Mexican mills to make gruel for my maintenance. That said Riley had swept out the jail in order that he might in [the] future have it to say that he swept out the room in which I was incarcerated. That said Brady expressed himself in the presence of E. A. Dow and others to the effect that Tunstall and I had reported that he (Brady) was a defaulter to the Territory, but that he meant to show us that he would not make a default in exposing this deponent in jail and taking the spirit out of him. That he may have allowed Baker, Evans and Hill to escape but that the would not allow deponent to do so.

Deponent further says that he found a writ of attachment had been issued out of the Third Judicial District Court in which the said Emile [Emilie] Scholand and Charles Fritz were plaintiffs. That it was dated the 7th of February 1878 and that the Sheriff commenced to attach there under on the 8th it having been sent a distance of about 154 miles in an almost unprecedented short time for this Territory. That he not only attached my personal property but also my real, together with the property of J. H. Tunstall and others, even pictures of the family of the latter as also a notarial seal belonging to D. P. Shield. He (the Sheriff) was commanded to attach and safely keep so much property as would secure the sum of $8000, but he attached property both real and personal worth over $40000. At this time I was not Mr. Tunstall's partner though I would become such by articles of agreement in May 1878. I was his attorney and took an active part in the management of his business. For this I was to have one half the profits of the business up to May 1878 after the deduction of 8 per cent on the capital invested.

In May 1878 articles of co-ownership were to be signed by us by which Mr. Tunstall was to furnish the capital, I to pay 8 per cent interest per annum for my share. At the time (February 1878) Mr. Tunstall owed me over $4000 as appears by the copy of account hereto attached marked 11, being a true and full account of all money transactions had by and between us from the time indicated until his death other than that stated. I had no other financial interest in Mr. Tunstall's business. He does business in the name of J. H. Tunstall only. No resistance of any kind or character was offered by deponent to the Sheriff Brady in the execution of said writ of attachment nor by any other person so far as this deponent knows of him.

Deponent further says that on or about the 14th of February 1878 Mr. Tunstall was informed that one J. B. Mathews (who was in the employ of Murphy and attended to any thing Dolan and Riley desired done) was at his (Tunstall's) ranch with said Baker, Evans, Hill and Davis as Sheriffs posse to attach Tunstall's cattle and horses as the property of the deponent. That said J. B. Mathews as Sheriff Brady's deputy was informed that deponent had neither cattle or horse there but that he could "round up" and if he found any he could take them. That he could not take Tunstall's property without an order from him or process against him. That said J. B. Mathews then and there stated that he would return to Lincoln and report to Brady. That he would return in a day or so probably but that he would bring only one man with him.

R. M. Brewer who was Tunstall's foreman told him that when he came he would "round up" the cattle and horses & he could see if there were any of McSween's horses or cattle there. On or about the 14th of February 1878 Robert Widenmann came in from Tunstall's cattle ranch and informed Tunstall in my hearing of what had taken place as theretofore related. That he was satisfied that Mathews intended to raise a large posse and take the cattle by force. That for this purpose said Baker had gone down to Dolan & Co's cow camp on the Pecos with instructions to Wm. Morton their foreman to raise all the men he could and meet Mathews with his horse at Turkey Springs a few miles from Tunstall's cattle ranch on the evening of the 16th of February 1878.

Mr. Tunstall was informed in my hearing by George Washington that Murphy, Riley & Dolan had helped Mathews to raise a force to the number of 43 men, that said Riley informed him (Washington) that there was no use in McSween's and Tunstall's trying to get any from them this time as they had them completely in their power. That they could not possibly be beat as they had the District Attorney (meaning Rynerson), the Court and all the power in Santa Fe to back them, that their plan was to take the cattle from Tunstall's ranch was [sic] by sending two Mexicans they had in their force to make a sham round up of the cattle and horses, so as to draw the men in Tunstall's house out of it, then the balance of the posse were to take possession of the house and "get" Tunstall's men. Upon this information Mr. Tunstall concluded to go to the ranch and induce his men to leave and allow Mathews and posse to take the property and seek his remedy in the Courts. For this purpose as he informed me he left Lincoln on the night of the 16th. This was the last time I saw Tunstall alive.

I have been informed by R. M. Brewer (deceased), John Middleton, W. Bonney, R. A. Widenmann, F. T. Wait [Waite] and Henry Brown that Mr. Tunstall reached his cattle ranch on the night of the 17th and commanded them all to leave the ranch and come to Lincoln which they did.

McCloskey (deceased) informed me that Mr. Tunstall sent him to get one Martin who was a good cattle man to come to the ranch to turn the cattle over to Deputy Sheriff J. B. Mathews and posse who were now said to be at said Turkey Springs numbering 43 men and see that the cattle were property tallied and that he (Tunstall) would seek his remedy at law. That he would not sacrifice the life of one of his men for all the cattle for they would all be killed if they remained at the ranch. Said McCloskey informed me further that he not only delivered that verbal message to said Martin, but told the same to said J. B. Mathews and informed him that Mr. Tunstall would offer no resistance to the taking of the property, though some of it belonged to this deponent.

Deponent further says that on the night of the 18th of February 1878 he was informed by R. M. Brewer, W. Bonney, J. Middleton and R. A. Widenmann that said J. H. Tunstall was murdered on the road to Lincoln about 30 miles from his cattle ranch by Jessie Evans, Frank Baker, J. J. Dolan, W. Morton, T. Coccoran [Cochrane], P. Gallegos, O. L. Roberts, Tom Hill, George Davis, Robert W. Beckwith, Tom Green, George Hindman, J. Hurley and others to the number of 18 men. My informant further stated that at the time of the murder they were some distance from Mr. Tunstall, but that he endeavored to make his escape but failed to do so.

I am informed that Tom Green who was present when the murder was committed, that Morton who was acting as Deputy under orders from said Deputy Mathews called out to Tunstall to stop that he wanted to see him and that they did not want to hurt him, and that thereupon Mr. Tunstall dismounted and walked towards Morton and delivered him a colts pistol carried by him (Tunstall) and that a few minutes thereafter Jessie Evans aforesaid took aim at Mr. Tunstall and shot him, the ball taking effect in his breast. and that as he (Tunstall) fell on his face, said Morton fired another shot at Mr. Tunstall out of Tunstall's revolver, the ball entering the back of his head and coming out in the forehead and that thereafter Morton walked to Tunstall's horse and shot another shot out of Tunstall's pistol at said horse whereupon the horse dropped dead and that the murderers carried the corpse of said Tunstall and laid him close by the side of said horse putting his hat under the dead horse's head.

On the night last above mentioned, this deponent wrote a note to John Newcomb requesting him to go to where Tunstall's corpse was and bring it into Lincoln that it might have a decent burial. That on the night of the 19th of February 1878 said John Newcomb with others brought into Lincoln the lifeless body of said Tunstall. Said Newcomb informed me then and there that he found said Tunstall dead at the place indicated by me.

That when he found the body it was lying close by the side of a dead horse belonging to said Tunstall and that Tunstall's hat was lying under the head of said dead horse. That on the night of the day last mentioned a corner's inquest was held on the body of the said Tunstall, a copy of the-findings are hereto annexed and marked 12.

That on or about the 20th I caused the body of said Tunstall to be embalmed and a post mortem examination made by Drs. Ealy and Appel. That not only was the body shot as already stated, but the skull was broken into pieces by a blow from some instrument after being shot as aforesaid. That on the 19th day of February 1878 I caused affidavits to be filed before J. B. Wilson Justice of the Peace within the said town of Lincoln charging the murder of Mr. Tunstall on the parties named upon which affidavits a warrant of arrest for such parties was duly issued on said affidavits and placed in the hands of Atanacio Martinez Constable in and for said town of Lincoln for execution. Copies of said affidavits and warrant are hereto annexed and marked 13.

That upon the 20th day of February 1878 said Constable Martinez called upon W. Bonney and F. T. Waite to help him serve said warrant. That it was well known that ten or twelve of the murderers of Mr. Tunstall were then and there in the house of L. G. Murphy, Dolan and Riley aforesaid. That as this deponent is informed by said Constable, said Constable proceeded to the house of Murphy, Dolan and Riley to make arrests as directed.

That at said house he met the said Sheriff Brady who without any warrant or authority of law took the said Constable, said Bonney and Waite prisoners and refused to aid or allow them to arrest any one though the majority of said murderers where [were] then and there with said sheriff. That on the evening of the day last mentioned said Constable was released and Bonney and Waite retained for two days more.

That after the burial of Mr. Tunstall on the 22 of February 1878 a meeting of the citizens of Lincoln County was held to prevent further blood shed if possible. That at such meeting Hon. Florencio Gonzales Probate Judge of said County, Isaac Ellis, merchant, Jose Montaño, merchant and John Newcomb farmer were appointed a committee to wait upon Sheriff Brady to ascertain why he prevented the said Constable from executing said warrant and making arrests as therein directed and took said Constable and posse as aforesaid prisoners and still held Bonney and Waite as such.

They informed me on their return that Sheriff Brady said he held both the Constable and posse prisoners because he had the power. They further informed me that they asked said Sheriff Brady to set a value upon the property (he having failed to appraise the property attached) and that deponent would give a bond to be approved by said Brady. That the property so attached would be forth coming to answer any order or decree that might be made in the premises by the Hon. District Court for said Lincoln County and that if this deponent failed to give such bond, then he (Brady) could do with the property aforesaid as he thought fit, and they informed me that Brady replied that he would not take a bond of any kind from deponent for said property.

Deponent further says that five or six deputies were put by said Brady in charge of the store of J. H. Tunstall, dec'd, with its stock of general merchandise attached as the property of deponent and that three of that number were non residents of the County, to wit C. [sic] Morton, J. Long, and J. Longwill [Longwell] and all irresponsible and notorious tools of Murphy, Dolan & Riley. That said Brady acknowledged to this deponent in the hearing of several persons that his deputies last above mentioned, had abstracted goods from said store and appropriated the same to their own use.

That on or about the 18th day of February said Sheriff Brady had a detachment of United States soldiers from Fort Stanton stationed at the house of Murphy, Dolan & Riley aforesaid and that he cause [sic] to be issued for their horses belonging to such detachment, the hay belonging to Mr. Tunstall in his life time without authority or permission, other than the fact that he had attached it as the property of this deponent.

That at the time of such issue as aforesaid, the said Brady refused as I am informed by S. Corbet to allow any of the hay so attached to be fed to Mr. Tunstall's horses and that in consequence of this refusal, Mr. Tunstall's horses had to be fed elsewhere at great expense. That on the 19th day of February 1878 an affidavit was filed with said J. B. Wilson Justice of the Peace charging said Brady deputies as aforesaid with the appropriation of goods &c as aforesaid and that as a result of an examination had on said matter on the ___ day of February 78, said Brady was held to await the action of the Lincoln County Grand Jury for April 1878. A certified copy of such proceedings are hereto attached Marked 14.

Deponent further says that on the 11th day of February 1878 he made and executed an appearance bond as required by Judge Bristol and sent the same by Registered Letter to W. L. Rynerson District Attorney as aforesaid. A copy of said bond is hereto annexed marked 15. Said bond was refused as will appear by the copy of the endorsement on said copy bond hereto attached. Jose Montaño merchant of the said town of Lincoln volunteered to become one of my bondsmen as aforesaid. Subsequently he informed deponent that he was threatened with ruin by J. J. Dolan & Co. if he became one of my bondsmen. The said sheriff as said Montaño informed deponent used all his influence with said Montaño to prevent his becoming one of my sureties as aforesaid so as to prevent me from bonds and to oblige me to go to jail. Subsequently said Montaño became one of my bondsmen as appears by said copy of said bond. Joseph H. Blazer informed me that J. J. Dolan & Co. had also threatened that if he became one of my bondsmen they would have him prosecuted for cutting timber on the Public Lands as I understood in U.S. Courts by T. B. Catron U.S. District Attorney at Santa Fe.

A few days after the execution of said bond said Sheriff Brady called upon said Jose Montaño as the latter informed me with a letter purporting to be from said W. L. Rynerson to the effect that though a friend to said Montaño he could not accept him on bond of this deponent and requested that he with draw his name from said bond. After such representations and coaxing by said sheriff, said Montaño signed a letter complying with said request of withdrawal, written by said Brady. The sureties on said bond justified in different sums amounting to the aggregate sum of $34500. Deponent was informed by G. Washington that he heard Brady and Riley aforesaid say that there was no use in trying to give bonds as W. L. Rynerson aforesaid would not approve of any that he (deponent) would give & that he would have to go to jail.

Deponent now learnt that J. J. Dolan went to Mesilla to get an alias warrant for this deponent, said Deputy Sheriff Barrier having failed to deliver me to said Brady he having been induced to that course by the representatives of the best citizens in said county that if he delivered this deponent to said Brady, deponent would thereby loose his life. That this deponent informed the said Deputy Sheriff from Las Vegas in San Miguel County that as a matter of law he would be guilty of contempt of Court by failing to comply with his warrant, but that from that species of offenses he could purge himself but at no time did I ask or request said Barrier not to comply with his warrant, though I believed then as I do now that had I been delivered to Brady aforesaid I would have been murdered. For though I knew Brady to be the tool of Murphy, Riley & Dolan aforesaid, I in no way suspected that they would undertake to use him as an instrument to murder me at that time, at the time I was first imprisoned as elsewhere stated. I sent for Brady to take me before said Judge Bristol not knowing even then that Murphy, Dolan & Riley were the movers in prosecuting me.

Deponent further says that a day or so after the death of Tunstall, Col. Purington, Lieutenants, Delaney, Pague and Humphreys U.S.A. Fort Stanton N.M. called at the residence of deponent (where a large number of men all farmers or stockmen had congregated of their own free will and armed as they expressed it to protect the life of deponent), in order to ascertain in a friendly unofficial way the the state of affairs. That Col. Purington then and there in the presence of said Brady informed me of their mission and that they had called on Murphy, Dolan and Riley previously on the same office. That I gave them a concise statement of my views, giving names, places and and referring to for contradiction or conformation of the facts stated by me. That said Brady acknowledged so far as deponent was concerned my statements was correct. Said Col. Purington then and there in a private interview informed me that he was satisfied that Tunstall was brutally murdered at the instigation of "The House," a term here to mean Murphy, Dolan & Riley aforesaid. That it was a fact that could not be disputed. That they supported thieves and murderers by buying stolen cattle from them (the thieves) and that there was no doubt but that they brought Evans, Baker, Hill and Davis aforesaid into the county this time for a bad purpose. That there was no doubt in his mind that if said Barrier would [have] turned me over to Brady aforesaid I would be killed.

Deponent further says that on or about the 24 of February 1878 he was informed that said J. J. Dolan went to Mesilla to see W. L. Rynerson aforesaid for the purpose of obtaining an alias warrant for my arrest and another for the arrest of said Barrier and that thereupon I was entreated by the citizens both Americans and Mexicans to quit the town of Lincoln at once for a while. That I done so first remaining at one farm house and then another. That on or about the 9th day of March I returned to the town of Lincoln with the determination to remain there and submit to any order that Brady might get against me even if I lost my life.

Upon my arrival at Lincoln about 2 p.m. of the day last mentioned I learnt that his Excellency S. B. Axtell Governor of New Mexico had been at Lincoln and had left a short time before my arrival and that he had removed J. B. Wilson Justice of the Peace aforesaid.

Every body with whom I conversed appeared to be very much disheartened owing to the refusal of the Governor to hear them in relation to the troubles and in removing Wilson claiming that the Governor had espoused the cause of Murphy, Dolan & Riley aforesaid and cited the fact (aside from his statements here) that he had procured troops for said Brady by order of the President. D. P. Shield, I. Ellis and R. A. Widenmann informed me that the Governor positively refused to hear any thing from the people about the troubles. That when they asked him to visit the people and give them an opportunity to be heard he replied that he was posted as well as he wanted to be and that he did not want to hear any more from them.

Hon. F. Gonzales, I. Ellis, J. Montaño and J. Newcomb aforesaid and many others insisted that I absent myself under the circumstances as hereinbefore stated until the meeting of the District Court to which I reluctantly consented.

On or about the ____ day of ____ 1878 R. M. Brewer was specially deputized by J. B. Wilson Justice of the Peace to serve a warrant for the arrest of W. Morton and Frank Baker, two of the alleged murderers of Tunstall. A copy thereof is hereto attached and marked ____ [exhibit not with statement].

That said Morton and Baker were then at the cow camp of J. J. Dolan & Co. aforesaid on the Pecos River a distance of at least 150 miles. That on or about the night of the 10th of March 1878 R. N. Brewer came to see me before I should leave the town of Lincoln that then and there he informed me that he and posse arrested said Morton & Baker and that when within 30 miles of Lincoln, W. Morton snatched the pistol of one McCloskey already referred to, now one of said Brewer's posse, and shot said McCloskey in the head and then put to the mountains with said Baker, neither being in any way shackled. That thereupon the posse chased and killed said Morton and Baker.

Said Brewer after relating the death of said three persons as above stated & requested me to advise him as to how to make his return. Deponent then informed Mr. Brewer of the Governor's visit, his removal of J. B. Wilson, his forbidding said Wilson in person not to exercise the functions of such Justice of the Peace any longer and that he was about to issue a proclamation, the contents of which I did not then know – but which I afterwards saw a copy of which is hereto annexed marked Exhibit 16. I further informed Brewer that I understood that Murphy, Dolan and Riley had taken steps to have him and posse arrested for undertaking to arrest Morton & Baker by virtue of warrants issued by said J. B. Wilson. I advised Mr. Brewer to keep away from Lincoln and out of the way of Brady, Murphy, Dolan & Riley until the District Court convened when I was satisfied we could get justice. I parted with Brewer on the night last aforesaid and not seen him since and am creditably informed that he is dead.

I knew Mr. Brewer since I came to this County of Lincoln. He was a man who never drank any kind of liquor nor quarreled with any one and was thoroughly honest. He was a hard working farmer and stockman. Our people (as the paper hereto attached and marked Ex 17 will show) considered him one of our best citizens. He was not on good terms with Murphy, Dolan & Riley, he often expressed himself to the effect that he knew they wanted to kill him. He strongly opposed the organization of the Vigilant Committee referred to elsewhere in this statement. I know of my own knowledge that he paid them in two years $1000 rental for a piece of unsurveyed public lands and when he refused to continue to pay they wanted him killed or out of the way.

Deponent further says that from the time he returned from Mesilla until he left Lincoln Nov 10 1878 nearly every person who came to see him urged him to leave the town until Court met, stating that unless deponent done so he would loose his life. That on or about the 10 of March 1878 deponent left the town of Lincoln in company with G.

Washington, G. Robinson and Deputy Sheriff A. P. Barrier aforesaid for South Spring River in said County of Lincoln a distance of 70 miles from said town of Lincoln where I remained until on or about the 29 of March 1878 when I left in company with J. S. Chisum, R. M. Gilbert, Dr. M. R. Leverson, Jake Harris, C. Sampson and my wife for the town of Lincoln to attend Court.

On the 28th day of March 1878 said Sheriff Brady with a posse of soldiers went to South Spring River to summons jurors. John S. Chisum informed me that Brady then and there assured him that he did not want to arrest me and would not as he knew I would be at Court. By a clerical mistake the venire was made returnable on the 1st Monday of April whereas the term set by law for the holding of the District Court at said county of Lincoln is the second Monday of April. This more freely appears by the letter hereto attached and marked ____ [exhibit not attached to statement].

But for that fact that the sheriff stated as I am informed that court was to have begun on the first Monday I should not have left South Spring River for another week, having no faith in the guarantee of Brady that he would not arrest me for I am informed by Hon F. Gonzales Probate Judge aforesaid that Brady assured him that he would not arrest me no matter how many alias warrants he got for the purpose. On the first day of April 1878 in company with the aforementioned persons I went to the town of Lincoln and then and there learnt for the first time that said Brady and Geo Hindman had been killed on said day. On said day in the evening at Lincoln one George W. Peppin, a tool of Murphy, Dolan & Riley with Smith and a few soldiers from the fort arrested me on the alias warrant already referred to, said G. W. Peppin claiming to be acting as the Deputy of the dead Sheriff Brady.

Seeing that Peppin aforesaid, J. B. Mathews aforesaid and three of Tunstall's alleged murderers were endorsed in all they done by Col. George Purington with the U.S. soldiers, I applied to Col. Purington for protection. He acknowledged that if he left me in the custody of said Peppin, Mathews et al, he believed that I would be killed by them, but he claimed that he had no place for me at the post. My friends insisted that W. Dowling [Dowlin] Post Trader at Fort Stanton had a room that I could secure. Purington contended that he had not. After much intriaty [entreaty] he consented to take me up to the fort where subsequently he came near preventing me from securing a room as aforesaid.

He appeared to be anxious to leave me in the custody of Peppin aforesaid though he heard one of Peppin's posse say that I was the man they wanted, that they wanted him (Purington) to turn me over to them, that they would care for me.

Deponent further says that G. W. Peppin went to said Col. Purington and asked him (Purington) if he would allow him (Peppin) to search the house of deponent for arms. Purington replied in the affirmative. Peppin and posse then went to the house to search. Deponent forbade them to enter unless they had a warrant for that purpose. I used these words on that occasion, "Peppin you know that you are not an officer, but were you, you can't search without a warrant for that purpose," whereupon Mathews aforesaid replied, "We can't aye we'll show you what we can do." Then said Peppin replied that Col. Purington gave him (Peppin) permission to search the house. I then applied to Purington who replied that he allowed every one to do as he pleased. Dr. Montague R. Leverson of Colorado was then my guest. He pleaded with Purington to prevent such an out-rage and sanctioned it by the presence of himself, Lieut Smith and 25 soldiers all of whom were in close proximity to said Peppin and so remained until Peppin and posse completed their search, and taking with them one pistol and one double barreled shotgun.

During all this Dr. Leverson said to Purington that the Constitution of the U.S. guaranteed a man immunity from search seizure &c, whereupon Purington used these words "Damn the Constitution and you for a fool." Lieut Smith afterwards addressed Col. Purington, "This is the damn fool I saw at the Pecos." Purington replied, "Ah! Is this the damn fool you were telling me about." Col. Purington cursed fearfully and insultingly abused Rev T. F. Ealy, a Presbyterian minister then not a month from Pennsylvania, who with his family was then my guest.

Deponent further says that D. P. Shield, G. Washington, Geo. Robinson and R. A. Widenmann were arrested by said G. W. Peppin & posse without warrant charging them with being implicated in the murder of Brady & Hindman. That Col. Purington was appealed to by said parties for protection and that he consented to take them to the post with this deponent. That deponent and said four persons went to Fort Stanton in a private conveyance. That said Geo. Washington & G. Robinson were placed in the military guard house at Fort by said Purington and obliged to work during their stay there. That said D. P. Shield, R. A. Widenmann and deponent secured a suite of rooms from said W. Dowling [Dowlin] and said Purington placed a guard at each door thereto with orders to shoot any and all of us who left the rooms without permission. That even our friends could not see us without permission though we were in confinement at our own expense.

That after Lieut Col. Dudley assumed command at said Fort Stanton he inquired as to the circumstances under which we were held and as a result of that inquiry he said that we would have to apply to him for military protection if we desired to remain at the post.

This Shield and deponent did and remained at Fort Stanton having the liberties of the post until the District Court convened April 8, 1878. On or about the 8th day of April A.D. 1878 I was again arrested on the alias warrant for the offense of embezzlement already referred to. The said Judge Bristol then and there said that he or W. L. Rynerson District Attorney aforesaid would approve my bond. Sheriff Copeland newly appointed was instructed to give me every reasonable facility to give bonds. I made out a new bond the sureties thereon justifying in amounts aggregating $10000 only, their bond on presentation was approved by the said W. L. Rynerson who had refused my other bond for $34,500.00, though the sureties on this latter bond being the first ones offered were known to every body to be worth more money then those on the one accepted.

Deponent further says that the Grand Jury for the April (1878) term of said District Court for the County of Lincoln examined the charges of embezzlement against this deponent and their findings thereon is hereto attached marked Ex 18.

That on or about the 18th day of February J. H. Riley aforesaid came to the residence of this deponent in a drunken condition, that at this time Mr. Riley was anxious to show that he had no weapons about his person and to convince persons in the room of this fact [he] turned out his pockets. That in doing so he threw out a memorandum book and after asking the men in the house, one by one, if they wanted to kill him and receiving a reply in the negative, took his departure leaving said memorandum book on the table at the residence of deponent.

Deponent says that he examined said book with great care. That he found a letter in it in the handwriting of said W. L. Rynerson addressed to Dolan & Riley a copy of which [is] hereto attached and marked Exhibit 19. That said book showed the amount of sugar [and] coffee hauled by one Stephen Stanley from the Indian Agency in said County on a particular date. That said memorandum book showed a lot of memorandum against this deponent from time to time and before he was arrested at Las Vegas as aforesaid.

There was also a memorandum of cattle received by said Dolan & Riley from the notorious cattle thieves who names were given. That it also contained a list of names of persons well known in this county for their friendship for or in opposition to said Dolan & Riley. Opposite each name was a nome de plume, Catron being "Grapes," Godfroy "Hampton," Bernstein (Indian Agent clerk) "Soapweed," Indians "Trees," DeLaney (A.A.Q.M. at Fort Stanton) "Warwick," Murphy aforesaid "Box," Rynerson (Dist Atty aforesaid) "Oyster," Dowling [Dowlin] (Post Trader Fort Stanton) "Pimp," and McSween (this deponent) "Diablo" – Devil &c &c.

This deponent further says that he has often expressed himself to the effect that he was determined to use all lawful means to bring the murderers of Tunstall to justice if it cost him every Dollar he possessed or could earn. That after the adjournment of the April 78 Term of the said District Court for Lincoln County deponent learnt from the Sheriff of the County that the Prosecuting Attorney said W. L. Rynerson had failed and refused to place warrants in his hands for the arrest of parties indicted for the murder of said Tunstall, but had placed warrants in the Sheriff's hand for the arrest of all indicted persons supposed to sympathize with feeling against Murphy, Dolan and Riley.

That thereupon and on or about the 27th day of April 1878 deponent addressed and sent a letter to said W. L. Rynerson asking him to place warrants in the hands of the Sheriff for the arrest of all persons indicted by said Grand Jury for the murder of said Tunstall, if any were indicted. That afterward, to wit on or about the 4th day of May 1878 deponent received from said W. L. Rynerson an answer to said letter dated April 27 1878, a copy of which is hereto annexed marked 20.

Deponent further says that from all he can gather the recent troubles in Lincoln County are owing to the determination of Murphy, Dolan and Riley to prevent opposition to their business and that and nothing else in the cause of Tunstall's death. That this deponent has been well satisfied that the parties named (Murphy, Dolan and Riley) have been working to take the life of this deponent for the last two years, and that to do that said Dolan offered one Stephen Stanley (as deponent is informed) and believes $1000.

This deponent declares in the most solum [solemn] manner that he knows of no reason for the hatred of Murphy, Dolan and Riley towards him other than deponent has professionally and as a neighbor helped people to throw of [off] the yoke of said Murphy, Dolan & Riley, informing parties of their rights when requested so to do, and by encouraging emigration and helped those who were in the County to remain, whether acceptable to Murphy, Dolan & Riley or not.

That I have done all in my power, a poor man and citizen to stimulate our people and energy and independence of action and character and that this course caused Murphy, Dolan & Riley together with their way of dealing with _____. Their way of dealing with the people caused them to loose their power. This loss of power having finally culminated in the death of Tunstall. That a petition of which a copy is hereto annexed marked Ex 21 was signed by every resident of Lincoln County to whom it was presented, asking them [Murphy, Dolan and Riley] to leave the County giving as a reason that our people might have permanent peace.

Deponent further says that on or about the 4th day of April 1878 Richard M. Brewer aforesaid and A. L. Roberts, one of the alleged murderers of Tunstall, were killed at Mescalero Apache Indian Agency in this County under the following circumstances as was related to me by one who was present and saw all the shooting from beginning to end.

Frank Coe who affidavit is hereto annexed marked _____ [this affidavit is not in the Angel Report file]. Brewer, Coe and others went to the agency – some to look for stolen stock – some on business – all to talk to the Indian Agent for harboring alleged murderers and thieves who were helping Murphy, Dolan & Riley against the people. There they met A. L. Roberts one of Tunstall's alleged murderers who drew his gun on Chas. Bowdre and fired as he approached said Roberts, the bullet grazing Bowdre's abdomen, whereupon Bowdre fired at Roberts, the bullet entering the stomach of Roberts. Roberts now shot Middleton & Coe, not fatally, and killed Brewer aforesaid.

That on or about the 1st day of May, I was informed by Saturnino Baca that five men had wanted to enter his house to secret themselves for the purpose of killing me and others. That they said they had killed a man or two a few miles below belonging to the "Regulators." We now received warnings to the effect that ten or twelve men were stationed at the house West of my house formerly occupied by Murphy, Dolan & Riley, but now controlled by T. B. Catron, U.S. District Attorney Santa Fe, being represented by his brother-in-law E. A. Walz. A copy of whose letter in relation to this matter is hereto annexed marked Ex 22 [this exhibit is not in the Angel Report file]. That there were 20 more well armed men on the East of my residence!

Upon this information the Sheriff (Copeland) placed 4 or 5 men on my house for the protection of my life and property and done the same as he and others informed me in the centre and at the East end of the town. Learning that these men numbered 30 or 40 men said Copeland as I am informed sent for a detachment of soldiers to aid him in resisting said bands of men.

From Frank Coe I learnt that when on his way home from said Lincoln to wit on or about the day ___ of May 1878 [April 29, 1878] in company with Frank McNab and James Saunders, they were fired at by different parties of men in ambush in different directions, killed McNab and dangerously if not fatally wounded Saunders in the left hip and ankle and holding said Coe until next day as a hostage. That the party after that came to the town of Lincoln and divided into parties as already stated. Just about noon of said day firing commenced but as to whether the firing was commenced by the Sheriff's party or by the murderers I cannot say, though I have been informed that it was commenced by the party lying in ambush at the East end of town.

About 3 o'clock in the afternoon of the same day Lieut Smith and a number of soldiers with Sheriff Copeland took about 22 men prisoner. Deponent has been informed that said 22 men after killing McNab and wounding Saunders as aforesaid desired to attack the store of I. Ellis & Sons but that after going near the building about day light next day, said posse found the doors and windows of said house were only kept closed for the purpose as they supposed of concealing armed men from their view and so abandoned the proposed attack.

That on or about the 3rd day of May 1878 an affidavit was filed with J. G. Trujillo Justice of the Peace of Precinct No 2 in said Lincoln County charging R. W. Beckwith, [William H.] Johnson and 20 others with the murder of McNab and wounding of Saunders as aforesaid. That a warrant was issued on said affidavit and placed in the hands of Sheriff Copeland for execution. That on or about the 4th day of May 1878 this deponent with several others went to Precinct No 2 for the purpose of testifying against the 22 men aforesaid.

That on or about the 6th day of May 1878 Lieuts. Goodwin and Smith with about 25 soldiers in charge of the said Sheriff came to said Precinct No 2 with warrants for the arrest of all 22 men. That the warrant on which affiant and others were sought to be arrested was issued by one D. Easton, Justice of the Peace for Precinct No 3, and that the offense charged was assault with intent to kill based upon an affidavit before some military officer at Fort Stanton by said G. W. Peppin and J. B. Mathews.

That this deponent was insulted by said Lieut Goodwin. That said Goodwin refused to obey the Sheriff and informed the Sheriff then and there that he would not allow any one to be arrested unless the Sheriff turned this deponent over to him (Goodwin) to be taken to Fort Stanton. That said positively refused to obey the Sheriff's orders. That by his words and acts showed himself to be a bitter partisan.

That after reaching Fort Stanton this deponent with I. Ellis & Sons and others were put in the guard house at Fort Stanton. That we were kept in confinement for two days. That we were taken from the guard house in order to have an examination before a Justice of the Peace. That the 22 men referred to as I am informed were turned loose and failed to be taken or go before a Justice of [the] Peace and so the charge of murder still remains against them with examination.

Deponent has been informed that said Johnson with the balance of said 22 men as posse was acting as the Deputy of Sheriff Brady, who has been dead at that time about two months, a fact well known to said Johnson & his party.

Deponent has been informed that that said 22 men were started from the Pecos for Lincoln for the purpose of killing I. Ellis, Sheriff Copeland and this deponent. Deponent further says that nearly all of said 22 men were the parties and tools of said Murphy, Dolan & Riley deriving their support chiefly from said Murphy, Dolan and Riley.

Deponent further says that he is informed that Sheriff Brady told his wife the night before he was killed that he knew that he wronged this deponent and over stepped the law and that he was going to see Murphy and unless Murphy receded from the position he had taken & do what was right with deponent, he would resign and leave Murphy to fight his own battles.

Deponent further says that Tunstall was one of the quietest and most inoffensive men he has ever seen, a man who neither offended by word or deed. He was industrious and thoroughly honest and truthful.

Deponent further says he has given a correct statement of the troubles in said Lincoln Co. that culminated in the death of Tunstall and of the disorder and violence that has followed so far as the knowledge and information of this deponent extends. That he has given a true statement of events without regard as to the light in which some may place him.

A. A. McSween (signed)
Read, subscribed and sworn to before me this 6th day of June 1878
Rafael Gutierrez
Probate Clerk
By Juan B. Patron
Dpty

McSween Statement Exhibit 1 - July 31,1877

[McSween's First National Bank check issued to Sheriff Brady for taxes dated July 31, 1877]

No 300
Lincoln N.M. July 31, 1877
First National Bank of Santa Fe N.M.
Pay to Mr. Brady Sheriff and Ex Officio Collector Lincoln Co. N.M. Fifteen Hundred and Forty Five 13/100 dollars In Territorial (N.M.) Scrip
A. A. McSween
1545.13/100 in Territorial Scrip

(Endorsement on Face)
First National Bank of Santa Fe N. Mex. Aug 23 1877

(Endorsed on back)
Wm. Brady
Sheriff & Ex Officio Collector
Jno. H. Riley

McSween Statement Exhibit 2 - October 19, 1876

[Agreement made by A. A. McSween with Emilie Scholand and Charles Fritz to act as attorney for the Estate of Emil Fritz dated October 19, 1876.]

Know all men by these Presents that Mrs. Emile [Emilie] Scholand had Charles Fritz, Administrator and Administratrix de bonis administrates [latin for of the goods administered] of the estate of Emil Fritz, late of the County of Lincoln in the Territory of New Mexico – deceased – have made, constituted and appointed and by these presents do make, constitute and appoint Alexander A. McSween of said County & Territory our true and lawful attorney for us, and in our name, places and stead to ask, demand, collect any and all moneys due said Estate; to sue for the recovery of the same; to receipt in our names for all sums of money so collected; to compromise and compound any claims due said Estate of Emil Fritz, deceased. To ask, demand and receive of the Mercantile Life Insurance Company of the City and State of New York the amount of the Policy #1058, dated July 12 1871 on the life of said Emil Fritz deceased in said Company and to compromise and compound the amount of said Policy and to give said compound full and complete receipt for the amount to be realized from said Policy when such settlement as he may make with said Company. Giving and granting to our said Attorney full power and authority to do and perform all and every act and thing whatsoever requisite and necessary to be be done in and about the promise as fully to all intents and purposes as we might or could do if personally present with full power of substitution and revocation, hereby ratifying all that our said Attorney or his substitute shall lawfully do or cause to be done by virtue hereto.

In Witness Thereof we have hereto set our hands and seals the nineteenth day of October in the year One Thousand Eight Hundred and Seventy Eight.

Emile [Emilie] Scholand (signed)
Administratrix
Charles Fritz (signed)
Administrator of the Estate

Territory of New Mexico
County of Lincoln

The following agreement entered into and between Alexander A. McSween Lincoln, Lincoln County, N. Mex. party of the first part and Emile [Emilie] Scholand and Charles Fritz of the County and Territory aforesaid parties of the second part.

Witnesseth that the party of the first part hereby promises and agrees in consideration of the promises to act as Attorney at Law of the parties of the second part in all matters and things concerning the estate of Emil Fritz, deceased, said parties of the second part having been duly appointed Administrator and Administratrix of said estate by the said Probate Court in and for the County of Lincoln aforesaid on the 19th day of September A.D. 1876. The said party of the first part further promises and agrees that as Attorney as aforesaid he will faithfully, diligently and to the best of his ability act as in his judgment may seem most conducive to the interest of said Estate, regardless of the interest of any other third party or parties. That he will at all times advise and council the parties of the second part when called upon so to do in relation to said estate.

The parties of the second part in consideration of the above promise to pay the said party of the first part a Retainer of Five Hundred Dollars out of the assets of said estate, it being agreed and understood by and between the parties hereto, that no part of said Five Hundred Dollars shall be paid to the said Alexander A. McSween unless the same is realized from said estate; the parties of the second part further promise and agree that the party of the first part shall have and receive as compensation for the collection the sum of ten per cent of all sums collected by him or reported to as collected.

Witness our hands and seals this 2d day of October 1876 at Lincoln, Lincoln County, New Mexico.

A. A. McSween
Attorney at Law (signed and sealed)

Emile Scholand
Administratrix (signed and sealed)
Chas. Fritz
Administrator,
of The Estate of Emil Fritz, Deceased (signed)

McSween Statement Exhibit 3 - December 21, 1876

[McSween's notification to Charles Fritz and Emilie Scholand through the Probate Court to present his legal fees to the Emil Fritz estate dated December 21, 1876 (incorrectly shows year as 1878). An itemized list of his charges to the estate is attached.]

Law Office
Alex. A. McSween
Lincoln, New Mexico
Dec 21 1878 [1876]

In the matter of the The Estate of Emil Fritz, Deceased

To Emile [Emilie] Scholand and Charles Fritz
Administratrix and Administrator of the Estate of Emil Fritz Dec'd

You and each of you are hereby notified that on the first day of the January 1878 term of said Court, I will present my account with the said estate of Emil Fritz, deceased, for the approval of said Court

A. A. McSween (signed)
Attorney for the Estate of Emil Fritz

We acknowledge service of the above notice
Emilie Scholand (signed)
Administratrix
Charles Fritz (signed)
Administrator
Of The Estate of Emil Fritz, Deceased

Lincoln New Mexico
12/18/1876
The Estate of Emil Fritz, Deceased

To Alex. A. McSween

The following accounts to be found on the list put in my hands for collection have been settled. Upon the accounts settled I charge ten per cent as per agreement hereto attached.

[Two pages of accounts, not reproduced here.]

Before the undersigned authority personally came Alexander A. McSween to me well known as the attorney for the Estate of Emil Fritz, deceased, who having been duly sworn according to law deposith and saith that the foregoing account is in all respects correct and just. That the indebtedness therein set forth accessed as therein stated, that the above and foregoing assessment of $3815.50 is justly due the claimant above all claims and offsets which the said Estate may have against him. That no part of the above and foregoing accounts claimed to be due has yet been paid or in any way satisfied, and deponent saith further that he has no further claim against the said Estate.

A. A. McSween (signed)
Atty for Estate of Emil Fritz Deceased

Sworn to and subscribed before me this eighteenth day of December A.D 1876

Ed Soto (signed)
Clerk of Probate Court
By Juan B. Patron,
Deputy Clerk

Territory of New Mexico
County of Lincoln
In the Probate Court
January 1877 Term

In the matter of Administration of Emil Fritz, deceased

On the regular January 1877 Term of the Probate Court of the County of Lincoln in the Territory of New Mexico, held at Lincoln in said County on Monday January 1st A.D. 1877, the foregoing account of Alexander A. McSween against the Estate of Emil Fritz, deceased, was presented for approval whereupon the same was examined in open Court by the Hon. the Probate Judge of said County in the presence of Charles Fritz, one of the Administrators of the Estate of said Emil Fritz, deceased, Emile [Emilie] Scholand Administratrix, being temporarily absent from said County, having acknowledged service of said notice of present action of said account for approval at this time as per Exhibit "A" made a part hereof. This account upon examination as aforesaid, having been found correct, it is ordered that the same be paid by the said Emile [Emilie] Scholand and Charles Fritz, Administratrix and Administrator (or their successor or successors) of the Estate of Emil Fritz deceased out of any moneys now or hereafter in their hands pertaining to said Estate.

Florencio Gonzales (signed)
Judge Probate of Lincoln County in the Territory of New Mexico

McSween Statement Exhibit 4 - May 1877

[L. G. Murphy's request (May 1877) to the Probate Court for examination of his company records for assessment of assets due him and Emil Fritz.]

The Territory of New Mexico
County of Lincoln
In Probate Court
May 1877 term

In the Matter of the Estate Of Emil Fritz, deceased.

To the Hon. Florencio Gonzales, Judge of Probate in and for the county of Lincoln, aforesaid.

Your petitioner, Lawrence G. Murphy would respectfully submit the following for your consideration and judicial action.

1st. That your petitioner is the surviving partner of Emil Fritz, deceased, and has therefore a paramount interest in the speedy and final settlement of said estate.

2nd. That in order that the rights of the deceased and living may neither be jeopardized nor sacrificed, your petitioner respectfully asks that you may nominate, and under and by your warrant appoint three persons competent and skillful in bookkeeping to examine the Books of accounts in which were recorded all the transactions in which the deceased and myself had a joint interest as L.G. Murphy & Co.

3rd. That all the Books, notes, receipts &c are still existing and capable of examination and explanation, and will be delivered for such examination to the parties your honor may appoint as aforesaid.

4th. That every facility will be extended such examiners by me that may elucidate the Records and bring their labors to a formal and satisfactory conclusion.

5th. That the examiners as appointed may report with minuteness within a specified time and by their finding disclose whether (and how much) the estate aforesaid owes me or vice versa.

Hoping your honor will grant my petition
I have the honor to be
Lawce. G. Murphy
Surviving partner of Emil Fritz

McSween Statement Exhibit 5 - May 1877

[Notice of the Probate Court (May 1877) to Emil Fritz Estate of having appointed three persons to comply with request of L. G. Murphy.]

The Territory of New Mexico
County of Lincoln
In the Probate Court
May 1877 Term

In The Matter of the Estate of Emil Fritz, deceased

Whereas Lawrence G. Murphy, a resident of the County of Lincoln aforesaid, surviving partner of Emil Fritz late of said County, deceased, filed his petition herein praying the Hon. Probate Court aforesaid to nominate and appoint three persons well learned in Book Keeping to examine the Books and papers in which the said Lawrence G. Murphy and Emil Fritz, deceased, recorded or caused to be recorded all transactions, receipts and disbursements in which they had a joint interest, in order that it might be ascertained whether (and how much) the said estate is indebted to the said L. G. Murphy or the said L. G. Murphy to the said deceased, promising that he would extend such persons as we might appoint every facility in elucidating the said books &c, and thus aid the persons so appointed in ascertaining finally the status of the said firm of L. G. Murphy & Co. at the time of the death of said Emil Fritz, to wit: the 26th day of June A.D. 1874.

Now, therefore, the said Judge of Probate hath appointed and by these presents does appoint you Juan B. Patron, Morris J. Bernstein and Alexander A. McSween to examine the Ledgers, Day Books, Journals, Cash Books, Bills Receivable, Bills Payable, notes and receipts in which said L. G. Murphy, surviving partner of Emil Fritz, deceased, and Emil Fritz as L. G. Murphy & Co., recorded their business transactions:

You will carefully, faithfully and diligently examine everything within your reach that will enable you to arrive at a final and correct conclusion: You will record your investigations with minuteness and precision from, the commencement of your investigation until its close and report the same to us immediately after the termination of your labors.

Witness the Hon. Florencio Gonzales, Judge of Probate and the seal of said Court at Lincoln, Lincoln Co., N.M. this 9th day of May, A.D. 1877.

Florencio Gonzales
Judge of Probate

Attest
A. A. Sedillo
Clerk

McSween Statement Exhibit 6 - May 25, 1877

[Record made from the examination of L. G. Murphy & Co. account books showing the business interests of Emil Fritz and L. G. Murphy prior to August 31, 1874.]

Amounts of debts due Lawrence G. Murphy & Co., constituted and composed of Lawrence G. Murphy (surviving partner) and Emil Fritz deceased as appears by their Books of accounts examined by us. We followed such accounts no further than the 31st day of Aug A.D. 1874, being the date at which said L. G. Murphy, surviving partner as aforesaid, was informed of the death of said E. Fritz as said L. G. Murphy testified before us.

[Seven pages of accounts, not recorded here.]

We the undersigned find that the sum of forty two thousand seven hundred and twenty eight 23/100 Dollars was due L. G. Murphy and the sum of Seventeen thousand four hundred and eighty three 67/100 Dollars was due Emil Fritz as capital stock in the firm of L. G. Murphy & Co. on the 31st day of August A.D. 1874 as appears by the books of said firm.

Witness our hands this 25th day of May A.D. 1877, at Lincoln, New Mexico

A. A. McSween (signed)
Juan B. Patron (signed)
Morris J. Bernstein (signed)

I, Charles Fritz fully concur with the above findings having been present aiding the said three examiners during the examination of the Books of L. G. Murphy & Co. as herewith set forth.

Witness my hand at Lincoln N.M. May 25, 1877
Charles Fritz (signed)
Administrator of the Estate of Emil Fritz deceased

We the undersigned commissioners appointed by your honor to examine the books and accounts of L. G. Murphy & Co. up to the time of the demise of Emil Fritz, to wit, the 31st day of August A.D. 1874, beg leave to submit the foregoing as the result of their labors & beg to be discharged from further duty.

Juan B. Patron (signed)
A. A. McSween (signed)
F. G. Christie (signed)

McSween Statement Exhibit 7 - July 19, 1877

[Letter dated July 19, 1877, from Donnell, Lawson & Co. to McSween giving notification of the Emil Fritz life insurance policy for $10,000, crediting McSween with $7,148.49, listing all fees incurred by Donnell Lawson.]

Donnell, Lawson & Co., Bankers
92 Broadway
New York
July 19 - 1877

Alexander A. McSween
Lincoln, N.M.

Dear Sir

We credit you $7,148.49 proceeds Life Ins. Policy Emil Fritz after deducting our com's [Commissions] as per agreement with you which we mention here, that the parties for whom you are acting may see it was the best could be done under the circumstances & has resulted greatly to the interest of all concerned.

The settlement offered you was $6500 less $700.00 charges, reducing the amount to $5800.00.

Our proposition to you was to advance this $700.00 & get possession of the policy & proof & guarantee you the $5800.00 ourselves & prosecute the case in the courts.

In consideration of this advance & guarantee [underlined] we were to receive one half the surplus after paying over to you the $5,800.00 & remembering ourselves for the outlay of $700.00 & attorneys fees &c. Under the old arrangement $5,800.00 is all you could have obtained, whereas now you get $7,148.49.

The following statement shows the whole transaction.

Received by our Lawyers – $10,000
From this deduct Advance – $700
Lawyers fees and telegrams – $803.03
Our 1/2 net profit – $1,348.51
To your cr. [credit] – $7,138.49

Thus – $10,000
Less Advance – $700
Fees and Tel [telegrams] – $803.03
Amt Guaranteed – $5,800.00
1/2 of this net profit to us – $1,348.48

The other 1/2 $1348.49 added to $5800 = $7,148.49

This we think must surely give great satisfaction to you and more especially to the parties you represent.

Merchants Life Insurance Company
In the matter of claim on policy of Emil Fritz
Messrs. Donnell Lawson & Co.

To Starr & Ruggles

To preparing special power of attorney from A. A. McSween to L. M. Lawson – $25.00

Examine papers with reference to claim of Merchants Life Insurance Company and advise Lawson as to same – $25.00

Conference with Messrs Beach & Brown Attorneys for Speigelberg as to proceedings taken for settlement with Hobbe for $5300, and settling with them and processing the papers in their hands for Lawson – $75.00

Investigating situation of the Estate of the Insurance Co. and proceedings for appointment of Receiver, apply to Insurance Dept at Albany and prepare and file claim – $50.00

Prepare to take proceedings for new Receiver in place of Alexander dec'd – $25.00

Prepare petition and papers to apply to Supreme Court to compel payment or for leave to sue Receiver, and making motion and obtaining leave to sue Receiver; beginning suit; preparing interrogatories to examine witnesses in Germany and New Mexico &c &c – $100.00

Negotiations with Receiver and his atty's for settlement and effecting settlement through order of court for $10,000 and withdrawing suit no costs chargeable to Receiver – 5%

Rec'd payment – $800.00
Starr & Ruggles (signed)

McSween Statement Exhibit 8 - August 1, 1877

[Letter from McSween to Emilie Scholand and Charles Fritz dated August 1, 1877, giving notice of the insurance money collection, and requesting he be released from the administrator bond.]

Law Office of
Alex A. McSween
Lincoln New Mexico
August 1, 1877

Mrs. Emilie Scholand, Administratrix, and Mr. Charles Fritz Administrator of the Estate of Emil Fritz, Deceased

I take this method of informing you that the Policy for $10,000.00 on the life of said deceased, issued by the Merchants Life Insurance Company of the City and State of New York has been paid and that I am now ready to settle you and account for said amount, together with other debts secured by me for said Estate.

Said sum should have drawn interest, and such would have been recovered but for the fact that L. Spiegelberg of N.Y. City, who had the matter in hand from the death of said deceased until Nov last when I took the matter out of his hands, failed to make the proper representation to the Company during its solvency or to its Receiver afterwards.

As you have both disregarded my advice and directions in the administration of said Estate, I desire to be relieved from further responsibility as one of your bondsmen; for this release I petitioned the Hon. Probate Court of the County of Lincoln N.M.

Before paying the money and other evidences of indebtedness over to you, the Record of the Court must show that am no longer responsible on said bond, but that [I] am fully discharged there from and that new Bonds approved by the Court are filed.

The knowledge that there are other parties than you interested in the management and final distribution of the assets of the estate induces me to exact the above.

Hoping the request will meet your approval and that you'll without delay, secure an acceptable Bondsmen in my lieu.

I am yours Respectfully,
A. A. McSween (signed)
Atty for Estate of Emil Fritz, Deceased

McSween Statement Exhibit 9 - Janury 18, 1878

[Letter from Tunstall to the *Mesilla Valley Independent* dated January 18, 1878, titled "A Tax-Payers Complaint."]

From Lincoln County – A Tax-Payers Complaint

Office of John H. Tunstall
Lincoln, Lincoln Co., N.M.
January 18, 1878

"The present Sheriff of Lincoln County has paid nothing during his present term of office." – Governors Message for 1878.

Editor of the Independent:

The above extract is a sad and unanswerable comment on the efficiency of Sheriff Brady, and cannot be charged upon "croakers." Major Brady, as the records of this County show, collected over Twenty-five hundred dollars, Territorial funds. Of this sum, Alex. A. McSween Esq., of this place, paid him over Fifteen hundred dollars by cheque on the First National Bank of Santa Fe, August 23, 1877.

Said cheque was presented for payment by John H. Riley, Esq., of the firm of J. J. Dolan & Co., this last amount was paid by the last named gentleman to Underwood and Nash for cattle. Thus passed away over Fifteen hundred dollars belonging to the Territory of New Mex.

With the exception of thirty-nine dollars, all the Taxes of Lincoln County for 1877 were promptly paid when due.

Let not Lincoln County suffer for the delinquency of one, two or three men.

By the exercise of proper vigilance the payer can readily ascertain what has become of that he had paid for the implied protection of the commonwealth. It is not only his privilege but his duty. A delinquent tax payer is bad, a delinquent tax collector is worse.

J. H. T.

McSween Statement Exhibit 10 - January 28, 1878

[Dolan's letter to the *Mesilla Valley Independent* answering Tunstall's letter to the newspaper titled "A Tax-Payers Complaint."]

ANSWER TO A TAX-PAYER'S COMPLAINT
Las Cruces, N. M., Jan. 29, 1978

Dear Sir:

In answer to a communication in reference to taxpayers of Lincoln County published in your issue of the 26th inst. and signed J. H. T., I wish to state that every thing contained therein is false. In reference to Sheriff Brady, I will state that he deposited with our house Territorial funds amounting to nearly $2000, subject to his order and payable on demand. Owing to sickness in the family of Sheriff Brady he was unable to be at Santa Fe in time to settle his account with the Territory. This I hope will explain satisfactorily how the Gov. in his Message had our County (Lincoln) delinquent.

If Mr. J. H. T. was recognized as a gentleman, and could be admitted into respectable circles in our community, he might be better posted in public affairs. For my part, I can't see the object of Mr. J. H. T.'s letter, unless it is to have the public believe that A. A. McSween is one of the largest tax-payers in our County, when in fact he is one of the smallest. Sheriff Brady is ready and willing at any time to show uneasy tax-payers what disposition he has made of the money paid by them; he can also show clean receipts from the Territorial treasurer of his account.

Respectfully,
J. J. Dolan

McSween Statement Exhibit 11 - Undated

[McSween business account record with Tunstall.]

Alex A McSween in acct with J.H. Tunstall:

[Three pages of charges and credits not reproduced here. The last line of the listing shows the total amount due McSween from Tunstall as $4157.46.]

McSween Statement Exhibit 12 - May 31, 1878

[Copy made by J. B. Wilson, May 31, 1878, of Coroner's Inquest Report on the body of J. H. Tunstall.]

Territory of New Mexico
County of Lincoln

We the undersigned Justices of the Peace and Coroner's Jury who say upon the inquest held this 19th day of February 1878 on the body of John H. Tunstall, here found in precinct No 1 of the County of Lincoln, Territory of New Mexico, find that the deceased came to his death on or about the 18th day of Feby 1878 by means of divers bullets shot and sent forth out of and from deadly weapons and upon the head and body of said John H. Tunstall which said deadly weapons were there and then held by one of more of the persons who are herewith written, to wit, Jessie Evans, Frank Baker, Thomas Hill,

George Hindman, J. J. Dolan, William Morton, and others not identified by the witnesses who testified before the Coroner's Jury.

We the undersigned to the best of our knowledge & belief, from the evidence of the Coroner's Inquest, believe the above statement to be a true and impartial verdict.

Geo B. Barber (signed)
R. M. Gilbert (signed)
John Newcomb (signed)
Samuel Smith (signed)
Frank Coe (signed)
Benj. H. Ellis (signed)
John B. Wilson, (signed)

Justice of the Peace in and for precinct No. 1 Lincoln, Lincoln County, Territory of New Mexico. I hereby certify that the above and foregoing is a true and and correct of the proceedings on the inquest of John H. Tunstall as appears by my docket.

Witness my hand this 31st day of May A.D. 1878 at Precinct No. 1 Lincoln Co. N. Mex.

John B. Wilson
Justice of the Peace
Precinct No. 1
Lincoln Co. N. Mex

McSween Statement Exhibit 13 - February 19, 1878

[Warrant issued by John B. Wilson for parties accused of murder of John H. Tunstall, based on affidavits made by R. M. Brewer and William Bonney, February 19, 1878. Affidavits not furnished. Copy carries date of August 31, 1878.]

The Territory of New Mexico
County of Lincoln

I, John B. Wilson, Justice of the Peace in and for Precinct No. 1, Lincoln County, New Mexico, do hereby certify that on or about the 19th day of February 1878, W. Boney [Bonney] and R. M. Brewer filed in my office affidavits charging John [James] J. Dolan, J. Conovaur [Cochrane], Frank Baker, Jessie Evans, Tom Hill, George Davis, O. L. Roberts, P. Gallegos, T. Green, J. Awly [Hurley], A. H. Mills, "Dutch Charley" proper name unknown [Charles Kruling], R. W. Beckwith, William Morton, George Harman [Hindman] J. B. Mathews, and others with having murdered and killed one Jno. H. Tunstall at the said County of Lincoln, on or about the 18th day of February, 1878, that on or about the 20th day of Feby 1878, issued warrants on said affidavits for the arrest of the parties above named and directed the same to the Constable of Precinct No. One in said County to wit: Atanacio Martinez.

That on or about the 22nd day of Feby 1878 said warrant was returned "not served." That on or about the said last mentioned day the undersigned issued an alias warrant for the apprehension of the above named persons, and there being then and there no officers to serve such warrant, the undersigned, as directed by law, in such cases specially empowered Richard M. Brewer to serve the same endorsing such deputation on said last mentioned warrant.

In testimony whereof, I have hereunto set my hand at Lincoln, Precinct No 1 Lincoln County, N. Mexico this 31st day of August 1878.

John B. Wilson
Justice of the Peace

Precinct #1
Lincoln Co N. Mex
Territory of New Mexico
County of Lincoln

Be it remembered that before the undersigned a Justice of the Peace in and for the County and Territory aforesaid, personally came R. M. Brewer & W. Boney [Bonney] who being duly sworn according to law deposeth saith that the County and Territory aforesaid on the 18th day of February

[Remainder of this exhibit is missing from Report.]

McSween Statement Exhibit 14 - May 31, 1878

[Statement by J. B. Wilson of act directed against Sheriff Brady for stealing goods from the J. H. Tunstall store. Copy record dated May 31, 1878.]

The Territory of New Mexico
County of Lincoln
Precinct Number One

I, John B. Wilson, Justice of the Peace in and for precinct number one in Lincoln County Territory of New Mexico, do hereby certify on the 20th day of February 1878 the following proceeding among others were had in and before me at my office in the town of Lincoln, as appears of record in my office to wit:

The Territory of New Mexico vs William Brady et al, February 19th, 1878 warrant issued returnable forthwith Feby 20th 1878. Atanacio Martinez, Constable of Precinct No. one, Lincoln County New Mexico and brings into court the bodies of William Brady and others charged with stealing and carrying away, hay, wood and merchandise from the store of J. H. Tunstall in said town of Lincoln New Mex., over the value of $20.00 on or about the 18th day of Feby 1878.

This court having heard the order and being duly advised in the premises ordered, considered, and adjudged that as named as charged with said larceny but said William Brady, be released and discharged and that said William Brady be held to give Bonds in the sum of $200.00 to appear before the 3d Judicial District Court at its April 1878 term to answer unto the Territory of New Mexico any indictment that may be found by the Grand Jury at the aforesaid term in and for the County of Lincoln with sufficient surety, said Bonds to be approved by the Constable of Precinct No. 1 Lincoln Co. N. Mex.

John B. Wilson (signed)
Justice of the Peace

I hereby certify that the above is a true copy of the entry of the above case as appears by my docket.

Witness my hand this 31st day of May 1878 at Precinct No one Lincoln Co. N, Mex.

John B. Wilson
Justice of the Peace
Precinct #1 Lincoln County N. Mex.

McSween Statement Exhibit 15 - February 9 and 11, 1878

[Bond issued February 9 and 11, 1878, in favor of McSween covering the embezzlement charge filed against him and Bond request denied by W. L. Rynerson.]

Territory of New Mexico
County of Lincoln

Know all men by these Presents that we Alexander A. McSween as principal and J. H. Tunstall, James West, John N. Copeland, Isaac Ellis, Francisco Romero y Valencia & Jose Montaño, his sureties are held and firmly bound unto the Territory of New Mexico in the penal sum of Eight Thousand Dollars, for the payment of which well and truly to be made we bind ourselves our and each of our heirs, executors and Administrators truly and firmly by these presents, signed with our hands and sealed with our seals this ninth day of February as One Thousand Eight Hundred & Seventy Eight.

The Condition of the foregoing obligation is such that:

Whereas he above bounded Principal Alexander A. McSween has been arrested on the charge of having embezzled the sum of Ten Thousand Dollars monies belonging to the estate of Emil Fritz deceased, and

Whereas, he was on the 10th day of February A.D. 1878 examined before the Hon. Warren Bristol, associate Justice of the Supreme Court and presiding Judge of the 3d Judicial District of New Mexico, in regard to committing by him of the said Alexander A. McSween of the said crime of embezzlement and

Whereas the said Judge being fully advised in the premises did commit the said Alexander A. McSween to answer any indictment that might be found against him, the said Alexander A. McSween by reason of the premises

Now therefore if the said Alexander A. McSween shall well and truly appear before the Hon. the District Court of the Third Judicial District of New Mexico, at the next ensuing term of said Court. to beholden in and for the County of Lincoln at the opening of said Court on the second Monday of April A.D. 1878 and shall remain in attendance upon said Court from day to day and from Term to Term there to answer any indictment that may be brought or found against him for committing the crime of embezzlement and shall so remain in attendance from day to day and from Term to Term until discharged by authority of Law, then this obligation to be void, otherwise to remain in full force and effect.

A. A. McSween (seal)
J. H. Tunstall (seal)
James West (seal)
John N. Copeland (seal)

Isaac Ellis (seal)
Francisco Romero y Valencia (seal)
Jose Montaño (seal)

Attest
Issac Ellis
John B. Wilson
Territory of New Mexico
County of Lincoln

Before me the undersigned authority personally came and appeared A. A. McSween, J. H. Tunstall, James West, John N. Copeland, Isaac Ellis, Francisco Romero y Valencia and Jose Montaño whose names are signed to the above instrument of wording and each known to me personally who acknowledged each for himself and that he executed the said instrument for the purpose therein specified and that the same is his true act and deed.

Witness my hand & national seal this 11th day of Feby A.D. 1878

D. P. Shield
Notary Public
Lincoln, N. M.

Territory of New Mexico
County of Lincoln

Before me the undersigned on shurity personally came and appeared on this the 9th & 11th days of February A.D. 1878 J. H. Tunstall, James West, John N. Copeland, Isaac Ellis, Francisco Romero y Valencia & Jose Montaño whose names are signed to the above instrument of writing who, each having first been by me duly sworn according to the law, upon his oath says that he is worth the amount set opposite to his name below in property situated within the Territory of New Mexico, over and above all his just debts and liabilities and property exempt by law from execution and forced sale.

J. H. Tunstall – $20,000.00
James West – $4,000.00
John N. Copeland – $3,000.00
Isaac Ellis – $4,000.00
Francisco Romero y Valencia (his mark) – $2,000.00
Jose Montaño – $1,500.00

Attest
Isaac Ellis
John B. Wilson

Sworn to and subscribed to before me by J. H. Tunstall, who executes in the sum of Twenty Thousand Dollars and by James West in the sum of Four Thousand Dollars and by John N. Copeland in the sum of Three Thousand Dollars on the 9th day of February 1878 and I further certify that Isaac Ellis subscribed said affidavit and justified in the sum Four Thousand Dollars and Francisco Romero y Valencia in the sum of Two Thousand Dollars and Jose Montaño in the sum of Fifteen Hundred Dollars on the 11th day of February A.D. 1878. All done in the County of Lincoln & Territory of New Mexico.

Witness my hand and Notarial Seal
D. P. Shield
Notary Public

Lincoln County
Territory of New Mexico

Endorsed

The within Bond is not approved for reasons as follows. Before approving the within Bond the sureties must justify before the undersigned as I have reason to doubt that the sureties for the most part are worth the amount set opposite their names. One of the parties had informed me that he is not worth more than one dollar and I think that some of the others on examination and upon fully understanding the justification may find they are mistaken. I may find the within sufficient and approve some upon examination and justification before me. Further the oath of one of the sureties who is a partner (said to be) of the principal, somewhat complicates the matter.

W. L. Rynerson
Dist. Atty.

McSween Statement Exhibit 16 - March 9, 1878

[Proclamation issued by Governor S. B. Axtell to citizens of Lincoln County dated March 9, 1878.]

Proclamation

To the Citizens of Lincoln County.

The disturbed condition of affairs at this County seat brings me to Lincoln County at this time; my only object is to assist good citizens to uphold the laws and to keep the peace to enable all to act intelligently, it is important that the following facts should be clearly understood.

1st

John B. Wilson's appointment by the County Commissioners as a Justice of the Peace was illegal and void, and all process issued by him were void, and said Wilson has no authority whatever to act as Justice of the Peace.

2d

The appointment of Robert Widermann as U.S. Marshal has been revoked and said Widermann is not now a peace officer nor has he any power or authority whatever to act as such.

3d

The President of the United States upon an application made by me as Governor of New Mexico has directed the Post Commander Col. George A. Purington to assist Territorial Civil officers in maintaining order and enforcing legal process. It follows from the above statement of facts that there is no legal process in this case to be enforced except the writs and processes issued out of the Third Judicial District Court by Judge Bristol and there are no Territorial Officers here to enforce them except Sheriff Brady and his Deputies.

Now therefore in consideration of the premises I do hereby command all persons to disarm and return to their homes and usual occupations under penalty of being arrested and confined in jail as disturber of the Public peace.

Signed
S. B. Axtell
Governor of New Mexico
Lincoln, March 9, 1878

McSween Statement Exhibit 17 - May 2, 1878

[*Cimarron News and Press* article relating to the death of Dick Brewer dated May 2, 1878.]

The following relating to the death of Brewer has been sent to us for publication:

We the undersigned residents of Lincoln county, in the Territory of New Mexico, deeply deplore the loss our county sustains by the death of Richard M. Brewer, a young man of irreproachable character, who commanded the respect and admiration of all who knew him. Some of us have been acquainted with him over eight years, and none ever knew his name to be associated with anything of a questionable character. He was a hard working, generous, sober, upright and noble minded young man. Cattle thieves and murderers, and their "kid-gloved" friends hated him, and promised him a violent death years ago.

In good faith, he went as special constable to arrest the murderers of John H. Tunstall, by virtue of a warrant issued by John B. Wilson, a justice of the peace in the town of Lincoln. Before he could make his return thereon, Governor Axtell issued a proclamation to the effect that Wilson was not a legal J. P., although the act of our legislature, by virtue of which said Wilson was appointed justice, was approved by his Excellency. Mr. Wilson had acted as such justice for over a year without having his authority questioned. Immediately after the issue of that proclamation, our late sheriff, and those who were interested in screening the murderers, obtained warrants against Mr. Brewer and posse for having made an effort to execute the warrants issued by Wilson. Brewer and posse knew well that if the late sheriff arrested them they would be murdered, so they took to the mountains.

We tender our heartfelt sympathy to the aged parents of the deceased Richard M. Brewer, and other relatives in Wisconsin, and we beg to assure them that, whilst they have lost a good son and relative, we fell that our county has lost one of her best citizens.

(Signed)

John S. Chisum
J. Ellis & Sons, Merchants
G. B. Barber, Surveyor and Civil Engineer
J. B. Patron, Speaker of the House of Representatives
Jose Montaño, Merchant
McSween & Shield, Attorneys
J. N. Copeland, Sheriff
J. Newcomb
T. F. Ealy, M.D.

Dow Brothers, Merchants

R. M. Gilbert

A. Wilson

W. Fields

C. Sampson

And ONE HUNDRED AND FITY OTHERS

McSween Statement Exhibit 18 - April 25, 1878

[Newspaper clipping quoting the report issued by the April 1878 Grand Jury. The clipping is incomplete. The source of the clipping is unidentified in the Report, but it is from the April 25, 1878, issue of the *Cimarron News and Press*.]

NEW MEXICO

Report Of The Grand Jury Of Lincoln County

Through the courtesy of Harry Whigham, editor of the Cimarron News and Press, we are enabled to give the following document to our readers at this date:

To the Hon. Warren Bristol, Associate Justice of the Supreme Court of the Territory of New Mexico and presiding Judge of the 3d Judicial District thereof:

The grand jury for the April, 1878, term of the District Court for the County of Lincoln, deeply deplore the present insecurity of life and property, though but the revival and continuance of the troubles of past years.

The murder of J. H. Tunstall, for brutality and malice, is without a parallel and without a shadow of justification. By this inhuman act our county has lost one of its best and most useful men – one who brought intelligence, industry, and capital to the development of Lincoln County. We equally condemn the most brutal murder of our late sheriff, William Brady, and George Hindman. In each of the cases, where the evidence would warrant it, we have made presentments.

Had his excellency, S. B. Axtell, when here, ascertained from the people the cause of our troubles, as he was requested, valuable lives would have been spared our community; especially do we condemn that portion of his proclamation relating to J. B. Wilson as J.P. Mr. Wilson acted in good faith as J.P. over a year. Mr. Brewer, deceased, arrested, as we are informed, some of the alleged murderers of Mr. Tunstall by virtue of warrants issued by Mr. Wilson. The part of the proclamation referred to virtually outlawed Mr. Brewer and posse. In fact, they were hunted to the mountains by our late sheriff with U.S. soldiers. We believe that had the governor done his duty whilst here, these unfortunate occurrences would have been spared us.

Under the impression that stealing the property of the United States was a crime against our territory, we heard evidence in regard to the administration of affairs at the Mescelero Apache Indian Agency in this county; but we are now informed by the District Attorney that crimes of the character thus investigated by us are not indictable in this court. We have, however, ascertained evidence that the Indians are systematically robbed by their agent of a large and varied assortment of supplies. We mention this here for the reason that it will explain why the Indians are migrating marauders and steal from and murder our citizens.

The witnesses by whom these facts can be proven are residents of this town and neighborhood, and a list of them has been furnished by us to the United States District Court clerk.

Your honor charged us to investigate the case of Alex. A. McSween [here the clipping in the Report ends; the missing portion is]:

[Your honor charged us to investigate the case of Alex. A. McSween, Esq. charged with the embezzlement of ten thousand dollars, belonging to the estate of Emil Fritz, deceased; this we did but were unable to find any evidence that would justify that accusation. We fully exonerate him of the charge, and regret that a spirit of persecution has been shown in this matter.]

McSween Statement Exhibit 19 - February 14, 1878

[Letter addressed to "Friends Riley and Dolan" and signed by W. L. Rynerson dated February 14, 1878.]

Law Offices of William L. Rynerson
District Attorney 3d Judicial N.M.
Las Cruces, N.M. Feby 14, 1878

Friends Riley and Dolan:

I have just received letter from you mailed 10th inst. Glad to know you (Dolan) got home O.K. and that business was going on O.K. If Mr. Widenmann interfered with or resisted the sheriff in discharge of his duties, Brady did right in arresting [him]. Any one who does so must receive the same attention.

Brady goes into the store in McSween's place and takes his interest. Tunstall will have same right there he had before, but he must not neither obstruct the sheriff or resist him in the discharge of his duties. If he tries to make trouble the sheriff must meet the occasion firmly and legally. I believe Tunstall is in with the swindlers with the rogue McSween.

They have the money belonging to the Fritz estate and they know it. It must be made hot for them all the hotter the better, especially is this necessary now that it has been discovered that there is no hell.

It may be that the villain "Green Bautista" Wilson will play into their hands as Alcalde [magistrate]. If so he should be moved around a little. Shake that McSween outfit up till it shells out and squares up and then shake it out of Lincoln.

I will aid to punish the scoundrels all I can. Get the people with [you]. Control Juan Patron if possible. You know how to do it. Have good men about to aid Brady, and be assured I shall help you all I can, for I believe there never was found a more scoundrely set than that outfit.

Yours &c
W. L. Rynerson (signed)

McSween Statement Exhibit 20 - May 2, 1878

[Letter from W. L. Rynerson to A. A. McSween dated May 2, 1878.]

Las Cruces, N.M.
May 2d, 1878

A. A. McSween Esq.,
Law Office of McSween & Shield
Lincoln, N.M.

Dear Sir, I am just in receipt of yours of date of 27th ulto, directed to me in which you say "If parties have been indicted by the last Grand Jury for the murder of J. H. Tunstall, I wish to ask you to place warrants in the hands of our Sheriff for their arrest. Please reply."

In reply I have to say that I will discharge my duty without let or hindrance from any one, and when warrants are necessary in every case they will be issued and placed in the hands of the proper officer. Just whom you mean by "<u>our Sheriff</u>" is not clear to me, as in the past few months it is said you had some interest in more than one sheriff. You may mean Martines [Martinez], you may mean Barrier, or you may mean someone else whom I don't know that you have reduced to possession and are pleased to designate as our (your) Sheriff and since you have undertaken the task of directing me in my duties I may be permitted to suggest that you seem to have forgotten to dictate or direct as to what should be done as to the warrants. "If parties have been indicted by the last Grand Jury for the murder" of Sheriff Brady, George Hindman, A. L. Roberts, and others in Lincoln County.

Passing Strange
Very Resp'y
W. L. Rynerson (signed)
Dist Atty

McSween Statement Exhibit 21 - Undated

[Petition request directed to Murphy, Dolan and Riley to "remove to some other county or state," with alleged 300 signatures of Lincoln County citizens. No names or date appears on the petition.]

To
Hon L. G. Murphy
J. J. Dolan and
J. H. Riley

Gentlemen, we the undersigned residents of Lincoln County New Mexico, being deeply interested in the development and upbuilding of this section of the Territory and the well being of all our fellow citizens without distinction, feel it is our duty to insure these in view of the troubles of past years now unhappily revived and continued with such irreparable loss of life and property.

That the people of this County desire you to remove to some other County or state in order that permanent peace may be restored. On conveying you this information we merely give expression to the earnest wish of all your neighbors and fellow citizens.

Your reputed business connections with murderers, outlaws and cattle and horse thieves has destroyed your business connections and endangered your personal safety and makes it our imperative duty in the interest of the peace and order to ask you to leave Lincoln County.

The request we make is as painful as it is Extraordinary but it is for the good of our people. We trust that you knowing the feeling of the people entertain towards you may find it consistent with your interest and that of the people to comply with this request.

We remain &c

Here follows the Signatures of over 300 of the Citizens of Lincoln County including that of the officers of said county [not provided with the Exhibit].

John Middleton - June 13, 1878

The Territory of New Mexico

County of Lincoln

Personally appeared John Middleton, who having been duly sworn according to law, deposes and saith. I have lived in the County of Lincoln, N.M., about one year. I follow the business of herding and driving cattle.

I knew John H. Tunstall in his lifetime. He was murdered on or about the 18th day of February, A.D. 1878, about ten miles from the town of San Patricio in said County.

I was in the employ of said Tunstall from the 20th day of October 1877 until the time of his death as aforesaid, caring for his cattle at his ranch on the Rio Feliz. Somewhere between the 12th and 15th day of Feby., 1878, whilst at said ranch with my fellow workers, R. M. Brewer, W. Bonney, F. T. Waite, G. Gauss, Martis [Martin], and R. A. Widenmann. J. B. Mathews, who represented himself as Deputy Sheriff of said Lincoln Co., with Jessie Evans, Tom Hill, Frank Baker, Frank Rivers [Long], notorious murderers, escaped prisoners and horse thieves, and John Hurley and George Hindman and Bill Williams <u>alias</u> A. L. Roberts, since killed at the Agency in said County, came to the said ranch.

R. A. Widenmann or R. M. Brewer, seeing Mathews & <u>posse</u> come towards the house, went out and asked Mathews to stop, asking Mathews to come alone and make his business known. Mathews said he had an attachment against the property of Alex. A. McSween and was looking for property belonging to said McSween. Brewer told him that McSween had no cattle or other property there. But that he could look through the cattle and if there was any he would help him and posse to round them up, but that he could not have Tunstall's or anybody else's cattle without an order therefor.

Mathews said that he would go back to Lincoln and get instructions from Brady, and that if he returned he would not have more than one or two men with him. Mathews & <u>posse</u> then left Frank Baker and Bill Williams, alias A. L. Roberts aforesaid, [and] went to J. J. Dolan's cow camp on the Pecos.

On or about the night of the 17th day of February, 1878, John H. Tunstall, deceased, arrived at his ranch, where I and others were as aforesaid, and told us to get ready to leave next morning for the town of Lincoln as he had learnt that J. J. Dolan & Co. had raised about 40 or 45 men for said Mathews as <u>posse</u> and intended to kill all of us at said ranch.

On the morning of the 18th Feby, 1878, said Tunstall, Widenmann, Brewer, Bonney and Waite and deponent left for Lincoln, Waite taking the main road, the balance taking a trail.

When about 30 miles from said ranch we scattered for the purpose of hunting some turkeys. While so hunting we heard yelling and saw a large crowd of men coming over the brow of the hill, firing as they were coming. Tunstall and I were on the side of a hill, about 700 yards from some horses we were bringing from the Feliz ranch to Lincoln, belonging to Tunstall, Widenmann, Bonney, Brewer and myself – the horses numbered nine. If they wanted the horses they could easily have got them without coming within 700 yards of us.

Not one of those I have named as being with Tunstall fired a shot. We endeavored to escape for our lives. I was within 30 steps of Tunstall when we heard the shooting first. I sang out to Tunstall to follow me. He was on a good horse. He appeared to be very much excited and confused. I kept singing out to him for God's sake to follow me. His last word was "What John! What John!"

With the exception of Tunstall, we all made an effort to join each other. Geo. Hindman, Jessie Evans, Tom Cochrane & Baker (Frank) were the only ones I can remember now who were of the posse that murdered Tunstall. I have been informed by Tom Green who was of that posse that Jessie Evans shot Tunstall first in the breast.

Tunstall before this had surrendered his pistol, the only weapon he had, to W. Morton, deceased. When Tunstall received the first shot in the breast, he turned, moved and fell on his face. Morton then, out of Tunstall's own pistol, fired a shot at Tunstall, the ball entering the back of his head. Morton then fired another shot out of Tunstall's pistol at Tunstall's horse and killed him. Sam Perry then proposed that they should carry Tunstall's corpse and lay it by the side of the dead horse, which was done. I saw the corpse of said Tunstall at the house of Alex. A. McSween in the town of Lincoln.

I attended the burial of said Tunstall on or about the 22nd day of Feby 1878. I was of the posse who arrested Frank Baker and W. Morton aforesaid at J. J. Dolan & Co's cow camp on the Pecos during the month of March, 1878. We understood an effort would be made by their friends, J. J. Dolan, J. H. Riley, L. G. Murphy et al to rescue them, so we took the Black Water road.

When within 25 miles of the town of Lincoln, Morton drew a revolver out of McCloskey's scabbard, they riding side by side, said McCloskey being one of the said posse, and shot said McCloskey in the head. Baker had a pistol concealed. Morton & Baker then made every effort to escape and refusing to halt were fired upon and killed about half a mile from were McCloskey was killed. I have related all I know about said affairs.

John Middleton
Sworn and subscribed before me this 13 day of June 1878
John B. Wilson
Justice of the Peace

Jose Francisco Montaño - June 6, 1878

Territory of New Mexico
County of Lincoln

Jose Montaño being duly sworn says he resides in Lincoln County Territory aforesaid and has resided there for the last ten years. That he is a free holder therein – and is by trade a merchant. That he has heard read in Spanish Juan B. Patron's affidavit verified June 6 1878 and that so far as the same refers to the cause of the trouble in this county, the action of Murphy, Dolan, and Riley, the characters of Baker, Evans, Hill and Davis, the same is true to the best of deponent's knowledge, information and belief.

That he has heard read in Spanish certain portions of the affidavit of A. A. McSween verified June 6 1878 and whereas it refers to the meeting and committee of citizens sent to Brady as to why he held the constables who went to arrest certain murderers [the same is true].

As to said McSween giving a bond to release the property attached is true. The same states the facts as they occurred and is true. That so far as the statements in said affidavits are made as to deponent's offering to go on McSween's bond and influence & coaxing by said Rynerson & Brady and as to the letter of withdrawal that the same is true.

Stephen Stanley told me I think last September that he had been drawing property from the Indian Agency for Dolan & Riley to Lincoln.

Saturnino Baca told me either in December or January or February that he had drawn a load of merchandize from the Indian Agency to Riley & Dolan at Lincoln.

Baca told me that when the inspector [William] Vandever was at the Agency inspecting, that the agent mixed good flour with the bad and that they knew just where to put their hand on the good flour & when it was inspected the agent Godfroy would take his knife and cut upon a bag of flour as by happhazzard [haphazard] and show him the good flour which had been mixed with the bad. And that fooled the inspector.

When Gov. Axtell was here investigating the trouble here, deponent tried to have an interview with him as to the troubles here and the Governor refused to see him or talk with him saying that he had not time to see him.

Jose Montaño
Read, subscribed and sworn to before me the 6th day of June 1878 and I further certify that I have truly, honestly and fairly translated the same into Spanish from English.
Rafael Gutierrez
Probate Clerk
By Juan B. Patron
Depty

Lawrence G. Murphy - May 14, 1878

Territory of New Mexico
County of Lincoln

Lawrence G. Murphy having been first duly sworn upon oath says that he has resided in the Territory of New Mexico since the year 1860 and that he has been a resident of Lincoln since the year 1866. That he was well acquainted with J. H. Tunstall in his lifetime and verily believe from what he knows that the killing was caused by the villainous conduct of his partner A. A. McSween in a attempt of the latter to swindle the estate of the late Emil Fritz deceased out of the sum of ten thousand dollars collected by said McSween.

That McSween took advantage of the prejudices of Mr. Tunstall and induced him to believe that the Courts were controlled by a ring and that he could not get justice therein and then incited him when their partnership effects had been levied upon to resist the officers of the law in a violent and unlawful manner that the interest of McSween might be thereby subserved.

He further testifies that at the recent visit of Governor Axtell to Lincoln County, that his [unreadable] was hailed by all law abiding citizens as an assurance that some measures would be inaugurated to enforce the authority of the law over the turbulent elements which under the direction of the said McSween continued the resistance to the constituted authorities in resisting the powers of the Courts by force and violence and if all was not done in that direction which was expected, he is satisfied from his knowledge of the facts that the falt [fault] is not that of the Governor's but of those who refused to give him their aid and assistance.

That to his certain knowledge, the governor visited the heads off the different parties, calling upon McSween & Shield, Ellis & Wilson, & J. J. Dolan & Co. and talked with them about the troubles and asked their assistance in keeping the peace & enforcing the laws and endeavored to find out all he could about the real origin of the troubles & the best mode of stopping further violence & blood shed.

That the governor exercised his well known ability and tact doing all that was in his power to this end of giving peace to the people and was only prevented from succeeding by the refusal of the McSween party to cooperate with him

What he has stated as to the Governor's conduct he knows from personal observation having been with him while he was in Lincoln County and seen the efforts that he made to bring peace to the distracted people. He is thus explicit because he knows the efforts that have been made to heap odium upon his name in relation to this transaction when he knows his cause was honorable and just and that he is one of the most efficient Governors this Territory has ever had.

Law. G Murphy
Subscribed & sworn to before me this 14th day of May 1878
W. W. Griffin
U.S. Commissioner

John Newcomb - June 8, 1878

The Territory of New Mexico
County of Lincoln

Personally appeared John Newcomb, who being duly sworn according to law deposeth and saith, that he has heard read an affidavit signed Florencio Gonzales, Probate Judge of said County, verified June 8, 1878, in relation to the troubles in said county. That he knows the statements made by said F. Gonzales in relation to L. G. Murphy, J. J.

Dolan and J. H. Riley to be as stated in said affidavit and substantially true. That so far as the name of this affiant is mentioned and said affidavit every statement therein is true.

Deponent further says that he has resided in said County since 1867 and that he is well acquainted with Murphy, Dolan & Riley aforesaid. That they have oppressed and ground down the people of said County and always through the courts which they claimed to control or murdering or driving people out of the County. "The House," here signifying parties last aforesaid, manage to control the people and keep out successful competition in business until John H. Tunstall started a store in Lincoln, N.M.

I know the way "the House" done business, I know the way they treated the people of this County; I knew Mr. Tunstall and how odious he was to "the House," owing to the fact that he had opened a store in Lincoln, and from all that has come within my knowledge, I am satisfied that the murder of Tunstall was brought about through the enmity of "The House" and executed by a Sheriff's posse as the tools of "The House."

In early and late years, the ruling desire of L. G. Murphy & Co. was to break up every one who had the courage to oppose them – they have tried it in my case; they have tried it in that of many others. They have always been unscrupulous and unscionable [unconscionable]. They had the power and they used it to [the] ruin of this county, the present troubles have been brewing for years and the anger of the people has now given way. "The House" had the reputation of surrounding themselves with thieves and murderers to accomplish their ends and filling their beef contracts with the Government with stolen cattle. They have had a monopoly of Government contracts, beef, wood, hay & corn.

They have tried a the Vigilance Committee in 1876 to get men competing with them in business out of the way so I am informed by parties who are said to have formed that Committee.

Everything mentioned in said affidavit of F. Gonzales in relation to the finding of the body of J. H. Tunstall, bringing it into the town of Lincoln, the circumstances under which it was found, burial &c and the meeting of citizens and visiting of the Committee on Sheriff Brady, deceased, is true.

John Newcomb
Sworn to and scribed before me this 8th day of June, 1878
John B. Wilson
Justice of the Peace
Precinct No. 1, Lincoln Co., N.M.

John Wallace Olinger - June 17, 1878

County of Dona Ana

John Wallace Olinger being duly sworn according to law says that he has heard read the foregoing affidavit of Samuel R. [B.] Perry and the same is true to the deponent's knowledge, information and belief.

That he was one of the posse that went from the Pecos and one of the men that followed after Tunstall's horses. I first saw Tunstall about 3/4 of a mile from where he was killed or at least his party. I never saw Tunstall to know who he was until after I saw him dead. I assisted in laying him out. I examined his pistol and found two loads out of it. It was reported that he [Tunstall] had shot it off as at Morton. The empty shells were in the chambers of the revolver and were left there by deponent & his party. The revolver was placed by the side of Tunstall. I heard I think two shots fired about this time. I heard the shots before I examined the revolver. I think that Hill fired these two shots. I do not know positively whether he did or not or whether they were fired out of a pistol or a carbine. There might have been three shots. I thought at first that perhaps the Tunstall party was firing at us – then I thought that the shots were fired to collect our party.

I, Baker, Evans, Hill were informed at the Feliz that they were not part of the posse. They were even informed before we arrived at the Feliz that they were not part of the posse & that we did not want outlaws with the posse & that Widenmann had warrants for their arrest. I did not see Tunstall's hat. I did not nor did any of our party put his hat under his horses head, to my knowledge. I would have been likely to have heard of it if they had. We thought it was a very serious matter. Tunstall's head was not mutilated. It was badly broken by the ball.

J. W. Olinger
Read, subscribed and sworn to before me this 17 day of June 1878
Frank Warner Angel
Special Agent
Depts Justice & Interior

Juan B. Patron - June 6, 1878

Territory of New Mexico
County of Lincoln

Juan B. Patron being duly sworn says, I have resided in said County since 1870. I was elected in Sept 1871 as clerk of the Probate Court and held that position either as clerk or deputy most of the time since then. In November 1877, I was elected to the legislature of this Territory – and was speaker of the House of Representatives of this Territory. I am well acquainted with the people of this County. I have conversed a great deal with the people as to the troubles that exist and have for some time existed in this county.

I am at the present time engaged in stock raising and am a free holder in this County.

I know a great many circumstances which lead me to believe that the cause of the present troubles is the result of oppression of the people for quite a number of years.

The first trouble that occurred in this county and out of which it may be said that the present trouble is the outgrowth was a dispute and persecution of this deponent by one Dr. Tideman [Tiedemann] U.S.A., who brought to his assistance the U.S. soldiers. Deponent had taken out a claim on some land on the Rio Ruidoso, supposing that no one had a claim to it. Dr. Tideman afterwards claimed that it was his land, and deponent was abused, arrested and all his acts and movements watched and misinterpreted. The result of this was that W. Brady who was a tool of L. G. Murphy and an U.S. Commissioner at the instigation of the Doctor & Murphy began a persecution of deponent and endeavored to influence the people against deponent. The result was that the people were divided into two parties, the Mexican element, standing by me, and the American, the soldiers & Murphy against me.

I can say that here first began the opposition to what is known as the house. Before this L. G. Murphy controlled every thing that there was any money in and dictated who should run for office and who should not. At one time, going into a convention of the people who were to select persons who were to run for office which the people had to give, knowing that said convention was opposed to him, overthrew the table, destroyed the stationary, and told them you might as well try to stop the waves of [the] ocean with a fork as to try and oppose me.

As a result of this determination to put down or out of the way those who opposed the will of the "House," the "Horrell" war, which was called the Texans against the Mexicans. Murphy & Co. aided and abetted the "Horrell" party and the result was that the Horrell party left the country leaving however all their property in the hands of Murphy, such as cattle, lands &c. There are people who say that this was one of the ends Murphy was working for.

From then on there has been although not concentrated opposition, but there has been enough of individuality among some of the people that Murphy, Dolan & Riley have been opposed in their schemes and plots. That in order to dispose any, get out of the way obnoxious parties, a vigilante committee was attempted to be organized of which Murphy was the prime mover, the real object of which was to kill this deponent and others.

The farmers have been complaining greatly as to the one-sided settlements had with the firm of Murphy & Co. That they had been induced to buy merchandise of them under an agreement that they should be paid a fixed price for their produce, but when a settlement was had, the goods were charged at exorbitant prices and the produce turned in at prices to suit them (M & Co).

Matters continued to go on in this way until Mr. H. Tunstall came to this County, opened a store and in straight forward course made friends with the people who preferred to trade with him rather than with Murphy, Dolan & Riley. This caused the enmity of them against Tunstall and this enmity has resulted in the death of Tunstall and the present blood shed in this County.

Some time ago Murphy told me that they would have to get rid of McSween & Tunstall.

I know the reputation of Jessie Evans, Frank Baker, Tom Hill, and George Davis. It is that of notorious horse thieves and murderers. I believe that Murphy & Dolan & Riley & W. Brady, our late sheriff, were friendly with them and assisted them.

Some time ago, some time in 1877, Mr. Tunstall and McSween lost some horses and mules. Baker, Evans, Hill, & Davis were arrested and lodged in jail for stealing the same and admitted to deponent that they had stolen the horses and mules. While they were in jail I received word from a person that had been confined in jail with them that they, Baker, Evans, Hill & Davis, had filed off their shackles & cut holes in the logs and were going to escape.

I came & told Mr. McSween this and then went & told Sheriff Brady.

After this they escaped. I went with others to the jail and found an auger, a knife, a file, and sacks with rocks in [them].

While at Santa Fe, I received telegram from W. L. Rynerson, during the recent trouble here, not to come home. After I returned to Lincoln, Rynerson told me that Dolan had told him that if I returned, that Baker and his companions would try and kill me. Brady told my brother that he and the "house" had made it alright with "the boys" and that I could come home. I believe that Dolan & his party told me this to obtain my influence on his side.

Brady admitted to me that he had let Riley have the territorial tax money and could not get it back from him.

Deponent further says that he was one of the Grand Jury of the April Term of the District Court Lincoln County. That no intimidation, bribery or threats were used by or against or with deponent nor was any outside influence, threats or bribes used to influence deponent or any of the grand jury. I was subpoenaed by Copeland.

There is no U.S. District Court held in this County.

I have seen sugar which I believe came from the Indian Agency. The sugar is different from the sugar that is generally sold here. It is darker [in] color and merchants do not see that kind of sugar here.

I have heard read the affidavit of A. A. McSween verified June 6th, 1878, and so far [as] it refers to me, the statements made by me, it is true.

Juan B. Patron
Read, subscribed and sworn to before me this 6th day of June 1878
Frank Warner Angel
Special Agent
Depts of Justice and Interior

John R. Patton - May 22, 1878

John Patton being duly sworn says that he resides in Lincoln County Territory aforesaid. That about a month ago he had a conversation with A. H. Howe who told deponent that George B. Kitt told him (Howe) that Tunstall was murdered in cold blood by Morton & Hill. That Tunstall was some distance off and was coming towards them, that Morton wished to shoot him and Hill said hold on wait till he comes nearer.

That after Tunstall came a little nearer, Morton shot him in the breast and then Hill shot him in the head. That both Hill & Morton told Tunstall that if he would give up, he would not be hurt, that not withstanding this promise they shot Tunstall.

John R. Patton
Subscribed and sworn to before me this 22 day of May 1878
Morris J. Bernstein
Notary Public

Samuel B. Perry - June 16, 1878

Territory of New Mexico
County of Dona Ana

Samuel R. Perry [Samuel B. Perry] being duly sworn according to law says I was one of the Sheriff's posse that went to attach Tunstall's property. I reside on the Pecos at Seven Rivers and am and have been in the employ of Dolan & Riley.

On or about the 16th of February 1878, I was informed that W. S. Morton had been deputized by J. B. Mathews, and that the papers had been brought to Morton by Jack Rivers [John Long]. I was on or about said day summoned on said posse.

On the night of the same day I left for the Penasco at Paul's ranch, the place where the whole posse was to meet. We arrived there on the night of the 17th. The next morning we started for Tunstall's ranch on the Feliz. On our way we met Henry Brown. He did not say that there would or would not be resistance. He did say that there was no one there.

McCloskey was at Paul's before we started. I did not hear him say any thing about resistance or not resistance. He might have without my hearing him.

We arrived at the Feliz on the morning of 18th about 8 am. We found there Martin Martz who was in charge of the cattle (he was either there or came before we left, I am not positive), and a cook by the name of Gauss. We inquired for the horses & they told us they had gone but did not know where they had gone. They had left about light & thought they had gone to Lincoln but did not know.

Mathews then gave the attachment papers to Morton & told him to take some men and attach the horses. Morton selected Robert W. Beckwith, Wallace Olinger, Sam Perry, Charles Kruling, Thomas Cochrane, Thomas Green, P. Gallegos, John Hurley, Charles Marshall, Manuel ____ [Segovia], Kit [Kitt], Ramon Montoya, & Geo. Hindman, Frank Baker, Jessie Evans, Thomas Hill.

The three latter were not called upon, they volunteered saying that they had a horse among the horses Tunstall had taken away & that they wished to go after it. I do not remember whether there was any objection made by anyone to their accompanying us except that Dolan said to either Mathews or Morton that they (Baker, Evans & Hill) had better not go. Either Baker, Evans or Hill replied that a person had a right to go for their property or something to that effect.

I am positive that Dolan did not go with us.

And we with Morton started after the horses. Myself, Hindman and George(Charles) Marshall having tired horses, brought up the rear. We had gone about 30 miles when Manuel appeared in front of us becking [beckoning] to us to come on. We trotted on & when we were about one half a mile from our party who were ahead & had overtaken Tunstall's property & party, Hindman said I heard a shot. I replied I guess not, it was a horse stumbled. I hear another, he said.

When we reached the top of the hill, we saw the horses rounded up & some of our party rounding up some of the horses. When we reached the horses, Morton came up and said Tunstall was killed. I said it could not be, for I did not believe that Tunstall was there. He said that he had followed after Tunstall whereupon Tunstall turned & came riding up to him. He (Morton) commenced to read the warrant, whereupon Tunstall drew his pistol and fired two shots at him. Before Tunstall had fired, Jesse Evans called to him to throw up his hands & he would not be hurt. Tunstall disregarded this and fired as above set forth whereupon he (Morton), Jesse Evans, & Hill fired at him and the result of the firing was that Tunstall and his horse were killed.

After the above statement had been made to me, Evans and most of our party being present, I went to the place where Tunstall was laying. I found him lying on his face, his horse was close beside him, their heads being in the same direction. The horse was still alive but nearly dead. Tom Hill thereupon to put the horse out of misery shot him with his (Hill's) carbine. I took his blankets and myself, Tom Green, Wallace Olinger & Geo. Hindman, Charley Kruling laid him out by the side of his horse. We did not see his hat nor did any one put it under the horse's head.

Tom Hill had Tunstall's revolver which he had found eight or ten feet from where the horse fell. Tom Hill handed it to Montoya and Montoya handled it to me & I placed it by the side of Tunstall. I did not examine the pistol. Tunstall's face was bruised by his fall, nor was it or his head was mutilated by any of our party.

We thereupon returned to the Feliz with the horses. We found Dolan at the camp about 500 yards from Tunstall's house. I am sure and positive that Dolan was not with our party that went after Tunstall's property.

After our return to the Feliz, I either heard Baker, Evans or Hill say the death of Tunstall was a small loss, that he ought to have been killed, or something that effect. I cannot say which one of the three said this of the three. One of these three said that Tunstall had tried to have them killed while they were in jail at Lincoln. Except as above I heard no threats against Tunstall either directly or indirectly. I believe that under the circumstances above set forth that Tunstall met his death while resisting a legal process.

Frank Baker was with Rivers [Long] when he (Rivers) brought the papers deputizing Morton & I with the other persons on the Pecos were summoned.

Dolan told Morton as we were starting after Tunstall's property to be very careful and to do nothing but what was according to law. While I was laying out Tunstall, I heard two or three shots, I will not be positive. I inquired what they were shooting about & they said they were shooting at that tree. There was some talk at this time that either Hill or Morton or Evans had fired off Tunstall's pistol. I thought it little strange that they were shooting at a mark, I did not think it was an appropriate time to be shooting at a mark. I do not know who were shooting at the mark. I was busy laying Tunstall out.

Samuel R. Perry
Read, subscribed and sworn to before me this 16th day of June 1878
Frank Warner Angel
Special Agent
Depts Justice & Interior

George A. Purington - June 25, 1878

Fort Stanton, N.M.
June 25, 1878

Mr. F. W. Angel,
Special Agent, Department of the Interior and Justice

Sir:

Referring to the affidavits of A. A. McSween and R. A. Widenman reflecting on my Official conduct while in command of Fort Stanton, New Mexico, during that period known as the "Lincoln County troubles," I have the honor to submit the following statement of facts which are confirmed by affidavits, letters and statements of citizens, Officers and soldiers, and by McSween and Widenman [Widenmann].

A day or so after Tunstall's death I went to Lincoln with Lieutenants Delaney, Pague, Smith, and Humphries [Humphreys], and saw in McSween's house from 35 to 50 armed men, a large majority of whom were men of reputed bad character. Most of these men, McSween said were in his employ, some of whom he was paying as much as four dollars per day.

I never stated to McSween in a formal conversation that I believed that Dolan and Riley, or "the house," was responsible for Tunstall's death. Every statement made in his affidavits concerning this conversation is false. None of the acts of G. W. Peppin Deputy Sheriff were endorsed by me, neither did I disapprove of them. I informed every one that whatever the Deputy did was on his own responsibility (see his affidavit and others marked A [Peppin Statement]).

The soldiers were there only for the preservation of life, and property, and were not directed to assist the <u>Deputy Sheriff</u> or Posse in searching houses.

I did not advise any citizens either directly or indirectly, nor did I use the words, "<u>damn the Constitution and you for a fool</u>" as sworn to by McSween and Widenman [Widenmann], and others. Mr. Levison [Leverson] was very much excited and commenced harranging[haranguing] my troops about the <u>unconstitutionality</u> of the Sheriff's acts; telling them that they would get into trouble if they allowed the Sheriff to proceed &c. Fearing that in the then great excitement some one might shoot him, I did say to him that he was making a "damned fool of himself," and suggested the propriety of his "shutting up" or words to that effect. See affidavits marked A & B [Peppin and Lust Statements].

On his arrival at this Post McSween secured two rooms of Mr. Dowlin Post Trader. McSween & Wife occupied one of these rooms, and Widenman [Widenmann] and Shields [Shield] the other. Mr. Dowlin not wishing to take the [Black] men, not having rooms or beds for them, they were sent to the guard house (see affidavit marked C [Dowlin Statement]). I would have confined the whole party in the guard house had it been large enough. It was understood that they were to be confined before they left Lincoln and when I promised the Sheriff to be responsible for their appearance at court. The Official report referred to in Widenman's [Widenmann's] affidavits as false is true to the best of my knowledge and belief (see his letter marked D & E upon which said report was based) [Letter from Widenmann and Goodwin's Statement].

Every act done by the troops in these troubles was with a view to save life and property. No support was given to either party. See Exhibit F [Orders to DeLany].

So far as I know all of my acts have met the approval of my military superiors and the Governor of the Territory. See Exhibits G & H [Letter from Loud and telegram from Hatch].

Very Respectfully
Your Obedient Servant
Geo. A. Purington
Captain 9th Cavalry

[Attached to Purington's statement are nine exhibits, the first one not assigned an identification letter, the others identified as Exhibits A to H.]

Purington Exhibit - Letter Purington to Sheriff Brady - February 18, 1878

Lincoln NM
Feby 18th 1878

Col G. A. Purington
Comdy Fort Stanton NM

Colonel

I have the honor to represent that I cannot find in this County a sufficient number of armed men to assist me in the execution of my duty though I have done all in my official Capacity to obtain such.

I therefore respectfully request that an officer and fifteen mounted men be immediately detached me to come to Lincoln – only for the preservation of the peace.

I am Colonel
Respectfully Your Obedient Servant
Wm Brady
Sheriff of Lincoln Co N M

Purington Exhibit A - George W. Peppin - June 22, 1878

Territory of New Mexico
County of Lincoln

Personally appeared before me the undersigned authority G. W. Peppin who being duly sworn according to law deposes as follows and says that he is Sheriff of Lincoln Co NM and that on the 10th day April 1878 he was Deputy Sheriff to Lieut Wm Brady, then Sheriff of said County. That on the 10th day of 78 he applied to Capt. G. A. Purington Comdy [Commanding] Ft Stanton N.M. for troops to assist him in serving warrants & arresting parties implicated in the assassination of Sheriff Brady and Geo Hindman. Deponent further says that he informed Capt Purington that he had warrants for the arrest of McSween and other persons. That he arrested McSween, Wideman [Widenmann], Shields [Shield], Geo. Robinson & Geo. Washington, and at Capt Purington's request he turned said persons over to said Purington to be confined at Fort Stanton NM.

Said Purington pledging himself to be responsible for their appearance before the District Court to be holden the following week. That he on his own responsibility went into the house of A. A. McSween and J. H. Tunstall for the purpose of finding the murderers of Brady and Hindman, reported as being concealed therein, and securing the arms and ammunition of Widerman [Widenmann], McSween, Washington & Robinson. That no doors were broken in or property destroyed, that no soldiers accompanied me or my posse.

That Capt Purington did not insult or use insulting language to any citizen. That Capt Purington did say to a Mr. Leverson who was haranguing the troops and my posse to shut up, that he was making a damn fool of himself or words to that effect. That the words, "damn the constitution, and you for a fool" was not used by Capt Purington or any one else in my hearing and I was present during the conversation between Purington and Leverson.

That at the time these arrests were made there was great public excitement and the presence of the troops had a good effect and went far towards allaying the excitement and restoring order.

> Geo. W. Peppin
> Sheriff of Lincoln County
> Sworn to and subscribed be me this 22nd day of June A.D. 1878
> Thos. Blair
> Capt 15 US Inf

Purington Exhibit B - Houston Lust - June 13, 1878

> Territory of New Mexico
> County of Lincoln

Houston Lust being duly sworn says he is 1st Sergeant Company H 9th Cavalry. That on the 1st day of April 1878, the day that Maj. Brady was killed, I went to Lincoln in company with other soldiers. When we arrived at Lincoln we saw Deputy Sheriff Peppin. He informed us that Sheriff Brady had been killed beyond McSween's house, by an armed party concealed about the premises of said McSween.

We thereupon rode down in front of McSween's house formed into line and dismounted. Peppin came up with his party and went around the house. Peppin informed Col. Purington that he had a warrant to arrest McSween and was going to arrest him and called on the Col. for men to assist him in arresting McSween. The Col. informed him that he had men enough. Peppin said that he had not, whereupon Lieut. Smith, myself and another soldier went with Peppin.

We went down to Ellis's house. We all went into the store of Ellis, an entrance to the house being from the store. Mr. Ellis senior went in to inform McSween that Peppin was there to arrest him and brought back word that McSween said he would not surrender to Peppin for the reason that he was not a legal officer, Brady being dead, whereupon Lieut Smith went into the apartment where McSween was and returned with said McSween. That McSween said, I surrender to you Capt. Smith. I consider I am under your protection.

He willing went with Lieut Smith up the street until we met Col. Purington. McSween then requested of Col. Purington to be carried as prisoner to the Fort and kept there as their lives (meaning Widenmann, Shield, Washington, Robinson, & said McSween) would not be safe with Peppin's party.

Col. informed them that if they went to the Fort that they would have to go into the guard house as he had no other place to keep them. They replied that they were willing to go there provided he would take them away from Peppin. Col. then informed them that he would take them only on permission of the Sheriff and on their own request. Col. then left and talked with Peppin & returned and informed them that it is an agreement. I will take you up to the Fort at your own request and keep you there but you must understand that it is your own request that I take you there.

Peppin then came up with a posse of men and started to go into McSween's house. McSween then called out to him not to go into his house to search it, that he was not a legal officer and that he had no right to search his house. Peppin then replied the Col. allows me to do it, whereupon Col. replied I did not do any such a thing. McSween then called out again to Peppin not to go in. Peppin replied Col. allows me, whereupon McSween inquired of the Col. if he had allowed Peppin to search the house, and Col. replied I don't care what Peppin says I have not allowed him. Whatever he does he does on his own responsibility.

At this time a man came out of the crowd, an Englishman [Leverson], and said Col. you must not allow this, it is not lawful for this man to go into the house and search for arms. Col. replied I have nothing to do with this man (meaning Peppin). What he does he does on his own responsibility. I have orders from the President to assist the civil authorities in preserving peace, and this man was Deputy Sheriff to Brady.

This Englishman then said to Col. that the Deputy had no authority to act, Brady being dead and commenced to talk to the soldiers informing them that they would get into trouble in obeying orders, whereupon Col. turned to him and said shut up you are acting like a damned fool. He (the Englishman) kept talking to the soldiers, that the people were a lot of unconstitutionalists and that he was going to leave the country as soon as he could. The Col. then turned to him and bowing said, "Sir, you have my permission to go now."

About this time McSween said that if the soldiers were not here that Peppin & his party would not dare to search his house, whereupon the Col. gave the order to mount and McSween & his party broke for their wagons to accompany the soldiers, fearing the soldiers would go off and leave them.

No soldier or soldiers accompanied Peppin in his search, or assisted him in it. Deponent further says that McSween, Widenmann, Robinson, Shield & Washington were taken to the fort at their and Mrs. McSween's earnest solicitation and request.

Deponent further says that no doors or windows were broken open to deponent's knowledge and I was present all the time. But on the contrary, the doors were standing open.

I did not hear any one use the words, "0 damn the constitution of the United States and you for a fool." I know that I would have heard them if they had been used. I did not hear Col. Purington use language unbecoming an officer & a gentleman. The only words used at the time when the Englishman was trying to induce the soldiers to disobey the Col. and not to obey any orders the Col. might give, and on which occasion the Col. informed him that he was acting like a damned fool.

I am positive that no order or orders were given to the soldiers either directly or indirectly for them to assist or aid Peppin in his search. No one has talked to me as to what testimony I should give. I did not even know until Mr. Angel commenced questioning me that my testimony was desired.

Houston Lust
1st Sgt Co "H" 9th Cay.
Read, subscribed and sworn to before me this 13 day of June 1878
M. A. Upson
Notary Public

County of Lincoln

George W. Smith being duly sworn says that he is 2d Lieut 9th U.S. Cavalry, and that he is the officer referred to in the above affidavit as Lieut Smith. That he has heard read the above affidavit and knows the contents thereof and that the same is true.

G. W. Smith
2d Lt 9th Cav
Read, subscribed and sworn to before me this 13 day of June 1878
M. A. Upson
Notary Public

Purington Exhibit C - William Dowlin - June 24, 1878

Territory of New Mexico)
Lincoln County

Personally appeared before me the undersigned authority Mr. Will Dowlin, who being duly sworn according to law deposes & says that he is the Mr. Dowlin Post Trader at Fort Stanton New Mexico referred to in the affidavit of Mr. A. A. McSween and R. A. Widenmann verified June 6, 1878.

That when asked by A. A. McSween for rooms on the 1st day of April 1878 when he was brought to the post under arrest I refused at once to give them rooms on the grounds that I did not want to get mixed up in the then existing troubles. Col. Purington did not influence me in any way or even suggest that I should not give them rooms. As for Geo. Robinson and Geo. Washington I said that I had no more room and would not take them in. Col. Purington then ordered the guard to take them to the guard house. As for the remark that he had need of their labor I heard nothing of such remark and am positive that it was not used at that time.

Will Dowlin
Post Trader
Sworn to and subscribed before me this 24th day of June 1878
Thos. Blair
Copt 15th Infantry
J.A.G.C.M.

I certify that Par 1031 R.A.R. has been complied with
Geo. A. Purington
Copt 9th Cav

Purington Exhibit D - Letter Widenmann to Purington - February 20, 1878

Fort Stanton NM
Feby 20d 1878

Col Geo Purington
Fort Stanton

Dear Sir

Being informed by reliable and trustworthy men that they have good reasons to believe and do believe that Jessie Evans, Frank Baker, Tom Hill and Geo Davis are at the house of J. J. Dolan & Co at Lincoln I would politely request you to furnish me sufficient men to surround and search said house and capture said men.

Very respectfully
Robt. A, Widenmann (signed)
Deputy US Marshall

P.S. It is impossible to get a civil posse to execute the warrants for the arrest of the above men.
Robt. A. Widenmann (signed)

A True Copy
G W Smith (signed)
2d Lieut 9th Cav U.S.A.

[Exhibit E is Millard F. Goodwin's Statement, June 24, given on pages 84-86]

Purington Exhibit F - Orders to Lieutenant DeLany - February 22, 1878

Post of Fort Stanton N.M.
February 22, 1878

Orders #18

It having been represented to the Commanding Officer of this Post by the Sheriff of Lincoln County that a state of lawlessness beyond his control exists in Lincoln N.M., 1st Lieut. C. M. DeLany 15th Infantry with all the available men of Co. "H" 15th Infantry will proceed at once to the town of Lincoln N.M. and will use his best endeavors to prevent the destruction of life and property by the bands of armed men in the town and vicinity.

Until instructions are received from the Hon Judge W. Bristol Judge U.S. Court no interference will be made with the civil authorities in the execution of their duty farther than the protection of life and property.

2d Lieut M. F. 9th Cavalry with detachment of 9th Cavalry now at Lincoln N.M. will report or Lieut. C. M. DeLany 15th Infantry.

By order of Captain Purington
Samuel S. Pague (signed)

Purington Exhibit G - Letter Loud to Purington - March 24, 1878

Hdqrs. District N.M.
A A A Genls Office
Santa Fe N.M.
March 24th 1878

To the
Commanding Officer
Fort Stanton, N.M.

Sir

Referring to your endorsement of 14th inst. on letter of U.S. Marshal of Dec 3d 1877.

The District Commander directs me to say that in view of the conflict of authority now existing in Lincoln County between the Deputy U.S. Marshal and the Sheriff of the County and as writs must issue from the same Judge requiring assistance of the troops to serve the same, and also from the fact that on the application of the Governor of the Territory the President has authorized the employment of troops to preserve the peace and enforce Civil law in Lincoln County hereafter until this conflict of authority ceases the Sheriff of the County will be considered by you the proper power to render assistance to when required by him to preserve the peace and sustain the laws.

Acknowledge receipt.

Very Respectfully
Your Obdt Servant
John S. Loud (signed)
1st Lieut and Adgt 9th Cav
A.A.A. Genl

A true copy
M. F.
2d Lieut 9th Cavalry
Post Adjutant

Purington Exhibit H - Telegram Purington to Edward Hatch - March 5, 1878

Telegram Sent
Santa Fe, NM
March 5th 1878
Comdg Officer
Fort Stanton N.M.

Comdg. Officer

(Operator at Las Cruces will forward without fail by tomorrow's mail, and report mailing this telegram.)

The District Commander directs that you upon proper application therefor assist Territorial Civil Officers in maintaining order and enforcing legal process.

Acknowledge receipt by telegraph by Las Cruces and report fully by mail.

By Command of Col. Hatch
Loud (signed)
A.A.A. Gen.

Official Copy
John S. Loud (signed)
1st Lieut and Adgt 9th Cavly
A.A.A. Gen.

A True Copy
M. F.
2nd Lieut 9th Cavalry
Post Adjutant

Berry Robinson - First Statement - June 13, 1878

The Territory of New Mexico
County of Lincoln

Personally appeared Berry Robinson, who having been duly sworn according to law deposeth and saith, that he is a private soldier in the 9th Cavalry, U.S.A.

That on or about the 1st day of April 1878, Capt Purington and Lieut. Smith in command of Co "H" were in the town of Lincoln in said County. That said Capt. Purington then and there arrested R. A. Widenmann. Said Widenmann asked Purington to tell him by what authority he arrested him and that said Purington's only reply was, "Widenmann, don't put on any frills."

That I heard said Capt. Purington say to one Leverson: "Damn the Constitution and you for a fool." That he was very abusive to citizens generally. That one Longwill [Longwell], claiming to be Deputy of Sheriff Brady, then deceased, [entered] a door in the house of J. H. Tunstall, deceased, being accompanied by a detachment of soldiers. That Geo. Robinson & Geo. Washington, and said Widenmann and D. P. Shield and A. A. McSween were taken to Fort Stanton, NM for military protection.

That I heard said A. A. McSween say to Capt. Purington, "I want those two men to be used as I am used. We can occupy the same room, [they] having served me at my expense."

Purington said he would, and did, put the men aforesaid in the Guard House. He did and put them in Territorial service. I was one of the guard over said McSween, Shields, Widenmann.

[Last two lines of statement are illegible and partly missing.]

Berry Robinson (his X mark)
Sworn to and subscribed to before me this 13 day of June 1878
John B. Wilson
Justice of the Peace

Berry Robinson - Second Statement - June 22, 1878

Territory of New Mexico
County of Lincoln

Pvt Berry Robinson Company H 9th Cavalry being duly sworn according to law deposes and says that the affidavit which he signed before John B. Wilson on the 13th of June 1878 is not at all in words or meaning as read over to him by Mr. A. A. McSween.

The statement read over to him by Mr. McSween and to which he supposed he was swearing was only that he saw one Longwill [Longwell] and Johnny Hurley breaking open the doors of the houses of Mr. Tunstall (then deceased) and George Washington. That Mr. McSween asked him if he could not swear that Capt. Purington had sworn at and abused the citizens to which he positively replied that he had not as he was not present.

That the only statement made by him to Mr. McSween was in regard to the breaking open of the before mentioned doors of Tunstall & Washington by Longwill [Longwell] & Johnny Hurley. The Deputy Sheriff Mr. Peppin having taken him with them, or another told him to go with them, and that he was not ordered nor sent with them by Captain Purington nor Lieut. Smith.

The Deponent further testifies that he can neither read or write and that any thing else contained in the aforesaid deposition than the statement in regard to the breaking into the houses of Tunstall & Washington by Longwill [Longwell] & Hurley is false & was not knowingly sworn to by him.

Berry Robinson (his X mark)
Pvt Co "H" 9th Cavy

Sworn to & subscribed before me this 22nd day of June 1878
Thos Blair
Capt 15th Inf
J A G C M

I certify that par. 1031 R.A.R. has been complied with
Geo. A. Purington
Capt 9th Cavy

Calvin Sampson - June, 1878

Be it remembered, that before the undersigned personally came Calvin Sampson who being duly sworn according to law says that he is and has been for the past nine years a resident of Las Vegas New Mexico. That on the 1st day of April 1878, he was in front of McSween's house and Geo. W. Peppin, J. B. Mathews & others were about to enter said house without showing any warrant or authority. That McSween ordered him not to go in his house. That he [Peppin] said Col. Purington had authorized him so to do. McSween called Purington's attention to the statement of Peppin and appealed to him for protection. That Purington said Peppin could do as he pleased.

That about that time Dr. M. R. Leverson coming up called the attention of Purington to that part of the Constitution of the United States which provides for the security of persons & property from seizure or search without warrant. That Purington in reply said, "Damn the Constitution and you for a fool."

That I am in no way interested in the troubles of Lincoln County, other than as a citizen of the territory, desiring that the laws may be enforced and criminals punished.

C. Sampson

Sworn to and subscribed before me this ___ day of June A D 1878 and I further certify that said affiant is a credible and reliable citizen whose statements are entitled to credit and belief.

J. Felipe Baca
Clerk of the Probate Court

David P. Shield and Adolph P. Barrier - Undated

Territory of New Mexico
County of San Miguel

Be it remembered that before the undersigned within and for the County and Territory aforesaid personally came Adolph P. Barrier [and] D. P. Shield, residents of San Miguel County who I certify to be respectable and credible witnessed & who each being duly sworn for himself says that they were present at Mesilla N.M. at the residence of Judge Bristol on the 2nd & 4th days of February last at the time of the investigation of the charges against A. A. McSween. That they were present during the entire examination and heard all the evidence.

That A. A. McSween was not sworn as a witness nor did he make in person a statement of his defense. That Mr. Tunstall made oath that no articles of copartnership was ever executed by and between him and said McSween. That the following statement purporting to have been made by the Judge as reported in the *Mesilla News* of its issue dated July 6th [is false].

In the case of Jesse Evans charged with the Murder of J. H. Tunstall in application of Jesse Evans for action of Habeas Corpus, R. A. Widenmann, being on witness stand:

"Court. Q by Court: Mr W. you swear positively that no papers had been made out, and that no partnership existed between Tunstall and McSween?"

"A. Yes Sir: I know all about all their transactions."

"Court. Well Mr. Widenmann when Mr. Tunstall and Mr. McSween were down here in an examination before me, they both swore positively that there was a partnership existing between them and that all the papers had been made out."

Affiants state that the said statement is false and untrue.

A. P. Barrier
D. P. Shield

[Here is the *Mesilla News* article referred to in this statement. The newspaper article is a report on the Habeas Corpus hearing of Jessie Evans at Mesilla, on July 2, 1878. The following abbreviations are used: def't – defendant; McS – McSween, N – Simon B. Newcomb, one of Evan's two attorneys; T – Tunstall; R – Rynerson, District Attorney. Widenmann is misspelled throughout. The inserted editorial comments in brackets in the article are by Ira M. Bond, the editor of the *Mesilla News*. Bond was a vociferous supporter of the Santa Fe Ring party.]

[Rich, Rare, Racy
Weidemann (sic) Takes the Stand
Who Swears to Lies?
Conflicts with Tunstall's and McSween's Testimony
Court Politely Tells W. He Lies
W. Disarmed by Sheriff in Open Court]

[Tuesday July 2nd, Jesse Evans was brought before Judge Bristol on a writ of Habeas Corpus; being charged with being one of the party that killed Tunstall in Lincoln Co, Col. Rynerson for the Territory, Judge Newcomb and Mr. Jones for the defense.]

[R. A. Weidemann, being sworn testified in substance: We, Tunstall, Weidemann, Brewer, Middleton, Bonny (alias the Kid), were going to the Plaza with horses, about 5 to 6 o'clock p. m. Feb 8, saw a large party coming after us, we started to run to get out of their way, did not see Sheriff, or deputy Sheriff. When they caught up within 300 yards of us they fired shots, they were in a whole bunch together, while running (on horseback). I looked back and recognized Jesse Evans, Frank Baker, J. J. Dolan, Tom Hill, Geo. Hindman, A. L. Roberts, and Billy Morton as being with the party, which was 15 to 20 strong. I ran into ravine to left of mountain. Tunstall run into ravine to right of mountain, the party followed T. I had run some distance when I heard shots on the other side of the mountain, there were trees and brush on the mts. The shots was a distance of 700 to 800 yards from me, could not see Tunstall or defendant at this time.]

[Question by Rynerson. Then you did not see defendant shot at all? Ans. No, I could not see him at all.]

[Q. by R. Did you ever hear def't. [defendant] use threats towards you? A. A man said he heard – (Judge Newcomb, if the Court please, he says he heard that a man said he heard &c. – Ruled out by Court as not proper.)]

[Witness {Widenmann}. The party rode after Tunstall into the ravine, they must have found him and I know they killed him; do not know whether T. fired first or not, do know that shots were out of his pistol when found.]

[Q. by Judge Newcomb. Mr. Weidemann, you did not see T. killed? A. No. Q. You did not see def't. shot? A. No. Q. You did not see T. after the shooting? A. No. Newcomb. Then you don't know of your own knowledge that T. was killed at all. A. Well I think he was killed.]

[Q. by Court. Mr. W. you say you was running horseback, dust flying, balls whistling around, you could casually look back, see a large party of 15 or 20 coming at full speed 300 yards behind, that you recognized Mr. Dolan in the party, when everybody knows that a number of reliable witnesses swear positively that Mr. Dolan was 25 miles from there at the time. A. Yes, I know a number of men swear Dolan was at another place, but I recognized Dolan there.]

[Court. Well Mr. W. I know by experience something about riding at full speed under such circumstances and looking back at a party 300 yards off and recognizing persons.

Mr. Weidemann your testimony in this matter will be taken with a very great deal of allowance.]

[Q. N {Newcomb}. What did you tell the officers at Stanton when you reached there {nearly out of breath}. A. I told them that they had killed Tunstall. I said Dolan must come before the courts, that he must do so, or I would hunt him up and bring him there myself. I never saw Tunstall at any time after death. {We are informed W. told the officers at Stanton that the party followed Tunstall down the ravine, that he could not see anything, but heard shots and he was afraid his friend T. was hurt. Ed.}]

[Q. by Court. What was you doing there? Was it McSween's property you was driving off? [Here W. was so anxious to make his point that he goes voluntarily outside the case and record to tell more – whoppers.] A. W. I was driving no property of McSween, he only had at this time 2 carriage horses, one of those was dying, there was no partnership agreement between T. and McS., no paper of any kind had been made out, and no papers were to be made out until this June, so I know positively there was no partnership existing.]

[Q. by Court. Mr. W. you swear positively that no papers had been made out, and that no partnership existed between Tunstall and McSween. A. W. Yes, sir, I do, and I know all about all their transactions. Court. Well Mr. Weidemann, when Mr. Tunstall and Mr. McSween were down here in an examination before me {February 2-4, 1878}, they both swore positively that there was a partnership exiting between them, and that all the papers had been made out. Do you think you know more about Mr. Tunstall's business then he did himself? A. W. No. I don't suppose I did, but I knew pretty near as much.]

[Court. Well Mr. Weidemann your testimony in all this matter will be taken with a very great deal of allowance.]

[Rynerson. I wrote you Mr. W. a letter saying I wanted to prosecute the murderers of Tunstall, wanted you to help me, to give me the names of witnesses, &c.; you did not even answer this letter to wit.]

[Lincoln Co. N. M., April 11, 1878]

[Robert Weidemann, Esqr.]

[Sir: I have seen a letter purporting to have been written by you in which among other things you state that Mr. J. H. Tunstall was murdered and make serious charges against the Courts of this Territory, to wit said "murder was committed in the interest of the New Mexico Ring and as the Ring controls the Courts of the Territory it is difficult to bring the murderer to Justice." I consider the charges you have made against the Courts as wholly unwarranted. I presume you intended to include me (as I am the prosecuting attorney of this District) as your language certainly does, as one being under the control of what you term the "New Mexico Ring." I write this to state that I am under the control of no "Ring," clique or party whatever and that you know that I am not nor have been under such control. I am in all matters pertaining to my official duties "controlled" by my oath of office; my sincere desire is to discharge my duty fully and faithfully. And if Mr. J. H. Tunstall or any other persons have been murdered no one will labor more diligently and faithful than I to bring the murderers to Justice. So anxious am I to bring the persons connected with the recent murders in this vicinity to Justice, that I here state to you and though you to the friends of Mr. Tunstall, that I shall be pleased for you and them to indicate to me the name of some capable attorney to assist me in the prosecution of persons connected with the killing of Mr. Tunstall.]

[I am Sir, Very Respectfully,
W. L. Rynerson,
Dist. Attty. 3rd Jud. Dist. N. M.]

[A. W. If I gave you the names of witnesses now they would not open their mouths, they would be killed.]

[Q. N. Please tell us about your meeting def't. at a ranche a day or two before the trouble and what happened there. A. I saw def't and Frank Baker at Brewer's ranche, I asked them to come with me to take diner, they did so. Mr. Brewer invited the sheriff's posse to dinner. Brewer said "Boys you come into dinner;" def't said he come over to look on, come over to see me, I don't know how long they stayed. I saddled up and left; I had a U.S. warrant to arrest def't and tried to serve it. Brewer and others said they would not help me. I had the warrant 3 or 4 weeks. I got assistance from the military. I went to Murphy's ranche but found nobody.]

[R. I am willing under the circumstance to take the responsibility to admit def't to bail, a pretty good bail, to secure attendance of def't at court.]

[Court. The party we hear fired, a circumstantial fact, beyond that Mr. W's testimony don't amount to much, in fact Mr. W's testimony at 300 yards, riding fast, shooting all around, such testimony must be taken with a good deal of allowance, I know by experience a good deal about such matters. There is no testimony as to the killing, no person here that saw the killing; yet we don't feel hardly justified in discharging the def't as there may be other witnesses appear at court, we think we will hold the def't to bail.]

[At request of Judge Newcomb def't {Evans} made a statement as follows:]

[I was not one of the posse, I was behind traveling with another party, did not see W. the day T. was killed, don't know of any parties that went up to fire at W., was behind did not see T. that day, had nothing to do with the shooting, don't know how many there were in advance, F. Baker was with me, I did not go with the sheriff's posse, was traveling same road, think it was the 2nd, day after I took dinner with Weidemann at his invitation, saw Dolan before I left about 20 miles from there that morning, did not see T. shoot or see any one shoot at him. Weidemann's man "The Kid" had a horse of mine and I was going to Ruidoso to try and get him, finally got him after the sheriff's posse got him, did not see T. that day, I had a colt's pistol and Winchester gun, do not know who killed T., did not get my horse shod at Brewer's, was laughing and talking with W., said I don't believe you have warrant for me, W. said you are right in your belief, W. asked me in to dinner, it was first time I ever saw W., sheriff's posse was ordered away when I was invited to dinner.]

[Court. Unless it can be proven that the entire party were there for a particular purpose, because 1, 2, or 3 shoot is no proof that all are implicated. I do not consider that Weidemann's testimony under the circumstance should be received with much weight; balls flying as he say, W. running.]

[Rynerson. I recommend bail in $5,000.]

[Court. Bail will be fixed at $5,000 and the Sheriff of this Co. directed to deliver the prisoner to the Sheriff of Lincoln Co.]

[At about this time Weidemann, who by his actions had convinced nearly every body that he had concealed weapons in his pocket by his manner of holding his hands in his outside linen coat pockets, had leaned against the inside casing of the door, when Sheriff Barela, who was standing in the door, said what right you got to carry concealed weapons in your pockets, put his hands in W's pockets, pulled out his weapons and placed them in his own pockets. W. changed colors but said nothing.]

[E. H. Wakefield was appointed special deputy by Sheriff Barela to deliver Evans to the Sheriff of Lincoln Co. and started in 20 minutes with his charge.]

[End of newspaper article.]

George Washington Smith - June 13, 1878

County of Lincoln

George W. Smith being duly sworn says that he is 2d Lieut 9th U.S. Cavalry, and that he is the officer referred to in the above affidavit as Lieut Smith. That he has heard read the above affidavit [the statement by Houston Lust] and knows the contents thereof and that the same is true.

G. W. Smith
2d Lt 9th Cav
Read, subscribed and sworn to before me this 13 day of June 1878
M. A. Upson
Notary Public

George VanSickle - June 12, 1878

The Territory of New Mexico
County of Lincoln

Personally appeared George VanSickle who having been duly sworn according to law deposeth and saith that he has resided in the County of Lincoln over twelve years and by occupation a farmer and stock raiser.

I am well acquainted with L. G. Murphy, J. J. Dolan and J. H. Riley and have been so since they commenced business in said County. Their reputation for honesty and fair dealing has been uniformly low. As a matter of business they done as they pleased. They intimidated, oppressed and crushed people who were obliged to deal with them. They were a gigantic monopoly. If they done wrong, there appeared to be no redress as they were reported to control the courts.

The present troubles are the result of their tyranny and determination to put down competition in business. The people generally complain of their surrounding themselves with murderers, thieves and desperadoes to carry out their ends; complain that they have ruined farmers by exacting and collecting unjust amounts by obligating them to part with their produce to pay such debts at prices to suit them; complain that they have to take contracts for corn &c at rates at which the required supplies cannot be raised; complain that they have swindled those who dealt with them.

"The House," as they are called here, never suffered competition if they could help it. I believe that it was Tunstall's competition with them for public patronage that caused his death; for they always managed to get rid of men who would take a formable opposition to them, either by running them out of the country, by legal persecution or by getting them killed by some tool.

Tunstall I know to have been a straightforward businessman and as such to have had the confidence of the Public, a fact that told heavily, in my judgment, on the business of "The House."

Sometime after the murder of Tunstall, three fellows came to my house and asked me for some milk pans they saw. I told them that the pans were the property of Mr. Tunstall, deceased. They replied that that made no difference as Major Murphy wanted them and that unless I sent them to him when his wagon came for them, I would have to look out, but that if I did send them, I would have friends.

S. W. Lloyd came for said milk pans, valued at $70.00, and I informed him that they belonged to Tunstall, deceased. I let him have the pans for Murphy without pay or promise of pay to save my life. There is no mistaking the threats of these men.

It is notorious that since the death of Tunstall that the house have offered a reward for Alex. A. McSween's life. They are now surrounded by desperate characters who will do any deed they are asked to perform provided they get the chance, having no interest in this county of any kind or nature, being simply wandering murderers and thieves.

I live 35 miles from the town of Lincoln and have no chance of saving my life from the attack that would be made upon me if it were known that I would unfavorably comment on the character of Murphy, Dolan & Riley. The men constituting their gang are non residents and can leave here when they choose.

George VanSickle
Sworn to and subscribed before me this 12th day of June 1878
Rafael Gutierrez
Probate Clerk
By Juan B. Patron
Dpty

Robert A. Widenmann - First Statement - June 6, 1878

Territory of New Mexico
County of Lincoln

Robert A. Widenmann being duly sworn says that he resides in Lincoln County aforesaid and has resided there for a year and a half. My occupation is that of merchant.

I was acquainted with John H. Tunstall, deceased. I had known him for about two years.

A little over a year ago I was at Santa Fe New Mexico and received at that place a letter from John H. Tunstall in which he said that he considered this County the best part of the Territory and that I had better come down here. Acting on that advice I came down to Lincoln about the middle of February 1877. When I arrived at Lincoln Mr. Tunstall was not here and I met Major L. G. Murphy who told me when I asked for Tunstall that he was not here and in conversation he said I had chosen rather a bad friend, that he and the people here did not have a very favorable opinion of Tunstall. I answered him that they did not know him to which he said well that is our opinion anyway.

In speaking with J. J. Dolan afterwards he made in substance the same remarks, while at the house of J. J. Dolan & Co, Mr. R. M. Brewer came in to settle his account. After considerable talk I heard him say that he knew that their account was not correct. That they had not given him credit for over five hundred dollars worth of corn, but rather than have a quarrel he would settle the account as it was.

After Mr. Tunstall returned to Lincoln, I told him what Murphy & Dolan had said of him. He laughingly replied that he could explain that very easily. That Murphy had tried to sell him other ranches to which he also had no title as he Tunstall had been informed by various parties living at Lincoln. That Tunstall declined to purchase from him without title, and from that time the animosity of Murphy, Dolan & Riley dated. That as soon as they saw that they could not draw him in they began abusing him.

Afterwards Mr. Tunstall & I went to Brewer's ranch & while there J. J. Dolan accompanied by Wm. Morton (the latter having the reputation of a desperate character in this county) came. He demanded that Brewer either leave the ranch or buy it of them, although it was known that Dolan had no title to it. Brewer repled that they had no title to the ranch, that he was living on it & had his crop in, but that if they would pay him for his improvements he would be willing to turn the ranch over to them rather than have trouble with them.

Dolan declined the proposition & told Brewer that if the ranch was not turned over he would make it a personal matter with him, laying stress on the words "personal matter with him." Brewer said that he knew his rights and if necessary knew how to defend them. That he was not hunting any fuss but that he did not run away from it. Dolan replied that if the ranch was not turned over Brewer would d–- soon find what the fuss would be. At this time both Dolan and Morton were armed to the teeth. This was the substance of the conversation at that time.

Deponent further says that subsequently Brewer obtained title to the ranch under the Desert Act, the papers being now in deponent's possession.

Deponent further says that this is only one of many other instances of L. G. Murphy, Dolan & Riley's attempts to force titles from the people of this county as deponent is informed and believes and as the general report exists in said county.

Sometime during September 1877 horses and mules of J. H. Tunstall and others, then at the ranch of R. M. Brewer, were stolen by Jessie Evans, Tom Hill and I think Frank Baker. R. M. Brewer, Charles Bowdre, [and] J. G. Scurlock started after the thieves and at Sheds [Shedd's] ranch (also called San Augustini [Augustine]) the party parted, Brewer going to Mesilla while Bowdre & Scurlock remained at Sheds [Shedd's] Ranch.

Brewer obtained warrants for the arrest of the thieves sworn out before I think Justice Rosencranse. In the meantime, the thieves arrived with the horses at Sheds [Shedd's] ranch. Bowdre & Scurlock asked them to return the horses and mules, especially those of Brewer, he being a poor man, to which they answered that they would do no such thing, that they had been to too much trouble to get the horses to return them again & the thieves went to Las Cruces where they arrived with the horses while Brewer was still there. Brewer could not induce the sheriff to arrest them because he had not the force to do so.

All the above was told me by Brewer when I met him near Tula Rosa [Tularosa] on his way back in company with Bowdre & Scurlock, I with F. T. Waite who heard the above facts stated to me by Brewer. Waite returned with Brewer & his party while I went on to Mesilla in company with Lieut. Pague.

Subsequently Baker, Evans, Hill and Davis were arrested by Sheriff Brady & posse at Seven Rivers, at Beckwith's [Ranch], and brought to Lincoln, and lodged in jail from which they afterwards escaped. Mr. Tunstall took an active part in having them pursed and arrested, he furnished funds, horses, saddles and arms, and the thieves knew that he did it.

That subsequently deponent was appointed Deputy U.S. Marshal and warrants were placed in his hands issued out of the U.S. Courts for the arrest of Evans, Baker, Hill, Davis & Nicolas Provencio for stealing government mules. In trying to execute those warrants I tracked them to the Ranch of L. G. Murphy at the Caresosa [Carrizozo] Spring. I was informed by Mr. Murphy personally that they were not at his ranch and had been there but once when they sold a horse to Mathews.

Deponent further says that the horse referred to above was sold to Mathews prior to their arrest last above mentioned and this conversation with said Murphy was had four months after the sale of said horse referred to aforesaid.

Afterwards and on or about the 13th day of February 1878 Evans admitted to deponent that at the time deponent was at Murphy's ranch referred to aforesaid he Evans was in the hills near the ranch sleeping there nights and being at the ranch during the day time and that he saw me when I left the ranch.

That on or about the 9th day of February 1878 Sheriff Brady entered the business house of J. H. Tunstall of which I was there in charge and read to me a writ of attachment attaching the property of A. A. McSween, a copy of which attachment is hereto annexed marked ___. [document not with statement]. I told him that the property belonged to J. H. Tunstall, that I protested against any attachment & would hold him and his bonds men responsible for any loss or damages.

Sheriff Brady said that he knew better, that the property belonged to A. A. McSween [and] he would attach it as such. He proceeded to take an inventory, without placing a value on any article or thing attached. He demanded the keys of different doors, leading from the store and upon my refusal to deliver the same had me arrested and searched without warrant or legal process and forcibly took the keys from me. He was at the time accompanied by G. W. Peppin, Jack Long, James Longwill [Longwell], and F. G. Christie.

On the 10th of February 1878 Mr. Tunstall & McSween arrived at Lincoln from Mesilla [according to McSween, he arrived on the 11th]. On the 11th of February Mr. Tunstall & I came to the store which was then in the possession of the sheriff and again protested against the attachment. We succeeded in getting all the horses released (2 mules and six horses) and at once started a man named G. Gauss with three horses for the ranch I think, and on the afternoon of the same day [we] started William McCloskey & John

Middleton for the ranch on two other horses and subsequently I followed in company with F. T. Waite and William Bonnie [Bonney] and arrived at the ranch on the morning of the 12th. R. M. Brewer was there in charge of the ranch as well as the above named persons who had been sent on and who were employed at the ranch then & prior to this.

On the morning of the 13th of February, J. B. Mathews (claiming to be Deputy Sheriff) rode up to the ranch of Tunstall's on the Rio Feliz in company with George Hindman, John Hurley, and Indian, Roberts, Evans, Baker and Hill. Seeing the last three in the party and knowing that they had threatened to kill me on sight I stepped out and asked the party to stop where they were (which was about 50 yards from the house) and asked Mathews to come forward and state his business. Mathews said he was Deputy Sheriff and had come to attach the cattle of A. A. McSween, to which I answered that McSween had no cattle there but if there were any he might take them. I offered no resistance nor did the people with me. Nor did we make any threats.

R. M. Brewer told Mathews in my presence and the rest of the party that he could round up the cattle and if he (Mathews) claimed that Brewer's (there being some of Brewer's cattle on the range) belonged to McSween, he could leave a man there to take care of them until the courts could settle the question. I then told Brewer that I was agoing to arrest Evans, Baker & Hill under my U.S. warrants, whereupon Brewer and the rest of the parties that were at the ranch with me said that it could not be done, that they were all ranch men and living at their places and if they assisted in arresting Evans, Baker & Hill, Dolan, Riley & Murphy would have them killed as soon as they got back to their ranches, and positively refused to aid me in the arrest.

Brewer then asked the party up to get something to eat and Evans advanced towards me swinging his carbine catching it at full cocked towards me, and asked me if I was looking for him. I told him that he would find out when I was looking for him.

He asked if I had any warrant for him to which I answered that was my business. He then said if you ever come after me you are the first man I am agoing to shoot at, to which I said that was all right, that I could also play a hand at that game too. He also told me in the presence of Brewer that Murphy, Dolan & Riley were the only ones in this section who payed them money.

Mathews told me that Evans has come over to see me to find out if I had any warrant for him. He said this in the presence of all. While Mathews was saying this I heard Baker say to Roberts, "what the hells the use of talking, pitch in and fight and kill the sons of b — s."

I asked Evans what he came over here for and he said that Mathews wanted him to come along, and that besides that he wished to see me, this was said to me alone. During part of the conversation which the others heard, Baker walked up in front of me with a pistol in his hand as though handing it to me swinging it on his finger, cocking it at the same time, pointing the muzzle towards me.

After most of the party had eaten, Mathews said he would go back to town to get further instructions as to holding Brewer's cattle and would come back with one man.

On the way to town I rode with them several miles (I mean by them, Mathews, Hurley & the Indian [Segovia]). The rest of Mathews' party said they were going to the

Penasco to the ranch of Paul's, and while riding with Mathews, he asked me if they attached Tunstall cattle too, whether we would resist. I told him not if he left them there, but that if he attempted to drive the cattle to the Indian Agency as they had said they would do, in order to kill them for beef, that we would do all that was in our power to defeat them, since if the cattle were driven there and killed we could not collect a cent from Sheriff Brady's bonds men who were known to be insolvent.

On my journey to the town I had Waite and Bonney with me, part of the time we rode ahead and part of the time Mathews and his party last above mentioned rode ahead.

Deponent further says that Brewer and Middleton were employed at the ranch continually, McCloskey had been employed there and was was [sic] there employed as he had been for several weeks previous at rounding up and branding cattle and had made arrangements to work a ranch. Waite had been in the employee of Tunstall. He went out with me as company & from Tunstall's ranch he and Bonney were going up to the upper Penasco to work a ranch. We had about 400 or 500 head of cattle at Tunstall's ranch.

I arrived at the town (Lincoln) on the night of the 13th and left on the morning of the 14th to be there when Mathews rounded up the cattle and to count them, Waite and Bonney and no others returned with me.

In the meantime Mr. Tunstall had heard that Mathews with a large party were going to the ranch. The Mexicans were to round up the cattle while the rest of the party were to kill all of us. He at once started for the ranch alone and arrived there the night of the 17th.

We decided upon his informing us all of this that rather then risk the lives of the men we would leave every thing as it was, send McCloskey over to the Penasco to inform Mathews and his posse that they could take the cattle and that we would seek our remedy by the law. We did this because we did not wish trouble & to show them that no resistance would be made. We sent McCloskey because he was a friend of a great number of the party that was reported to be with Mathews.

McCloskey left the ranch at three o'clock in the morning and he had orders to tell Mr. Martin on the Penasco to come over and stay at Tunstall's ranch to count the cattle with the Deputy Sheriff and to stay at the ranch with [the] party the Deputy Sheriff left at it until the matter could be arranged through the courts.

Tunstall, Brewer, Middleton, Bonney, Waite and myself started for the plaza about 8 o'clock of the 18th. Waite driving the waggon [British spelling], the rest of us driving about eight horses besides those we were riding. The horses were the property of J. H. Tunstall, R. M. Brewer and myself. None of the horses then or ever belonged to A. A. McSween and all but three had been released by the sheriff and of those three horses one belonged to Brewer, one to Bonney and the third was traded by Brewer to Tunstall for one of the horses which the sheriff had not attached here.

About ten miles from the ranch, Waite took the road with the waggon while the rest of the party took the trail passing by the Pajarito Spring. About five o'clock in the evening of the 18th, Brewer, Tunstall and I were riding along driving the horses, Middleton and Bonney being about 500 yards in the rear, and we three had just come over the brow of the hill when a flock of turkeys rose to the left of the trail. I offered Tunstall my gun he having none with him to shoot some of them but he declined the use of it, saying that I was a better shot than he was. Brewer and I started off for the turkeys, leaving Tunstall with the horses, and had got about three hundred yards from the trail when I heard a noise behind me. Turning in my saddle, I saw a party of men come over the brow of the hill on a gallop. I said to Brewer, "look there Dick," and hardly spoken the words when a ball whizzed between me and Brewer and the attacking party all commenced shooting at us with out speaking a word to us. I said to Brewer we can't hold this place it being a perfectly barren and rocky hill side, let us ride to the hill over there and make a stand, the hill being covered with trees and large boulders.

We rode towards the hill the whole party coming after us, until they had reached the hill side we had been on, continually firing at us. When they reached the hill side, they evidently saw Tunstall, for they all turned down to where he was. In going to the hill, we were met by Bonney and Middleton, who had partly rode around us to get away from the attacking party.

When we were very near the top of the hill, we heard two or three solitary shots. Middleton then remarking to me that they had killed Tunstall. From the time the party turned from us & towards Tunstall and the firing of the shots last mentioned must have been from five to ten minutes. Not one of us fired a shot against the attacking party, nor had we fired at any turkeys or even had we or did we or either of us fire our guns off.

I was riding a bay horse, Tunstall was riding a bay horse, Brewer was riding a bay, Middleton was riding a bay, Bonney was riding a grey.

We rode to the top of the hill covered with trees for shelter and sopped [stopped] and the other party rode upon the hill we had just left. This was after the shots which we believed had killed Tunstall. They then rode around on the top of the said hill in full view of us and then disappeared.

I recognized Evans, riding a bay, Baker riding a grey, Dolan riding a sort of sorrel, P. Gallegos riding a bay, Hindman, Hurley, Hill, Morton. These are all that I now can recall by name as seeing on the top of said last mentioned hill. There were altogether nineteen persons with the sheriff's posse as I have been informed by Wm. McCloskey who rode with the party from Tunstall's ranch (and was with them from the Penasco) towards us about fifteen miles when his horse gave out and he remained behind, he being on his way to join Tunstall and the rest of us.

The following are the names given by McCloskey to me as being with the sheriff's posse and were taken down by me at the time he gave them to me. I now read from the original entry made by me in my memorandum book, Sam Corbet being present, viz William Morton (since killed), Jessie Evans (now at Fort Stanton now under arrest), Tom Hill (since killed), Frank Baker (since killed), Tom Green (now in the employee of Chas. Woolse at the Pecos), George Hindman (since killed), John Hurley (now with Riley), Ponceana [Ponciacho] (being one of the murderers of Benito Cruz for the murderers of whom a reward of $500 is offered by Gov. Ritch), Pantaleon Gallegos (now at Santa Fe), Charles Marshall (now in charge of Catron's or Riley's cattle herd at the Pecos), Tom [Samuel] Perry (I do not know now where he is), Tom Cochrane (now with Riley), Rivers [Long] (I do not know where he is I think in Arizona), Robert Beckwith (now at Seven Rivers with his father), Charley Kruling alias "Dutch Charley" (now in hospital at

Fort Stanton), Kitt (now I think in Arizona), J. J. Dolan (now at Santa Fe), and the Indian (since killed).

We had intended before Mr. Tunstall had come the last time to the ranch that if the sheriff's party rounding up the cattle should attempt to attack us, to resist and for that purpose had cut port holes in the house and had some sand bags before the door. They were to be used in no other case.

Deponent further testifies in answer to questions of Mr. Angel: Warrants were sworn out by Brewer, Middleton and I think Bonney, I being absent at the fort, before J. B. Wilson Justice of the Peace, but against whom the warrants were made out I am unable to say, never having examined them. There was only one warrant. All the persons were mentioned in it I believe.

On the 21st of February 1878, I think, I will not be positive of the date, new warrants were issued by J. B. Wilson, Justice of the Peace, and placed in the hands of Atanacio Martinez constable to serve them. The parties wanted under said warrant or most of them were at the house of J. J. Dolan & Co at Lincoln. Martinez went to serve them after summoning Waite & Boney [Bonney] to aid him to the house of J. J. Dolan & Co where the murderers were with the sheriff. [The warrants were issued February 18; the arrest attempt was made February 20.]

I saw them go there and am informed by said Martinez, Waite, & Bonney, that as soon they got to J. J. Dolan & Co's store, they were covered by guns in the hands of the Sheriff and Tunstall's murderers, disarmed, Waite & Bonney taken prisoners by the Sheriff Brady without warrant or legal process and held prisoners. Martinez was told by the Sheriff that J. B. Wilson had no power as Justice of the Peace, that his warrants would not be recognized by him Brady, and that he (Brady) would not allow any one to be arrested in the house, and then he Martinez was allowed to depart but without his arms. This last warrant I have been informed was the same as the first one mentioned aforesaid.

Robt. A. Widenmann
Read, subscribed and sworn to before me 6th day of June 1878
Rafael Gutierrez
Probate Clerk
By Juan B. Patron
Dpty

Robert A. Widenmann - Second Statement - June 6.1878

Territory of New Mexico
County of Lincoln

Robert A. Widenmann being duly sworn says that he resides at Lincoln, Lincoln County, Territory of New Mexico and is a merchant and banker.

On the first day of April 1878 Capt. Geo. Purington Co. H 9th Cavalry rode into the town of Lincoln with a company of soldiers and surrounded the house of A. A. McSween. I stepped out of the house, it being at the time my place of residence, and greeted Capt. Purington. He asked me whether I had had anything to do with the killing of Brady, to which I answered that I had not and that I had very nearly been killed myself. He then began cursing and using abusive language. I told him that I had thought he was impartial, to which he answered that he was. I said his present actions did not seem to show it when he turned to Lieut. Smith and ordered him to arrest me, which he did, though no warrant was shown or legal process taken.

Soon after one Geo. W. Peppin claiming to be deputy sheriff stepped up to me and said, "Widenmann I arrest you." I asked whether he had a warrant and he said he had. I then demanded to have the warrant read to me when Capt. Purington said, "Don't put on any frills now Widenmann." With and though the orders of Capt. Purington I was by force of arms arrested and held prisoner. Deponent further says that Capt. Purington with and through his soldiers aided and abetted said Geo. W. Peppin, claiming to be deputy sheriff, in searching houses though said Peppin had no search warrant and that under cover of said troops who were acting under the orders of Capt. Purington said Geo. W. Peppin broke in doors in order to search houses.

That when one Montegue R. Leverson, a stranger in this section and County told him the said Capt. Purington that houses could not be searched without a search warrant and called said Purington's attention to the provisions of he Constitution of the United States, said Capt. Purington said, "O damn the Constitution of the United States and you for a fool."

That said Capt. Purington cursed said Leverson and other citizens present in the presence of ladies and his subordinate troops using language unbecoming to a gentleman and an officer.

Deponent further says that D. P. Shield now at Las Vegas, Geo. Robinson and Geo. Washington, the later two residing in Lincoln, were also arrested without warrants or legal process by said Geo. W. Peppin, claiming to be deputy sheriff under the cover of U.S. troops who were under the orders of Capt. Geo. Purington. That the said deponent and the three other persons were forcibly taken to Fort Stanton and there detained and imprisoned and placed under guard without legal process or orders of commitment to the detriment of their business and were not given a trial or preliminary trial as provided by law.

That the said George Robinson and Geo. Washington were forced to do menial service and labour [English spelling] in company with military prisoners, in fact treated the same as military prisoners though held prisoners contrary to the provisions of the Constitution of the United States and the laws of the Territory of New Mexico.

That he and the said other prisoners above mentioned and held prisoners were released only after Lieut. Col. Dudley had taken command of Fort Stanton and turned them over to the sheriff of Lincoln County John. N. Copeland on a warrant issued by the District Judge the day they were so turned over.

Deponent further says that as per annexed copy of a report of Capt. A. Purington then commanding Fort Stanton to headquarters at Santa Fe, marked Exhibit ___ [Exhibit not attached to statement], said Capt. Geo. Purington made one false statement in said report and that many others therein are false.

That following is the false statement knowingly made. On the 20th day of February Mr. Widenmann again made applications for troops to arrest Evans, Baker, Hill and others whom he asserted were at the house of J. J. Dolan & Co. in the town of Lincoln.

Deponent says that on the night of the 19th to the 20th of February 1878 he was sleeping in the quarters of Lieut. S. S. Pague at Fort Stanton. That about one o'cl [o'clock] of the morning of the 20th of February Capt. Geo. A. Purington entered the room in which said deponent was sleeping and showed deponent a letter just received signed by a large number of respectable citizens of Lincoln, which letter stated that said citizens had good reason to believe and did believe that Evans, Baker, Hill and others were at the house of J. J. Dolan & Co. and requesting said Capt. Geo. A. Purington to send troops to arrest them. Capt. Geo. A. Purington then asked deponent what he would do under the circumstances, to which deponent answered that the representations of such citizens as had signed the letter could not be disregarded and that he would therefore have to ask for troops.

Deponent further says that he asked Capt. Geo. A. Purington three of four times [to] send then for a certified copy of said letter but was always put off and has not succeeded in getting a copy. That in examining and searching the house of J. J. Dolan & Co., he neither ransacked it nor opened a drawer or any drawers, nor examined any clothing or packets of clothing nor took any jewelry, letters or papers or any thing from the house nor did any one of the two citizens who accompanied him. That the letters and papers and jewelry referred to were lost by J. H. Riley when he came to the house of A. A. McSween while he, said Riley, was intoxicated, as per exhibit [exhibit not attached. It was at this visit to McSween's house that Riley lost the letter he had received from Rynerson, given on page 134].

That he, the said deponent, had nothing to do with the Constable and his posse who arrested the posse of the sheriff of Lincoln County who held the store of J. H. Tunstall under writ of attachment against one A. A. McSween, but that he, said deponent, positively told said Constable that he could not enter any building until the said deponent had withdrawn with the troops as per exhibit ____ [not attached]. That he, said deponent, never resisted the sheriff or any sheriff in the service of any legal process, and that he never used or did use the U.S. troops to serve his own purpose, but used them only in endeavoring to serve the warrants which had been placed in his hands.

Deponent further says that after he had been arrested by Capt. Geo. A. Purington said Capt. Geo. A. Purington said that he was going to leave the deponent and the other persons arrested in the jail at Lincoln because he had no room in which to confine them at Fort Stanton, though said Capt. Geo. A. Purington well knew that if deponent and the other prisoners were left there they would be murdered. This deponent told said Capt. Geo. A. Purington that as he has been arrested by him, said Capt. Geo. A. Purington, he also demanded to be protected. Said Capt. Geo. A. Purington seemed very unwilling to take deponent and the other so called prisoners to Fort Stanton and so expressed himself, but after much talking at last consented to do so.

Deponent further says that after arriving at Fort Stanton he and others succeeded in getting rooms at Fort Stanton from W. Dowlin Post Trader at their own expense. That he and others desired that Geo. Robinson and Geo. Washington aforementioned be confined in the same rooms with them, but that said Capt. Purington positively refused that saying that Geo. Robinson and Geo. Washington must go to the guard house had need of them and their labour and upon this they were taken to the guard house.

Capt. Geo. A. Purington afterwards acknowledged that had he had not brought deponent and the other prisoners to the guard house they would have been murdered. Capt. Geo. A. Purington placed two guards over D. P. Shield, A. A. McSween and deponent and said guards had orders to shoot any of the above persons who should they leave their rooms without permission and said guards also had orders to not allow any person or persons to speak with the above named D. P. Shield, A. A. McSween and deponent.

Robt. A. Widenmann
Read, subscribed and sworn to before me this 6 day of June 1878
Rafael Gutierrez
Probate Clerk
By Juan B. Patron
Dpty

Chapter 5 | Letters

Introduction

Included with the Angel Report report in the National Archives file are a number of letters. Here are the letters relevant to the issues address by the Report.[1]

Section of N.M. Territorial Law Governing J.P. Vacancies - January 13, 1876

Translated

Sec. 40. In the event that any vacancy exists now in any County office, or that it may hereafter occur in any County precinct or demarcation in any County by reason of death, resignation, or removal, or in any other manner, the County Commissioners of said County shall have the power to fill such vacancy by appointment until an election be held as now provided by law approved January 13, 1876.

Actos de la Assemblea, Legislativea del Territorio de Nuevo Mejico, 1875-1876, p. 28.

Given under my hand this 16th day of March A.D. 1878.

Juan B. Patron
Chairman Board Co. Commissioners

John B. Wilson's Appointment as Justice of the Peace - February 14, 1877

Translated

February 14, 1877

James H. Farmer, Justice of the Peace elect of precinct No. 1 of this county and Territory, having resigned, giving as reasons for doing so the distance of his residence from the seat of the precinct, and occupations that incapacitate him to faithfully discharge his duties as Justice was accepted, and John B. Wilson was appointed in his place, and the Clerk is authorized to issue his Commission to that effect, to said John B. Wilson.

I certify that the foregoing is a correct transcript and translation of the record of the appointment by the County Commissioners of Lincoln County, Territory of New Mexico, of John B. Wilson as Justice of the Peace in and for said County, made at a regular and special meeting after the Court of the said Commissioners of said County held at the County seat, Lincoln, the 14th day of Feb. A.D. 1877.

Juan B. Patron
Chairman Board Co. Commissioners

Edward Thornton to Secretary of State William M. Evarts - March 9, 1878

Washington March 9th 1878
[To William M. Evarts, U.S. Secretary of State]

Sir:

My attention has been called to the murder of John H. Tunstall a British subject, which is stated to have taken place in the County of Lincoln, New Mexico eleven miles from the town of Lincoln, on the afternoon of the 18th ultimo, and to have been committed by one James J. Dolan, and others. It is also affirmed that an informal investigation of the circumstances which led to the murder will show a disgraceful state of affairs as regards not only the Territorial, but the United States officials.

It appears that after the murderers arrived in the town of Lincoln, Mr. A. M. [sic] McSween obtained warrants for their arrest, and put them into the hands of a constable in order that the criminals might be apprehended. He did not deliver them to the Sheriff of the County because he believed that that officer was indirectly connected with the murder.

When the Constable and posse went to serve the warrants, he was met by the Sheriff, who made them prisoners, and refused to allow them to make any arrests, though the alleged murderers of Mr. Tunstall was then and there with the Sheriff.

If the above mentioned statements be true, it would appear that a most inexcusable murder has been committed and that the Sheriff of the County instead of assisting in the arrest of the murderers, as he is in duty bound, is impeding the course of justice. Under these circumstances I cannot doubt that the Government of the United States will promptly cause enquiries to be made into the matter, and will take such measures as it may deem expedient for investigating the conduct of the Sheriff of Lincoln County and for ensuring the arrest of the accused, and their being brought to trial.

I have the honor to be with the highest consideration, Sir
Your obedient servant
Edwd Thornton [Sir Edward Thornton, British Ambassador]

William M. Evarts to Attorney General Charles Devens - March 13, 1878

Department of State
Washington
13 March 1878

The Honorable Charles Devens,
Attorney General

I have the honor to invite your attention to the enclosed copy of a note of the 9th instant [March] from the British Minister of this Capital in relation to the murder of John H. Tunstall, a subject of Great Britain, said to have been committed by one James J. Dolan and others on the 18th ultimo [February], in Lincoln County, New Mexico.

I will thank you to cause the proper inquiries to be made into the facts of the case as represented in the Minister's note, and to advise this Department of the result.

I have the honor to be Sir
Your obedient servant,
Wm. Evarts [William M. Evarts, U.S. Secretary of State]

Enclosure: Sir Edward Thornton to Mr. Evarts, 9 Mrch 1878

S. F. Phillips to Thomas B. Catron - March 18, 1878

March 18th, 1878
Thomas B. Catron, Esq.,
U.S. Attorney, Santa Fe, New Mexico

Sir:

I enclose a copy of a letter of the 13th instant from the Secretary of State and a copy of the communication therein referred to from the British Minister in relation to the murder of John H. Tunstall a subject of Great Britain alleged to have been committed by one James J. Dolan and others on the 18th ultimo in Lincoln County, New Mexico.

At the request of the Secretary you will please make prompt inquiry into all the circumstances attending this murder and report fully to me with a statement of what measures have been or can be taken to bring to punishment the parties guilt of this crime.

Very respectfully,
S. F. Phillips,
Acting Attorney General

Montague R. Leverson to Rhode Island Senator Henry B. Anthony - March 20, 1878

Lincoln, Lincoln Co
New Mex
20 March 1878

My Dear Sir:

I will call myself to your recollection as the friend of our late friend Mr. Jeuches by whom I was introduced to you first in 1867.

I enclose the draft of a letter I have just sent to Mr. Jno. E. Sherman U.S. Marshal at Santa Fe & I entreat you to call on Mr. Schurz & ask him to let you see the letter I have sent to the President under cover to him as also the other letters on the same subject I have written to the President.

This County I am sorry to inform you is under the rule of a gang of thieves and assassins at the head of whom are the United States officials (excepting only U.S. Marshal & his deputies).

It is not the Mexican or Native population which is in fault but Americans & Irish.

If the President should fail to institute a searching inquiry I entreat you to procure a Congressional inquiry where a state of things will be brought to light compared with which even Old Mexico would be preferable.

The British government must demand satisfaction for the murder of Mr. Tunstall seeing that his murder was perpetuated under the direction of U.S. officials.

Address reply to me to Santa Fe.

Respectfully,
Montague Leverson
Of Denver Co. Colorado

[Enclosed with this letter was the following letter from Leverson to Sherman.]

Montague R. Leverson to U.S. Marshal John E. Sherman - March 20, 1878

[Letterhead of Office of John H. Tunstall crossed out.]

Lincoln N. M.
20 March 1878

Dear Sir:

As it is possible that I may not get back to Santa Fe quite as soon as I had hoped & things in this Co. are in a state that more bloodshed may be daily expected with the U. S. troops aiding and protecting the murderers, I have thought it best to communicate to you some of the facts in order that you may the more readily give credence to what I state. I will remind you that I am the person by whom the naturalization frauds of New York in 1868 were detected & exposed over my signature in the N. Y. Tribune. I having refused $3000 offered and shewn to me by an emissary from Tammany to suppress my report before it was published & then told to state what I would take & to remember that "Tammany never goes back on its friends."

You have I dare say already heard of & perhaps seen the really infamous proclamation issued by the governor.

In 1876 the present governor approved the bill which empowers & directs the County Commissioners to appoint J.Ps. to their offices and supply vacancies (see Sec. 40). Under this sec the Court of Lincoln have appointed various officers & among them they Mr. J. B. Wilson to be J. P. in which capacity he has acted continually from Feb. 1877.

Sworn informators were made before him about the murders of Mr. Tunstall on which he issued warrants & placed them in the hand of his constables appointed for that purpose to make the arrests &c. In case you should not have seen the proclamation of his Excellency I mailed you a copy by which you will perceive that the [governor] not only takes upon himself to decide what if his statement be true should be determined as good warrants, but actually ignores the fact of there being other Justices of the Peace elected by the people of the County.

While his protégé Brady is the very man who to the knowledge of the governor himself as shown by the previous message to the Legislature was until 9 July last a defaulter to the Territory & never paid in a dollar since he came into office!

The amount thus defaulted was paid by Mr. Catron on the 9 Jany out of the proceeds of Indian vouchers & moneys forwarded by Mr. Riley of the firm of J. J. Dolan of this place.

Under the warrants issued by Mr. J Wilson, 2 of Mr. Tunstall's murderers were arrested. While riding to jail they succeeded in shooting one of the guards and were then shot down.

Under the governor's proclamation the troops are now at the beck and call of the sheriff pursuing the men who made the arrest to the indignation and dismay of every honest citizen in the county.

Two more of the sheriff's posse by whom Mr. Tunstall was murdered stopped and were robbing a Mr. Wagner who was bringing a herd of sheep from California, when one of his hands – a German whom they had wantonly shot – shot & killed one of them & shot & wounded the other. Both of these men were "wanted" by the U.S. for robbery & and been generously furnished mules, saddles and arms by Mr. Riley of he firm of J. J. Dolan & Co being 2 of the men so kindly let out of jail last fall by the governor's protégé sheriff Brady.

I assure you I have done my very best to get at the truth and have listened to & questioned both sides. I am acquainted with the statements, denials and explanations furnished by the sheriff's lot, but they are too flimsy & too thoroughly contradicted by facts which are patent & can't be gainsaid to need further notice here.

So soon as I return to Santa Fe I will call & give you further information but in the meantime in the interests of justice & honesty & to avoid further bloodshed so far as possible, I earnestly recommend you to telegraph to Washington that orders be given for the troops to be retired to the fort and that they be ordered out only on the call of the U.S. Marshall or of his deputies and only in aid of U.S. process in their hands also & above all things do not fail to sustain our present deputy M. Widenman [Widenmann], the citizens can be relied on to do their duty so soon as the demoralizing spectacle of the U.S. troops aiding and abetting thieves and assassins under the orders of the government is put an end to.

[Here Leverson's letter in the Angel file ends. The following has been added to the end of Leverson's letter in a different handwriting. It was probably added by Sherman before he sent the letter on to Devens.]

"Justice" Wilson issued warrants of arrest for members of the Sheriff's posse who had been charged before him as the murderers of Mr. Tunstall.

The story of the shooting of the guard and the two men charged with the murder of Tunstall will be found to have quite a different coloring. McC. [McCloskey] the guard is claimed by Morton, one of the prisoners, to have been his friend. He so wrote to his friends in West Va. & in anticipation that he would be killed by the arresting party. McC. was simply shot & killed. Morton & Baker were badly mutilated with many shots. Such appears to be a well received & believed statement.

Morton counted McC. as his friend. The idea was that the arresting party (McC. being one of them) intended to kill Morton & Baker before reaching Lincoln, but McC. was opposed to it & acted friendly to M & B.

[The last page of Leverson's letter is missing from the file.]

[Here is the letter from Morton being referred to. It was mailed to a family friend, Judge Hunter H. Marshal of Richmond, Virginia.]

[South Spring River, N. M., March 8, 1878 {Chisum's Ranch}]

[Dear Sir:]

[Some time since I was called upon to assist in serving a writ of attachment on some property, wherein resistance had been made against the law. The parties had started off with some horses which should be attached, and I, as Deputy Sheriff with a posse of twelve men was sent in pursuit of same, overtook them, and while attempting to serve the writ our party was fired on by one J. H. Tunstall, the balance of his party ran off. The fire was returned and Tunstall was killed. This happened on the 18th of February.]

[The 6th of March I was arrested by a constables posse, accused of the murder of Tunstall. Nearly all of the Sheriff's posse fired at him [Tunstall] and it is impossible for any one to say who killed him. When the posse which came to arrest me and one man who was with me first saw us about one hundred yards distant we started in another direction, when they (eleven in number) fired nearly one hundred shots at us. We ran about five miles when both of our horses fell and we made a stand, when they came up they told us if we gave up they would not harm us; after talking awhile we gave up our arms and were taken prisoners.]

[There was one man in the party who wanted to kill me after I had surrendered, and was restrained with the greatest difficulty by others of the party. The constable himself said he was sorry we gave up as he had not wished to take us alive. We arrived here [Roswell] last night en-route to Lincoln. I have heard that we were not to be taken alive to that place, I am not at all afraid of their killing me, but if they should do so I wish that the matter be investigated and the parties dealt with according to law. If you do not hear from me in four days after receipt of this, I would like you to make inquiries about the affair.]

[The names of the parties who have me arrested are, R. M. Bruer [Brewer], J. G. Skurlock [Scurlock], Chas. Bowdre, Wm. Bonny (Goodrich!), Henry Brown, Frank McNab., "Walt" Sam Smith, Jim French, Middleton (and another named McClosky and who is a friend). There are two parties in arms and violence expected, the military are at the scene of disorder and trying to keep peace. I will arrive at Lincoln the night of the 10th and will write you immediately if I get through safe. Have been in the employ of Jas. J. Dolan & Co. of Lincoln for 18 months, since 9th of March 1877, have been getting $60 per month, have about six hundred dollars due me from them, and some horses &c. at their cattle camps.]

[I hope, if it becomes necessary, that you will look into this affair, if anything should happen. I refer you to T. B. Catron U. S. Attorney Santa Fe N. M. and Col. Rynerson District Attorney, La Mesilla N. M. they both know all about the affairs, as the writ of attachment was issued by Judge Warren Bristol La Mesilla N. M. and everything was legal. If I am taken safely to Lincoln I will have no trouble but let you know.]

[If it should be as I suspect, please communicate with my brother Quin Morton, Lewisburg W. V. Hoping that you will attend to this affair if it becomes necessary, and excuse me for troubling you if it does not.]

[I remain yours Respectfully,
W. S. Morton]

Telegram John Sherman to Attorney General Charles Devens - March 23, 1878

The Western Union Telegraph Company
Dated March 23, 1878
Received March 26, 1878
To Charles Devens, Attorney General Washington

I have U.S. warrants for four desperadoes in Lincoln County New Mexico which I cannot serve without assistance of troops. Commanding General here declines to furnish them except upon an order from the President. Respectfully asks instructions.

John Sherman, Jr.
U.S. Marshal

Charles Devens to U.S. Marshal John Sherman - March 26, 1878

Department of Justice,
Washington, D.C.
March 26th, 1878

John E. Sherman,
US Marshal
Santa Fe, New Mexico

It does not appear why arrest of four men cannot be made without troops.

Chas. Devens,
Attorney General

Edward Thornton to Attorney General Charles Devens - March 27, 1878

Washington
March 27, 1878

Sir:

With reference to my note of the 9th instant relative to the murder of Mr. J. H. Tunstall, a British subject, near Lincoln, New Mexico, I have the honor to inform you that I have received a letter from that place of the 16th instant, in which it is charged that the above mentioned crime was incited by the District Attorney of the Third Judicial District and that the murderers are being screened or attempted to be screened by the Governor of the Territory and the Judge of the District.

Without pretending that these charges are well founded until they shall be supported by further proof, it seems to me to be a case which demands prompt and searching investigation, and I am confident that the Government of the United States will not fail to give to the matter its early and serious attention.

It appears that when the murder of Mr. Tunstall took place, warrants for the arrest of the murderers were issued on sworn informations by Mr. John B. Wilson, a Justice of the Peace.

By the enclosed copy of a translation of the record, it appears that Mr. Wilson was duly appointed a Justice of the Peace on the 14th of February 1877 by the County Commissioners, who, as appears by the enclosed translation of the 40th section of the acts of the Legislative Assembly of the Territory of New Mexico 1875-76 page 28, were authorized to make such appointments.

Notwithstanding the apparent legalities of the appointment, a Proclamation, copy of which I have the honor to enclose, has been issued by the Governor of the Territory, declaring that Mr. Wilson's appointment by the County Commissioners was illegal and void, and that all processes issued by him were void.

It is therefore to be presumed that the warrants issued by Mr. Wilson for the arrest of the above mentioned murderers will have no effect and if it be true that some of the United States Authorities are in league with them, there seems to be but little prospect that the murderers will be brought to justice unless the government of the United States should take energetic measures to ensure their capture and trial.

I have the honor to be with the highest consideration, Sir,
Your obedient servant
Edw. Thornton

Robert Widenmann to Secretary of the Interior Carl Schurz - March 29, 1878

Lincoln County Bank
Lincoln, N.M.
March 29, 1878

Hon Carl Schurz
Secretary of the Interior
Washington, D.C.

Dear Sir:

Referring to my last letter I beg to inform you that S. Stanley returned from the Indian Agency last night with a large load of goods, and delivered same at the store of J. J. Dolan & Co. in this place, which store and business is in the hands and under the control of Thos. B. Catron U.S. District Atty.

Mr. Watkins [Department of Interior Indian Agency Inspector] has as yet not arrived here and if he delays much longer I fear I shall be under the sod before the investigation is commenced. Threats in this direction are daily made.

Very respectfully
Robt. A. Widenmann

Montague Leverson to President Rutherford B. Hayes - April 1, 1878

[Letterhead of Juan B. Patron, General Merchandise]

Lincoln, Lincoln Co. N. M.
1 April 1878

His Excellency Rutherford B. Hayes
President of the United States

Excellency.

I returned to this town from an inspection of the lower Country this morning & found that only a few hours previously two more of Mr. Tunstall's murderers have been killed, viz; the sheriff who employed the ruffians in his posse, & a noted cattle thief, who was also one of the sheriff's deputies on the occasion of Mr. Tunstall's murder.

More bloodshed will follow unless the governor be at once removed. He is the mainstay of the thieves and murderers. The state of affairs here is precisely that the two Sicilies before they were freed by Garibaldi. The administrators of the law were the criminals and the honest men were driven to the mountains and pursued as bandits.

I again urge on your Excellency the fact that the native element has nothing to do with these troubles and it is of no use looking on it as a Mexican anarchy. This County alone ought to have a population today of 30 to 40,000 persons & would have it but for the thieves being supported by the Government.

Only last year Mr. Jno Chisum was refused all aid by the sheriff, by the military and by the governor, to protect him from the bandits who in bands of twenty and thirty were stealing the cattle of his employer (Mr. R. D. Hunter of St Louis). I am informed that Mr. Watkins the delegate offered to pay him $5000 if he (Mr. Hunter) would give up a contract for supplying beef which had been awarded to him and would guarantee him that none of his (Hunter's) cattle should be stolen to supply the contract!

Mr. Hunter had only tendered in self defense because the year previously his cattle had been stolen and the Indian Agent (Godfroy) has knowingly received such stolen cattle from the contractors!

Respectfully
Montague Leverson

Montague Leverson to Secretary of the Interior Carl Schurz - April 1, 1878

Lincoln, N. M.
1 April 1878
Hon Carl Schurz

Sir:

Since I wrote my letter to the president this forenoon, some of the deputies of the late Sheriff aided by the Commander of the Post and a company of Cavalry have dared to search the houses of citizens here without warrant or authority of any kind and have arrested just whom they please being persons who had as much to do with the killings of the sheriff [Brady] as you had. Among them the deputy of the U.S. Marshal of New Mexico.

Montague Leverson

William M. Evarts to Attorney General Charles Devens - April 3, 1878

Department of State
Washington
3d April 1878

The Honorable Charles Devens
Attorney General

Sir:

Regarding the communication addressed to you by this Department, under a note of the 13th March ultimo in relation to the murder in New Mexico of Mr. J. H. Tunstall a subject of Great Britain, I have now the honor to enclose a copy of a further note [Evarts is referring to the March 27 letter from Sir Thornton to Devens given on page 177] and of its accompaniments upon the subject from the British Minister of this Capital and to invite your attention to his request that energetic measures may be taken to secure the arrest and conviction of the murderers.

I have the honor to be,
Sir, Your obedient servant,
Mr. Evarts

John Sherman to Attorney General Charles Devens - April 3, 1878

Office of the Untied States Marshal,
Territory of New Mexico
Santa Fe, N. M.
April 3d, 1878

To the Attorney General U.S.
Washington D. C.

Sir:

I have the honor to report the arrest of Nicolas Provencio and Jesse Evans, the former in confinement at La Mesilla and the latter in confinement at Fort Stanton. Jesse Evans is wounded and as receiving care and nursing at Fort Stanton for which I have authorized the commanding officer to pay one dollar per day.

Frank Baker and Hill [Morton] were killed while resisting officers in their official duties. There is every prospect of the early arrest of Davis.

All of the above are of the gang of desperadoes in Lincoln County before reported upon.

Very respectfully,
Your obedient servant
John E. Sherman, Jr.
US Marshal

Samuel F. Phillips to Secretary of State William Evarts - April 9, 1878

April 9, 1878
Hon. William M. Evarts
Secretary of State

Sir:

I have the honor to acknowledge the receipt of your communications of the 12th, of March last and the 3rd inst., with their enclosures in relation to the murder in New Mexico of Mr. J. H. Tunstall, alleged to be a subject of Great Britain.

Upon receipt of the first named communication I addressed a letter to the District Attorney for New Mexico [Thomas B. Catron] in which I directed him to institute a thorough inquiry into the circumstances of the murder and to report promptly to me whether from the facts any steps can of should be taken by the Government in the matter. I have not yet received a reply, but I have taken other measures to have the subject thoroughly investigated than through the officers of this Department now in New Mexico.

Very respectfully
Your ob't serv't
S. F. Phillips
Acting Attorney General

Thomas Catron to Attorney General Charles Devens - August 19, 1878

Office of T. R. Catron
Attorney at Law
U.S. Attorney
Santa Fe, N. M.
Aug 19, 1878

Hon Charles Devens
Attorney General

Sir:

Mr. Frank Warner Angel who has been here for some time, about one week since furnished me with some affidavits of parties which reflect somewhat upon me in my official character. I requested of him sixty days in which to answer them and furnish other affidavits. He declined but allowed me thirty days. The affidavits he has furnished except in a very few instances do not give me names, places, dates nor particulars, so that I am absolutely compelled to prove a negative. To do this I am compelled to travel over several counties and find all the persons who would know of such facts, at least a sufficient number to establish the folly of the charges.

I fell confident I can disprove every charge made against me in these affidavits. They are false as therein they reflect on me personally or officially, and I have at this time to attend to my professional and private affairs so that I cannot in thirty days without very great pecuniary loss to myself and clients get up my defense.

Mr. Angel was here in the Territory over three months, his first affidavit against me is dated May 9th and they were all given me August 12th over three months [later].

I am confident you would prefer that the officers under you should show that they are not guilty, rather than that the contrary should appear.

I have no complaints to make against Mr. Angel. He treated me in a kind and courteous manner and for my part I have no objections to his course although the affidavit s he took are mainly of persons of low character. He had to take such testimony as he could get, which I am perfectly confident I can disprove if I have sufficient time.

I therefore request that you will allow me sixty days in which to take testimony in my behalf from the 12th of this month.

I am very respectfully
Your obedient Servant
T. B. Catron
U.S Attny

G. C. Wing to U.S. District Attorney Thomas Catron - September 7, 1878

Department of Justice
Washington D.C.
September 7th, 1878

T. B. Catron
U.S. Attorney, New Mexico

Attorney General replies to your letter 19th ultimo, presented yesterday by Elkins, that you have had ample opportunity to answer charges and no extension of time can be granted.

G. C. Wing
Chief Clerk

Stephen Elkins to Attorney General Charles Devens, September 13, 1878

Dear Park, MD
September 13, 1878

Hon. Charles Devens
Attny General

Sir:

About the last of August Mr. Catron U.S. Attorney for New Mexico forwarded me to present in person with explanations as I was familiar with the circumstances an application for thirty days more time in which to answer affidavits furnished and interrogatories propounded to him by Special Agent Angell [sic] on the 12 day of August.

For this purpose I called at the Department of Justice three different times, but you were out of Washington.

Finding that the thirty days granted Mr. Catron by Mr. Angell in which to answer were about to expire and finding I would not be able to see you in person, I presented Mr. Catron's application to Mr. Phillips acting Genl. with some explanations, and he was willing to grant until Oct. first, but the Chief Clerk, Mr. Wing, thought owing to what had previously taken place in the premises, that the application had better be made to you and at my instance kindly framed a telegram to you, stating Mr. Catron desired a month extension, which was refused.

I telegraphed Mr. Catron that his application had been refused, whereupon he sent me an urgent telegram asking if possible to procure for him at least fifteen days from the 12th of this month, that it was necessary to proffer [a] defense. For which purpose I again went to Washington to see you on Thursday, but was informed you would not return to Washington probably before Saturday or Monday & not being able to remain in the city, I made a statement to the Chief Clerk and requested him to communicate the substance of it to you touching the last request of Mr. Catron, telling him that I would also write you on the subject.

I make this further effort to procure more time for Mr. Catron because in the telegram sent you it was impossible to state the reasons, which I will briefly do in addition to what Mr. Catron says in his letter.

In what I have to state now I will not attempt to defend Mr. Catron further than to say I confidently believe him innocent of the charges brought against him, and if he has the time he asks he can establish this fact to your satisfaction, and that the effort to secure his removal proceeds from his political enemies, who have used as their instrument men to make affidavits who are in nearly every instance without character, without veracity.

I was in Santa Fe when the affidavits were furnished Mr. Catron and read them and know the parties who made them.

In addition to what Mr. Caron has said in his letter, I desire to add in support of his application by telegram for fifteen days extension from the 12th inst.

1st. Not until the 12th day of August did Mr. Angel furnish Mr. Catron with any affidavits although one was made on the 9th day of May at the same time as I now remember he propounded to him. I now remember eight interrogatories. The affidavits and interrogatories refer to accusations covering a great space of time, and require him in order to make a proper answer to procure the affidavits of person residing in nearly every portion of the Territory and to refer to the records of the Courts in each of the three judicial districts which are very large, the third being distant from Santa Fe, Mr. Catron's place of residence three hundred miles and when you reflect that all traveling is by stage & private conveyance, you will see that in going from one district to another a great deal of time will be necessarily consumed.

2d. Since the 12th day of August to my knowledge Mr. Catron has been compelled to go to the State of Colorado on important professional business which has taken two weeks of his time.

3d. The five affidavits furnished by Mr. Angel which I saw were ex-parte, and contain statements and refer to names and dates that will compel Mr. Catron to go [to] the records of the various district courts to disprove or explain them, & get the testimony of disinterested person to show hey are false.

You know how hard it is to procure affidavits from disrespectable people who may have feeling against a public officer & how difficult it is to disprove the statement, but which with time can be utterly overcome.

4th. The charges are serious and involve Mr. Catron's reputation as an officer. He is the lead attorney in New Mexico, a man of position & standing among his fellow men. He enjoys the confidence of the members of the bar, the business men, the Civil & Military officers of the Territory, and having built up for himself a substantial reputation, he should have a fair hearing against those who are trying to destroy it.

He does not mean to ask nor do I for him any undue indulgence or any charitable consideration, but considering all of the circumstances & that there is no court in session, that no harm can come to the U.S. by granting him the fifteen days additional, I have not considered it improper to urge his request. I could furnish other & further reasons but fear I have already taken up too much of your valuable time.

Very Respectfully
S. B. Elkins

Thomas Catron to Attorney General Devens - September 13, 1878

Santa Fe, N.M.
Sept. 13, 1878

Hon Charles Devens
Atty General
Washington D.C.

Sir:

On yesterday I mailed to him Frank W. Angel Special Agent 62 Liberty Street New York my own answer to the several affidavits he had against me, or reflecting on me, also my own answers to the interrogations propounded by him to me, also affidavits of S. M. Ashenfelter, Jno. D. Bail, Samuels Davis, Francisco P. Abreu, Francisco Salazar, Frederick Grace, William Burden, W. F. M. Arney, Pedro Sanches, Franciso A. Mestas, and Diego Archuleta, in answer to the affidavits against me.

I am also getting other affidavits in till time as permits which these affidavits [unreadable] Mr. Angel. I will be able in about ten or twelve days to complete all my parts or at least such as I can get before election day. These affidavits against me are nothing more than electioneering defenses. The Democratic party are making many efforts to prevent me from getting any affidavits or recommendations until after the election, and if I should then be removed it will be taken as a Democratic victory and used in the present Campaign.

I have the honor to request that you will extend to me at least twelve days to take further affidavits. I would like to have until October the first, as by that time some of the fever of the Democratic leaders will be worn off and I will I hope be able to get other affidavits if [unreadable].

I need time however to get such other affidavits as I can get notwithstanding their efforts. I will continue doing so and send them to you or Mr. Angel.

I would invite your careful attention to my answers and affidavits in my defense.

Hoping that you will give me additional time to file additional testimony,

I am very truly
Your obedient Servant
T. B. Catron

Thomas Catron to Attorney General Devens - September 17, 1878

Sept 17th 1878
Santa Fe, N. M.

Hon Charles Devens
Attorney General

Sir:

On the 14th inst. I forwarded to Mr. Angel at New York by registered letter the affidavits of [unreadable] Vigil, Jose M. Garcia, F. A. Smith and a second one [unreadable] Smith taken by Mr. Angel which he said he had no use. Also Extract from the Grand Jury Report July Term 1876 and 1877 later being Exhibit "D." And on this date have forwarded to him registered letter the following affidavits of Juan Luna, Jose B. Ortiz, Thos J. Tucker, and Antonio Ortiz Salazar. I request that all these be taken in connection with previous affidavits and papers forwarded by me to Mr. Angel the 12th inst., as a part of my defense to the charges that have been made and [unreadable] evidence in my defense to the charges that have been made by him against me. I am still taking affidavits and getting evidence in my defense and hope that they all be duly considered by you before arriving at a determination in my case. The additional affidavits I am taking will be forwarded with all convenient speed Mr. Angel.

I am very respectfully
Your Obedient Servant
T. B. Catron
U.S. Attorney

Charles Devens to Stephen B. Elkins, September 18, 1878

Sept. 18th, 1878
Hon. S. B. Elkins
Dear Park, Md

Dear Sir:

I have read your application to me for an extension of fifteen days from the 12th, of the time when Mr.Catron has been informed his answer should be made to the charges against his official character.

I cannot promise that action will not be taken before a day certain; and I do not feel that Mr. Catron should require a longer time than he was given to reply with sufficient distinctness to all that has been inquired of him. Especially since he appears to have considered the matter of answering not of sufficient importance as to take precedence of his private matters, I cannot think that he now considers further time essential.

It is probable that no action will be taken until the return of the President. More than this I cannot say in the way of distinct information.

Very respectfully,
Chas Devens
Attorney General

Stephen Elkins to Attorney General Devens - September 24, 1878

Dear Park, Md
Sept. 24 1878

Hon Chas Devens
Attorney General

Sir:

I have just received from Mr. Catron a telegraphic message informing me that his testimony & answer have delayed in being forwarded until the 19th inst. & requested me to ask that no action be taken until they should be received. I think they will reach the Department by the 26th – unless there is some unusual delay & I hope you will permit his request in this respect.

Very Respectfully
S. B. Elkins

N.B.

I will be in Washington on Monday next & if it would be agreeable to you to honor me, I would like to make a statement in Mr. Catron's behalf, with the testimony this answers & the facts I know. I think it can be clearly established that only bitter political, personal enemies have assailed him & the charges are unfounded. I have written the President to day & hope the letter will be referred to you as in it I make a brief statement as to Mr. Catron & my opinion of the charges against him.

Thomas Catron, Resignation Letter - October 10, 1878

Albuquerque, N. Mexico
Oct 10th 1878
Hon. Charles Devens

Attorney General U.S.
Washington D.C.

Sir: In accordance with a purpose long entertained I hereby tender my resignation as United States Attorney for New Mexico to take effect November 10, 1878.

Very respectfully yours
T. B. Catron

Charles Devens to Thomas B. Catron, Resignation Accepted - October 19, 1878

October 19th, 1878
Thomas B. Catron, Esq
U.S. Attorney
Albuquerque, New Mexico

Sir:

Your resignation of the Office of United States Attorney for New Mexico is hereby accepted to take effect November 10th, 1878, as tendered in your letter of the 10th instant.

Very respectfully,
Charles Devens
Attorney General

Stephen Elkins to Attorney General Devens - November 10, 1878

New York City
Hotel Bristol
Nov 10 1878

Hon Charles Devens
Attorney General

Sir:

The U.S. Court for the 3rd Jud. Dist. of New Mexico begins to-day. Mr. Catron's resignation was made to take effect to-day. He writes me to ask of you it being too late for his successor to reach their train for the court, whether or not he shall appear for the U. S. at the present term.

If you desire him to appear a telegram to him at Mesilla New Mexico will reach him in time – if not & you will kindly notify me. I will telegraph him.

Very Respectfully
S. B. Elkins

Charles Devens to Stephen B. Elkins, November 12, 1878

Nov 12th, 1878
Hon. S. B. Elkins
Hotel Bristol
New York City

Dear Sir;

I am obliged to you for your note of he 10th inst., calling my attention to the fact that the Court for the 3rd District of New Mexico begins to-day, and that Mr. Catron would continue to act as attorney if so advised by me.

I had before telegraphed him that it would be convenient if he continued until the 30th inst. at Santa Fe.

By your note he has apparently not received that, and I have to-day accordingly telegraphed him that I desire that he should continue, as he has suggested until the qualification of his successor, and that his resignation will be changed to this extent.

Very respectfully
Chas Devens
Attorney General

Telegram Sherman to Attorney General - October 29, 1878

[Western Union Telegram]

Santa Fe N.M
October 29, 1878
Hon Charles Devens
Atty Genl Wash D. C.

Respectfully request authority to employ two detectives to follow leaders of Lincoln County Banditti into Colorado. Have writs against them for murder, robbery and larceny of Govt. property this at General Wallace's request.

John Sherman Jr.
U. S. Marshal

Charles Devens to U.S. Marshal John Sherman - October 20, 1878

Department of Justice
Washington D.C.
October 20th, 1878

John Sherman, U.S. Marshal
Santa Fe, New Mexico

I have not means to employ the detectives. Ascertain if possible the location of persons indicted, and then send to Marshal of Colorado, and secure their arrest.

Charles Devens
Attorney General

Charles Devens to Secretary of the Interior Carl Shurtz - January 10, 1879

Jan. 10th., 1879
Hon. Carl Schurz
Secretary of the Interior

Sir:

I have the honor to forward with this a report of Mr. F. W. Angel, who was dispatched by this Department to New Mexico to investigate certain matters affecting the Government's interests in that locality.

This report is accompanied by the written material upon which it is based, and relates to the so called Una De Grato grant, which upon the examination made by the agent, satisfies him that it was obtained through fraud and forgery.

If, after you have examined the findings submitted with this, you shall conclude that any action requiring the co-operation of this Department is necessary, I will, upon being so advised, endeavor to have every step taken that properly belongs to this Department.

Very respectfully,
Char. Devens,
Attorney General

Charles Devens to Secretary of State William Evarts - January 10, 1879

Jan. 10th., 1879
Hon. Wm. M. Evarts,
Secretary of State

Sir:

I have the honor to enclose printed copies of the letters which accompanied your communication of the 12th of November last in which communication you asked to be informed of the result of the investigation conducted through this Department into the circumstances attending the death of John H. Tunstall, an alleged British subject, in New Mexico.

Upon being advised by you that your attention had been called by the British Minister to the killing of Tunstall, and that information respecting it was desired, I immediately directed the United States Attorney for New Mexico [Catron] to institute a thorough inquiry and report to me.

It not appearing that that officer had at once undertaken such investigation, an agent of this Department [Angel] was sent to the Territory, charged among other duties with that of specially learning all the particulars of the murder as well as the causes which led to the same. The agent was for a considerable time engaged in executing this duty, and he has recently submitted to me his report, together with voluminous papers affidavits and statements which show the grounds upon which he has reached the conclusion stated.

I enclose a copy of his report and of the papers that appear by pages in the finding of Mr. Angel.

As will appear, the investigation does not establish that the death of Tunstall was due to the action of any United States officials, but that it is to be attributed to the private enmity which he had incurred of certain lawless characters, and further, that of the three persons by whom the murder was undoubtedly committed, two have been killed, and the third is an outlaw whose crimes against the Territory are notorious.

Very respectfully,
Your obt. Serv't,
Chas. Devens,
Attorney General

William Evarts to Attorney General Charles Devens - February 8, 1879

Department of State
Washington
Feb. 8, 1879

The Honorable
Charles Devens
Attorney General

Sir:

Referring to previous correspondence on the subject of the murder in New Mexico of Mr. John H. Tunstall, a subject of Great Britain, I have the honor to enclose herewith, a copy of a note of the 3rd instant from the British Minister of this Capital and to invite your attention to the request it contains for information as to what steps have been taken for ascertaining the whereabouts of one Jesse Davis [Jessie Evans], in order that he may be arrested and brought to justice. He is represented as being the only surviving one of three men who were charged with the commission of the crime in question.

I have the honor to be, Sir,
Your obedient servant,
Wm. Evarts

Enclosure
Sir Edward Thornton to Mr. Evarts, 3 Feb. 1879

Sidney M. Barnes to Attorney General Charles Devens - May 30, 1879

[Sidney M. Barnes was confirmed by the U.S. Congress to replace Catron as N.M. Attorney General on December 16, 1878.]
Los Lunas
May 30th 1879

Charles Devins [sic]
Atty Genl of the United States

Sir:

On the 21st day of June 1878, an Indictment was found by the Grand Jury of the United States in the 3rd Judicial District Territory of New Mexico against 9 person to wit, Charles Bowdre, Doc Scurlock, Henry Brown, Henry Antrim (alias) Kidd [sic], John Middleton, Stephen Stevens, John Scroggins, George Coe & Frederick Waite charging them with murdering Andrew Roberts in April 1878, on the Mescalero Apache Indian Reservation, N. M.

Three of the Defendants, Coe, Antrim, and Scurlock have been arrested. Coe is in jail at Santa Fe, Antrim & Scurlock are confined at Fort Stanton. I hope others will be arrested by the June day of commencement of Court at Mesilla 3rd District. Those arrested are reported to be terrible offenders. I am anxious to bring them to a speedy trial. I forward you herewith a copy of the indictments and Marshal Sherman's Deposition.

The Defendants will be represented by able lawyers. I believe the cause of Justice requires me to submit the case to you and ask you to clothe me with discretion & power to secure the aid of an additional Attorney in the event I come to the conclusion when I get to Mesilla & investigate the case fully that I need help. I do not desire to make expense unnecessarily. T. B. Catron former Atty offers to aid me if requested by you. I am not certain that I desire his services – wish the privilege to determine for myself.

If you conclude to obtain help advise at once by Telegram at Mesilla. Communications by mail will not reach me in time. I send newspaper also.

Respectfully
Sidney M. Barnes
United States Atty, New Mexico

[A copy of the Grand Jury indictments is given on page 133. No deposition by Marshal Sheriman is in the Report records.]

Chapter 6 | Attempt to Destroy the Report

Angel's verbal presentation of his investigations to Secretary Schurz on August 31, 1878, produced immediate results. The next day Schurz presented Angel's findings to President Hayes, and Hayes, accepting Schurz's recommendation, fired Governor Axtell. The Report also led to the firing of U.S. Attorney Catron, who failed to satisfactorily address the charges of misconduct leveled against him by Angel.

But there were no criminal charges laid against anyone in New Mexico – despite the explicit conclusion by Angel in his Report that:

> *"There was no object for following after Tunstall, except to murder him, for they had the horses which they desired to attach before they commenced to pursue him and his party." (Angel, p 62.)*

This allegation suggests that Deputy Jacob Mathews, for example, could have been charged with conspiracy to commit murder for authorizing the posse that chased after and killed Tunstall.

The Report was not made public, so no one in New Mexico – especially not the press – saw it. The anti-Ring press would have happily reported its contents. Instead, even after Governor Axtell was fired, the Ring press continued to disparage Angel.[1]

In early 1879, Secretary of State Evarts gave a copy of the Report to British Ambassador Thornton. Thornton gave a copy of the Report to his boss, Foreign Secretary Robert Arthur Talbot Gascoyne-Cecil, 3rd Marquess of Salisbury. Salisbury gave a copy of the report to Tunstall's father, John Partridge Tunstall, in London.[2]

Tunstall's father petitioned the British Government requesting it seek compensation from the U.S. Government for his son's death and property loss. On August 25, 1882, Tunstall senior died. Two years after his death, the family published a pamphlet entitled *"Resume of the Facts Connected With the Murder of J. H. Tunstall and the Plunder of His Property in Lincoln County New Mexico in 1878."* This pamphlet described the killing of Tunstall and the looting and loss of his store. It alleged that Tunstall's killing was premeditated and plotted by the Santa Fe Ring. As evidence of this premeditation, the family published the full text of District Attorney Rynerson's letter to *"Friends Riley and Dolan."* (McSween, Ex 19, p 134.)

The pamphlet included a plea to the British public for:

> *"Signatures... to the enclosed address of Lord Granville. The matter is one of national interest as affecting the respect due to the life and property of English men abroad."* [3]

George Leverson Gower Grandville had replaced Salisbury as British Foreign Secretary in 1880.

John Partridge Tunstall. Undated photo. Courtesy Maurice G. Fulton Papers, Special Collections, UA.

On April 25, 1885, the British Government made a formal request to the U.S. Government for compensation for the loss of Tunstall's property, estimated at 80,000 pounds. On June 1, 1885, the U.S. Government denied the claim, giving as its reason, that there was:

"No principle of international law which makes it the duty of one nation to assume the collection of the claims of its citizens against another nation, if the citizens themselves have ample means of redress without the intervention of their Government." [4]

That knowledge of the Report by government officials in the United States faded quickly was of great benefit to Axtell. After Chester A. Arthur became president on September 19, 1881, due to President Garfield's assassination, the Santa Fe Ring regained its power. Through the efforts of Stephen Elkins and Collis Huntington, President Arthur was persuaded to appoint Axtell chief justice of the New Mexico Territorial Supreme

Court, a stunning personal rehabilitation. A factor in Arthur's willingness to appoint Axtell was Arthur's extreme dislike for former President Hayes, who had fired him as Port of New York Custom Collector. Axtell's support by Huntington was also a formative factor in Arthur's decision. Huntington was an ex-railroad executive who at the time was the chief lobbyist for the Southern Pacific Railroad. When Axtell was governor of New Mexico, he had aided Huntington by supporting the blocking all railroads from building in New Mexico except the Southern Pacific Railroad.[5]

In 1892, Catron decided to run for New Mexico delegate to the U.S. House of Representatives. Well aware of the consequences if his opponent, Democrat Antonio Joseph, was to dig up the Angel Report, Catron wrote to good friend and fellow Ring member Elkins:

> *"I understand the democrats are desirous of obtaining a copy of that man Angell's [sic] report against me, made when I was U.S. Attorney, for the purpose of making use of it in this campaign. There is nothing in this matter except it may be his report, that I would care anything about being published. I never saw his report, and know nothing about its contents, but I suppose it is something dirty and filthy. I wish you would see the Attorney General and see that he does not allow any copy of that paper to be issued to any one, or any other part of these proceedings, as they are unnecessary here. They only desire it for political effect, and I would have no objection whatever to taking the judgement [sic] of the people on the merits of the case, but I do not desire any judgement upon Mr. Angell's report. Kindly see to this immediately."* [6]

Elkins was in a powerful government position, serving as Secretary of War under President Harrison. Seven days later, S. D. Mills, Elkins' secretary, replied:

> *"Yours of the 26th ultimo came to hand and was referred by Secretary Elkins to the Attorney General. It was in regard to Angel's report when you were U.S. Attorney. The Attorney General returns it this morning marked O.K. so I think you need have no further worry about it."* [7]

Catron lost to Joseph in an extremely close race that was not decided until 12 days after the election.[8] No information from the Report surfaced during the campaign.

Catron was still worried, however, as he intended to run again in 1894, and he was convinced he would win on that attempt. On February 3, 1893, he wrote to Elkins:

> *"First: Get Attorney General Miller to take out of the files in his office and deliver up to you that report made by Angell against me. That is a thing which they will want to use against me hereafter, simply as a piece of mudslinging. There is no use allowing them to have it. When Cleveland went out of office, every paper which was filed there against Judge Vincent was taken out and returned to Vincent. I do not care to have those returned to me, but you can get that report and destroy it."* [9]

Elkins replied in person on March 13, 1893:

> *"I have had a diligent search made for Angel's report in the Attorney General's Department, but it cannot be found."* [10]

Catron won the 1894 delegate race, and no information from the Angel Report emerged in that election. In fact, there appears to be no further public knowledge of the Report until English author and historian Frederick W. Nolan *"discovered a portion of one of the Angel reports in the archives of the British Foreign Office"* in the early 1950s – derived from the copy given to the British Government by Thornton.[11] This discovery prompted Nolan to search for the Report in the U.S. National Archives, where he found it in Department of Interior records.

Drawing upon the first-hand witness statements in the Report, Nolan published "A Sidelight on the Tunstall Murder" in the July, 1956, issue of the *"New Mexico Historical Review."* With this ground-breaking article, Nolan became the first Lincoln County War historian to give an account of Tunstall's killing based on what participants on both sides of the event saw and believed and told Angel.[12]

Catron asked Elkins to destroy the Report. Elkins replied that the Report could not be found. This statement implied that President Harrison's Attorney General William H. H. Miller had destroyed the report after Catron's first request – *"The Attorney General returns it this morning marked O.K. so I think you need have no further worry about it."*

Angel submitted the Report to the Attorney General Devens of the Department of Justice. Devens forwarded the <u>original</u> Report to Secretary of Interior Schurz (Devens, p 188), and on the same day sent a <u>copy</u> to Secretary of State William Evarts (Devens, pp 188-189). <u>It is very odd that Devens sent the original to Schurz.</u> The copy that was given to British Ambassador Thornton would have been made from Evarts' copy (or maybe it was the actual copy Evarts received from Devens).

The Angel Report that exists today in is multiple handwritings. Some of it is in Angel's handwriting, some in the handwriting of a deponent giving a statement, and some in the handwriting of the clerk or notary republic taking the statement. The statements, however given, are signed and certified. Because of the signatures, we know the existing document is the original Angel Report.

That Devens sent the original to Evarts indicates that there was never a copy in the Department of Justice files. So when Catron asked that the Report be destroyed, and Elkins replied that it could not be found, he was telling the truth, rather then being cagey because he did not want to record in a letter that he had destroyed an official government document. If the Report had been in the Department of Justice files, the author is certain it would have been destroyed at Elkin's instigation.

Because of Deven's astonishing and non-officious decision to <u>not keep a copy</u> of the Report for the U.S. Department of Justice, the Report exists today, and we can read the electrifying words of the participants in the event that kicked off the Lincoln County War, the unprovoked, sadistic murder of John Henry Tunstall on February 18, 1878.

<u>What a appalling crime against history it would have been if Catron and Elkins, who would go on to become the first two U.S. Senators from New Mexico, had succeeded in destroying the Angel Report.</u>

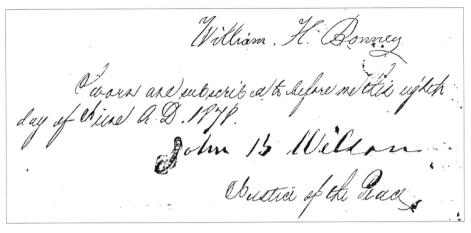

Signatures of William H. Bonney (Billy the Kid) and John B. Wilson on Bonney's statement to Angel, June 8, 1878. In other documents known to be signed by Billy, he signed as W. H. Bonney, Wm H. Bonney, W. Bonney, and William Bonney.

Signatures of Pantaleón Gallegos and Frank Warner Angel on Gallegos' statement to Angel, May 12, 1878.

Signatures of James J. Longwell and W. W. Griffin on Longwell's statement to Angel, May 14, 1878.

Signatures of Jacob Basil Mathews and Frank Warner Angel on Mathew's
statement to Angel, June 26, 1878.

Signatures of Alexander Anderson McSween and Rafael Gutierrez on McSween's
statement to Angel, June 6, 1878.

Signatures of Robert A. Widenmann, Rafael Gutierrez, and Juan B. Patron on
Widenmann's statement to Angel, June 6, 1878.

Cast of Characters

Here are brief biographies of the most important persons appearing in the Angel Report.

Angel, Frank Warner. Born May 28, 1845, in Watertown, New York. In June, 1868, Angel graduated from The Free Academy, now City College, of New York. A year later, after interning with the law firm of Barney, Humphrey, & Butler, Angel was admitted to the New York bar. He was appointed special investigator for the U.S. Department of Justice April 15, 1878, charged with investigating Tunstall's murder and corruption in Lincoln and Colfax Counties. He submitted his report on Tunstall's murder to the Justice Department on October 3, 1878, which charged Territorial Governor Axtell with 12 acts of corruption, fraud, and mismanagement that contributed directly to the death of Tunstall. His interviews with the participants in the Lincoln County War are of immense value to historians. On October 29, 1878, Angel was appointed Assistant District Attorney for the Eastern District (New York). Angel served as Assistant DA until February 4, 1886, when he resigned and entered private practice. Angel died March 15, 1906, in Jersey City, New Jersey.[1]

Antrim, William Henry "Billy the Kid." Most historians believe Billy was born in New York City in 1859, although no records documenting his birth or his paternal parentage have been found. Some authors have suggested he was born December 20, 1859.

Billy's real name was William Henry McCarty. His mother may not have been married. Billy, his younger brother Joseph, and his mother Catherine McCarty left New York in 1872 for Wichita, Kansas. There they lived with William H. Antrim, a farmer, who later would become Billy's stepfather. Catherine and her sons were probably taken on by Antrim as a charity case, and as free labor.[2] Within a few months, Antrim and his three wards left Kansas for New Mexico, where Antrim married Catherine in Santa Fe on March 1, 1873.[3]

Shortly after the marriage, the family moved to Silver City, New Mexico.[4] There, on September 16, 1874, Catherine died of tuberculosis. One year after his mother's death, Billy was arrested and jailed for concealing stolen property. Billy was manipulated into hiding the purloined items by George Schafer, a much older tough known around Silver City as "Sombrero Jack." [5] Billy escaped from the jail by shinnying up a fireplace chimney in the corner of his cell. Following his escape, Billy fled Silver City, beginning his now famous life as an adult.

During his life, in court records, Billy was referred to as William Bonney, alias "Kid,' alias William Antrim. It is unknown why Billy began calling himself Bonney. It is possible that his birth father's surname was Bonney. Billy went by Henry Antrim while growing up in Silver City. In letters, Billy signed his name as W. H. Bonney, or occasionally, W. Bonney. In his statement to Angel, Billy identified himself as William H. Bonney.[6]

Register, Corn Exchange Hotel, Mesilla, listing "Doc" Scurlock, Charles Bowdre, and Richard Brewer as hotel guests. September 22, 1877. Courtesy Archives and Special Collections, NMSU.

Billy was killed about midnight, July 14, 1881, by Sheriff Pat Garrett in Pete Maxwell's bedroom at Fort Sumner.[7]

Appel, Daniel Mitchell. Born October 28, 1854, in Pennsylvania. Appel graduated Jefferson Medical College in 1875 and entered the army a year later. Appel did the post mortem examination of Tunstall's body. On February 3, 1879, he married H. Kate Godfroy, the daughter of Frederick Godfroy, the Mescalero Apache Reservation Agent. That marriage did not last, for reasons unknown; on October 27, 1882, he married Sophia

Lindsay. During the Spanish American War was in charge of the U.S. Army Medical Department for the Philippine Islands. He died April 21, 1914, in Hawaii.[8]

Axtell, Samuel Beach. Born October 14, 1819, in Franklin County, Ohio. Axtell graduated from law school in 1843 and was admitted to the bar that year. He was elected to the U. S. Congress as a Representative from California in 1867, serving two terms. He was appointed governor of Utah February 2, 1875 by President Grant, but removed after only a few months in office due to extensive public criticism. He was appointed governor of New Mexico July 30, 1875. He was removed as governor September 3, 1878. He was appointed chief justice of the New Mexico Territorial Supreme Court in 1882 and served until he resigned in 1885. Axtell died August 6, 1891.[9]

Baker, Frank. Real name Frank Johnson. Baker may have been born in New York. He came to New Mexico from Texas in the mid-1870s and joined a gang of outlaws and cattle rustlers known as "The Boys." He was suspected of several unsolved murders. On September 17, 1877, Baker in company with Evans, Hill, and Davis stole valuable horses belonging to McSween and Tunstall. McSween, in a letter to the *Mesilla Valley Independent*, wrote:

> *"This forenoon my horses and those of Mr. Tunstall were stolen from a ranche on the Rio Ruidosa. I valued my horses at seven hundred dollars; Tunstall's cost over one thousand dollars. Two of mine were fine black American horses; among Tunstall's were one of the handsomest mules in this section of the country."* [10]

A posse consisting of Richard Brewer, Charles Bowdre, and "Doc" Scurlock went after the four men, and found them with the horses at Shedd's Ranch. Confronted with their theft, the thieves agreed to return all the horses except Tunstall's. Tunstall's they would keep *for expenses."* Brewer replied, *"If you can't give me the Englishman's, you can keep them and go to hell."* [11] The posse went to Mesilla to find men to help them arrest the thieves, but were unable to elicit any help. While in Mesilla, they stayed at the Corn Exchange Hotel (now the La Posta Restaurant).

Baker, Evans, Hill, and Davis four were arrested one month later at Hugh Beckwith's ranch at Seven Rivers by a posse led by Sheriff Brady and jailed in Lincoln. They escaped November 16, 1877, with the apparent connivance of Sheriff Brady. Baker was one of the members of the chase posse that killed Tunstall. Baker was arrested for Tunstall's murder by a posse led by Richard Brewer using warrants issued by Justice of the Peace Wilson. While being taken to Lincoln on March 9, 1878, Baker tried to escape and was shot and killed.[12]

Barrier, Adolph P. Born in 1843 in France. Original surname was probably Barrière. His life is a mystery prior to his opening a house painting business in Las Vegas in 1875. His newspaper ads list his services as *"gilding, frescoing, graining, glazing, marbling, calcimising, and paper hanging"* [13] On January 4, 1878, he was sworn in as a deputy sheriff and put in charge of delivering McSween to Mesilla for his embezzlement charge hearing. After the hearing, Barrier continued to *"protect and guard"* McSween until May 29, 1978. His body guarding of McSween made Sheriff Brady and Dolan furious, and Barrier was ordered to stop guarding McSween, which he refused to do until May 29, when he learned his business in Las Vegas was suffering. On his return to Las Vegas, he was arrested and charged with contempt of court for refusing to stop guarding McSween. The charges were later dropped.[14]

Barrier then disappears from history until October 14, 1901, when he was arrested for counterfeiting in San Antonio, Texas. *"He was found with counterfeit molds for silver dollars in his possession."* He was tried, convicted, and sentenced to the penitentiary in Leavenworth, Kansas.[15]

Beckwith, Robert W. Born October 10, 1850, in New Mexico, probably near Santa Fe. The Beckwith family moved to the Seven Rivers area about 1870. Beckwith was a member of the chase posse that killed Tunstall. He was killed July 19, 1878, the last day of the 5-day war in Lincoln, in the same riotous firing that killed McSween and three others. Which side killed him is unknown. He had two shots in his body, one in his head and one in his wrist. (For a detailed account of this war, see *"The Trial of Billy the Kid,"* by the author.[16]

Bowdre, Charles. Born about 1848 in Mississippi. Bowdre married Manuela Herrera, the younger sister of "Doc" Scurlock's wife, about 1879. Bowdre was in the posse led by Brewer that arrested Baker, Evans, Hill, and Davis for stealing McSween and Tunstall's horses. At the fight at Blazer's Mill, Bowdre fired the shot that fatally wounded Buckshot Roberts. He was killed December 23, 1880, at Stinking Springs by Pat Garrett's posse. Bowdre was buried the next day in the Fort Sumner Cemetery, in a new suit paid for by Garrett.[17]

Brady, William. Born August 16, 1829, in Ireland. Brady immigrated to the U.S. and joined the U.S. Army in 1851, serving two five-year terms. He joined the 2nd N.M. Volunteer Infantry August 19, 1861. He was promoted to Brevet Major and appointed commander of Fort Stanton April 29, 1864. He was replaced at Fort Stanton in October, 1865, by Emil Fritz and appointed commander of Fort Selden. He was transferred to Fort Sumner in May, 1866. He was discharged from the army October 8, 1866. In 1868, he purchased a large ranch east of Lincoln. He became a U.S. citizen July 20, 1869. He was elected sheriff of Lincoln County September 6, 1869. After serving two years, Brady was elected to the Territorial House for one term. In November, 1876, Brady was re-elected sheriff of Lincoln County.

Brady had a decisive and culpable role in Tunstall's murder. Based on Judge Bristol's order, he occupied Tunstall's Lincoln store, attaching its contents. Then, even though he had attached more than sufficient property to legally satisfy Bristol's writ of attachment, Brady decided to attach all of Tunstall's cattle. He organized the first posse that went out to Tunstall's ranch. When that posse failed in its appointed task, he ordered Deputy Mathews to gather a large second posse and return. He fully expected that the second posse would kill some of the men at the ranch, and probably instructed Mathews to do so if the opportunity arose. Members of that second posse, which included four known prison escapees, chased after Tunstall. Two of the escapees, Buck Morton and Tom Hill, caught up with and killed Tunstall before he could reach the safety of Lincoln.

Brady was himself killed April 1, 1878, by shots fired from Tunstall's horse corral. Billy the Kid was tried for the shooting and convicted of murdering Brady.[18] For details on the trial, see the *"The Trial of Billy the Kid,"* by the author.

The graves of Richard "Dick" M. Brewer and Andrew "Buckshot" Roberts in the Blazer's Mill Cemetery. 2017 photo.

Brewer, Richard M. Born February 19, 1850, in St. Albans, Vermont. Brewer arrived in Lincoln in 1870 and homesteaded a ranch on the Rio Feliz. In 1874, he bought a second ranch from James Dolan. When Tunstall arrived in Lincoln and began buying livestock, he hired Brewer as his ranch foreman. Brewer was with Tunstall when he was murdered by Buck Morton and Tom Hill. On April 4, 1878, Brewer was killed at Blazer's Mill by "Buckshot" Roberts.[19] (For details on how Brewer and Roberts' graves were rediscoverd and remarked, see *"The Trial of Billy the Kid."*)

Bristol, Warren Henry. Born March 19, 1823, in Stafford, New York. Bristol graduated from Wilson Collegiate Institute and studied law at Fowler's Law School. He practiced law in Minnesota from 1850-1872. He was appointed judge of the New Mexico Third District Court in April, 1872. He was a committed partisan ally of the Murphy-Dolan faction. He issued the writ of attachment on McSween and Tunstall's Lincoln property that initiated the chain of events that led to Tunstall's murder. Judge Bristol resigned from the court in 1885 and died January 12, 1890, in Deming, New Mexico. A few years later body was moved to Lockport, New York.[20]

Brown, Henry Newton. Born in 1857 at Cold Spring Township, Missouri. Brown left Missouri at the age of 17, drifted into Texas, and worked as a cowboy and buffalo hunter. He left Texas for Lincoln, New Mexico, in 1876, after reportedly killing a man. In Lincoln he worked for Murphy, then for John S. Chisum. When the conflict between Murphy and Tunstall started up, he aligned himself with Tunstall. Brown was behind

Mausoleum of Thomas Benton Catron in the Fairview Cemetery, Santa Fe, New Mexico. 2009 photo.

the corral wall with Billy when Sheriff Brady was shot, and was indicted for the killing. He was with Billy at Blazer's Mill when "Buckshot" Roberts was killed. Following the killing of McSween in Lincoln he, returned to Texas briefly, then moved to Caldwell, Kansas, were he became assistant city marshal and then full city marshal. He resigned after 16 months, spent some time in Missouri, and was rehired as Caldwell marshal. On April 30, 1884, Brown, his deputy, and two other men tried to rob the bank in Medicine Lodge, Kansas, killing the bank manager in the process. They were caught and jailed. A mob of 300 gathered to lynch the men. As they broke into the jail, Brown escaped, but was killed by a shotgun blast. The other three men were lynched.[21]

Catron, Thomas Benton. Born October 6, 1840, near Lexington, Missouri. Catron graduated from University of Missouri in 1860. During the Civil War, he fought for the Confederacy. He saw action in numerous battles, including Lexington, Vicksburg, Corinth, Lookout Mountain, Missionary Ridge, and Mobile Bay. He moved to Santa Fe in 1866, and then, after being appointed district attorney of the Third Judicial District, to Mesilla. In September, 1868, he was elected to the Territorial Legislature representing Dona Ana County. In January, 1869, he was appointed the Attorney General of New Mexico. In February, 1872, he was appointed U.S. Attorney for New Mexico. He resigned as U.S. Attorney on October 10, 1878 (to avoid being fired). In 1912, he was elected to the U.S. Senate as one of New Mexico's first senators. He died May 15, 1921.[22]

Chisum, John Simpson. Born August 15, 1924, in Hardeman, Tennessee. By 1873, he had a huge cattle operation in New Mexico. Many of the men who later fought in the Lincoln County War worked for Chisum at one time, as Billy did. Chisum sold most of his livestock holdings in 1875. The *Las Vegas Gazette* said of his ranch at the time of the sale: *"It contains 1,600 sections of land, on which Mr. Chisum has 80,000 head of cattle."* Chisum died in Paris, Texas, on December 22, 1884, and was buried on Christmas Day.[23]

Copeland, John N. Born in Kentucky. Copeland was in New Mexico by 1872, working as a butcher for the Mescalero Agency. He acquired a ranch in the Lincoln area. In February, 1873, Copeland killed two Hispanic ranch hands, justifying the killings by accusing the men of theft. After Sheriff Brady was killed, Copeland was appointed to replace him. He was not a Murphy-Dolan partisan. Copeland lasted 31 days as sheriff before he was fired and replaced by George Peppin, by order of Governor Axtell. On December 13, 1878, Copeland shot Juan Mes. He was tried and acquitted by Justice of the Peace Wilson. Copeland died June 26, 1903.[24]

Davis, George. Real name Jesse Graham. Also used the alias Tom Jones. Davis may have been a cousin of Jessie Evans. He was a member of the chase posse that killed Tunstall. He was indicted for the killing of Tunstall. In 1879, he was indicted for killing C. C. Eden. On May 19, 1880, he, Jessie Evans, and others robbed several stores at Fort Davis, Texas, reaping over $9,000 in cash. On July 3, 1880, a company of Texas Rangers sent after the robbers:

> *"Came upon the gang, who began to retreat. A running fight for a mile drove the robbers to the rocks, where, being fortified, they made a bold stand. The rangers charged, giving them a hand-to-hand fight. The robbers fought*

desperately, but soon surrendered, with the loss of Jesse Graham, alias George Davis." [25]

Devens, Charles. Born April 4, 1820, in Charlestown, Massachusetts. Devens graduated from Harvard in 1838 and earned a law degree from Cambridge University. He was elected to Congress in 1848 from Massachusetts. During the Civil War he fought for the Union and was wounded at the battles of Fair Oaks and Chancellorsville. He mustered out of the army in 1866. In 1873, he was appointed to the Massachusetts Supreme Court. He resigned that office when he was appointed U.S. Attorney General March 12, 1877 by President Hayes. He resigned as Attorney General in 1881. He died January 7, 1891. [26]

Dolan, James Joseph. Born May 2, 1848, in Ireland. Dolan served in 17th Regiment, New York Zouaves, during the Civil War. He reenlisted after the war and was discharged at Fort Stanton. He was hired by Murphy as a bookkeeper and clerk. He became a Murphy partner in April, 1874. When Murphy retired in 1877, the company became Dolan & Co. He was the master mover behind the events that resulted in Tunstall's killing. He was invited to accompany Deputy Mathews on his second trip to Tunstall's ranch, and he selected the possemen that chased after and killed Tunstall. On July 13, 1879, Dolan married Caroline Fritz, the daughter of Charles Fritz. A few days after the birth of their second child, Caroline died. On February 20, 1888, Dolan married a second time, to Eva Maria Whitlock.

A few years after the Tunstall's killing, Dolan purchased Tunstall's Lincoln store and his Rio Feliz ranch. By 1891, Dolan had built a six-room adobe house on the ranch, which still stands. Dolan died February 26, 1898, of cerebral hemorrhage, and was buried in the Fritz family cemetery. [27]

Ealy, Mary R. Born December 23, 1850. Mary trained as a teacher. She married Dr. Taylor Ealy October 1, 1874. She died May 31, 1935.

Ealy, Taylor Filmore. Born September 12, 1848, in Schellsburg, Pennsylvania. Ealy attended a theological seminary and received a medical degree from the University of Pennsylvania in 1874. He came to Lincoln as a Presbyterian medical missionary and school teacher, arriving February 18, 1878, the day Tunstall was killed. After the Lincoln 5-day war, he relocated to the Zuni Pueblo and worked as a school teacher. Two years later, he and his wife gave up missionary work and returned to Schellsburg where he established a medical practice. Ealy died February 20, 1915. [28]

Elkins, Stephen Benton. Born September 26, 1841, near New Lexington, Ohio. Elkins graduated from Columbia University in 1860. When the Civil War started he joined the Union Army, but his father and brother fought for the Confederacy. After the war, he moved to Mesilla and began practicing law. He was elected to the New Mexico Territorial Legislature in 1864. In 1866, he was appointed Territorial Attorney General, and the next year U.S. Attorney for New Mexico. In 1873, he was elected to the Territorial Legislature. In 1878, he moved to West Virginia. Until his move to West Virginia, he was viewed as the de facto leader of the Santa Fe Ring. Elkins served as Secretary of War under President Harrison from 1891 to 1893. He was elected West Virginia Senator in 1895 and served until his death January 4, 1911. [29]

Ellis, Isaac. Born in 1829 in Missouri. Ellis arrived in Lincoln in June, 1877, with his two grown sons, Ben and Will, and established the Ellis store, which was also the family residence. Isaac witnessed the shooting of Sheriff Brady and Hindman and testified for the prosecution at Billy's trial in Mesilla. Isaac moved to La Luz in 1890 and died there in obscurity in 1910.[30]

Evans, Jessie J. Alias Jesse Williams. Real name may have been Will Davis. George Davis may have been a brother or cousin. Born in 1853, in Missouri. Evans evidently grew up in Kansas. On November 10, 1871, in Topeka, Kansas, Evans was convicted of passing counterfeit 50-cent notes and fined $500. When Evans came to New Mexico, he worked for John Chisum as his foreman. On December 31, 1875, Evans, John Kinney, and several others killed three men at a dance at Fort Selden. No one was charged. On January 26, 1876, Evans killed Quirino Fletcher at Las Cruces. The killing was apparently a revenge killing. Fletcher had killed two Texans a few months earlier in Mexico, one of whom may have been a friend of Evan's. Fletcher's body lay in the street all night. When his father was informed of the killing, he responded, *"Well, he has killed two men, but will kill no more."* Evans was tried and acquitted of that crime.

Evans was in the chase posse that pursued and murdered Tunstall and was indicted for that killing. On March 14, 1878, he was badly wounded while trying to rob a sheep herder. His fellow robber Tom Hill was killed. Evans made his way to Shedd's ranch, where he was arrested and taken to Fort Stanton, then to Mesilla. In Mesilla, he was charged with the murder of Tunstall, but released on bond after his case was postponed to the next court session. That inexplicable action by Judge Bristol at the request of District Attorney Rynerson gave him his freedom just in time to permit him to return to Lincoln and fight in the Lincoln 5-day war. Following the Lincoln 5-day war, he went to Texas where he, George Davis, and others attempted to rob several stores at Fort Davis. He was caught and sentenced to the Texas penitentiary. In May, 1882, he escaped and disappeared from history.[31]

Evarts, William Maxwell. Born February 6, 1818, in Charlestown, Massachusetts. Evarts graduated from Yale College in 1937. He was admitted to the bar in 1841. From 1865 to 1868, Evarts was one of the lawyers that prosecuted Confederate President Jefferson Davis for treason. After two years of preparation, during which Davis was imprisoned, Davis was released on $100,000 bail. Davis' trial expected to begin shortly after he got bail; but on December 25, 1868, President Andrew Johnson issued a pardon for all Confederates accused of treason. In July, 1868, Evarts was appointed U.S. Attorney General. In 1877, he was appointed Secretary of State by President Hayes, serving for Hayes' full term. In 1885 he was elected New York Senator. As Senator, he led the fund-raising effort to raise the money needed to build the base of the Statue of Liberty. Evarts died February 28, 1901.[32]

Fritz, Carl Phillip Friedrich "Charles." Born January 19, 1831, in Egolsheim, Germany. Charles came to Lincoln in 1872, invited by his brother Emil Fritz, who probably regaled him with stories of the many financial opportunities in the area. When Emil died, Charles and his sister Emilie Scholand were the heirs to Emil's estate, which included a partnership in L. G. Murphy & Co., a ranch, livestock, and a $10,000 life insurance policy. Charles died December 2, 1885.[33]

Fritz, Emil Adolf. Born March 3, 1832, Egolsheim, Germany. During the Civil War, Emil served in the California Column. He reenlisted after the war ended and served as commander of Fort Stanton, leaving the service to become a partner with Murphy. On a return trip to Germany, he died June 26, 1874. McSween was hired to collect Fritz's $10,000 life insurance policy benefit from the Merchants Life Assurance Company. McSween only succeeded in collecting $7,148.49 of the benefit. After McSween charged his commission and expenses, less than one third remained for Fritz's heirs, which led to a lawsuit against McSween and, unfairly, against Tunstall. That lawsuit led to the confiscation of Tunstall's property, which was the spark that ignited the Lincoln County War.[34]

Fritz, Luise Marie Emilie (Scholand). Born February 20, 1847, in Oedheim, Germany. Emilie married William Scholand in New York City shortly after arriving from Germany in 1871. Following their marriage, they moved to Lincoln. When Emil Fritz died, Emilie and Charles Fritz were appointed administrators of his estate. On April 18, 1876, Emilie divorced Scholand. In 1880, Emilie married again. When her second husband died, she married a third time. She outlived her third husband. Emilie died September 7, 1930.[35]

Gallegos, Pantaleón. Born in 1857 in Los Corrales, Santa Fe, New Mexico. His birth surname was Sandoval. Gallegos was the name of his stepfather. In later life, he switched to Sandoval. His life before he became a clerk with L. G. Murphy & Co. in 1875 is unknown. He was a member of the posse that chased after and killed Tunstall. In 1885, Pantaleón joined John H. Riley, William L. Rynerson, and Thomas B. Catron to form the Tularosa Land and Cattle Company, a partnership. Pantaleón left the company in 1889, just before it was incorporated. He died July 20, 1910, in Tularosa.[36]

Galvin, John C. H. Born in May, 1840, in Ireland. During the Civil War, Galvin served in the Third Infantry Regiment of the California Column. He mustered out in New Mexico November 12, 1865. He was in the posse that chased after and killed Tunstall. He was one of the first settlers in Deming, which was founded in 1881, where he built one of the first buildings in town, the Galvin Building, which operated as a saloon. On March 29, 1895, Galvin got into a drunken fight with William Smith. Smith suffered a broken leg and other injuries from which he later died. Galvin was indicted for assault with intent to kill. In his defense:

"Galvin brought witnesses to prove it was not his hitting Smith but Smith's hitting the floor that broke his [Smith's] leg and caused his death. The jury found Galvin to be guilty of assault and battery [and let him off with a fine and the costs of prosecution]." [37]

Galvin died June 3, 1908, and was buried in the Fort Bayard National Cemetery.[38]

Gauss, Gottfried G. Born in Germany about 1825. Gauss immigrated to the U.S. in 1853. He served thirteen years in the U.S. army, the last two during the Civil War. After arriving in Lincoln, he worked for Murphy. He was working for Tunstall at his ranch when Deputy Mathews arrived to confiscate Tunstall's cattle. He saw the second posse leave the ranch to chase after Tunstall. He was an eye-witness to Billy's famous escape from the Lincoln courthouse jail. He heard Billy shoot Deputy James W. Bell. Bell then ran out of the courthouse and fell into Gauss' arms. He saw Deputy Marshal Robert Olinger emerge from the Wortley Hotel and get shot by Billy. The likely reason he was outside and able to observe Billy's escape was because he was taking care of a large garden on land behind the courthouse. Gauss left Lincoln in the late 1890s, and may have died in 1902.[39]

Gonzales, Florencio. Born in November, 1843, in Spain. Gonzales trained as a priest in Spain and arrived in New Mexico in 1863 (probably sent by the Church). He settled in Missouri Plaza (La Plaza de Missouri) in 1865, which had just been founded. According to family history, he performed one mass at Missouri Plaza and then left the priesthood. He married Remunda Sanchez shortly after his arrival (which is probably why he left the priesthood). In 1867, he homesteaded a ranch which was stolen from him by Murphy. He homesteaded a second ranch and opened a mercantile near San Patricio. In 1875 he was elected Lincoln County Probate Judge. The next year he was appointed county commissioner. Gonzales was one of the four men that recovered and brought Tunstall's body to Lincoln. In 1882, he was elected to the Territorial Legislature, and served two terms. He died December 8, 1897, at San Patricio.[40]

Goodwin, Millard Fillmore. Born May 25, 1852, in New York. Goodwin graduated from the Military Academy June 14, 1872. He saw extensive service in Texas before being assigned to Fort Stanton. He left the army August 1, 1882, due to tuberculosis. Goodwin died July 19, 1888, in New York.[41]

Hayes, Rutherford Birchard. Born October 4, 1822, in Delaware, Ohio. Hayes attended Harvard Law School and was admitted to the bar in 1845. By 1850, he was specializing in criminal law. When the Civil War began, he joined a volunteer company, even though he had been opposed previously to using military force to retain the Union. He was wounded several times, including once at the Battle of South Mountain. In October, 1864, he was promoted brevet major general. Hayes was elected to the U.S. House in 1865. In 1868, he was elected governor of Ohio. In 1877, in an election with many disputed and fraudulent votes, he was elected President, after a series of election challenges. A special commission was appointed to decide the election. The commission contained 7 Republicans and 7 Democrats and one "Independent." The commission voted 8 to 7 that Hayes had won. In a concession to the Democrats, whose candidate Samuel J. Tilden had had more electoral votes going into the commission decision, President Hayes agree to withdraw Union troops from all occupied Southern states, ending reconstruction. Hayes' final electoral vote after the commission decisions was 185 to 184. Hayes died January 17, 1893.[42]

Hill, Tom. Real name Thomas "Tom" Chelson. Hill arrived in New Mexico in the mid-1870s. He began riding with the outlaw group known as "The Boys." He was in the posse put together by James Dolan to pursue Tunstall. He and Buck Morton murdered Tunstall. Hill was killed March 14, 1878, when he and Jessie Evans attempted to rob a sheep herder.[43]

Hindman, George W. He arrived in Lincoln in 1875. Hindman was crippled, having been mauled in earlier life in both the arms and legs by a bear. Hindman was in the posse that chased after Tunstall. He and Sheriff Brady were killed April 1, 1878, by firing from behind Tunstall's corral wall.[44]

Howe, Albert. Born in 1852 in Georgia. Howe was in the posse that chased after Tunstall. His account of the killing of Tunstall, based on what he was told by George Kitt, is the best available. Howe was a merchant near South Fork at the time he was selected for the posse. By 1885, Hill was residing in Dona Ana County. The census of that year shows him to be a widower living alone. His death date is unknown.[45]

Hurley, John. Born in 1845 in New York. Hurley moved to Lincoln in 1872. He was with the first posse that went to Tunstall's ranch to attach his cattle, and was with the posse that chased after and killed Tunstall. At the time he was working as a "laborer" and deputy sheriff. A few years later he opened a saloon in Lincoln called "Johnny's Place." He sold the saloon in 1884 and went to work for John C. DeLaney's billiard hall located just outside of Fort Stanton. Hurley was killed by Nicolas Aragon on January 25, 1885, while serving as a deputy for Sheriff John W. Poe, at Chaperito, near Anton Chico. Poe and his deputies were trying to arrest Aragon, who had escaped from jail at Puerto de Luna. Aragon was acquitted of the charge of murdering Hurley, but later sent to the penitentiary for killing Deputy Jasper Corn. DeLany, a staunch friend, was said to have cried when he learned of Hurley's death.[46]

Kruling, Charles "Dutch Charley." Almost nothing is known about Kruling, other than he went by the assumed name Dutch Charley (a not-uncommon alias) and was living in Lincoln in 1878. He was a member of the posse that chased after and killed Tunstall. In 1880, he was living in White Oaks. Kruling was killed November 30, 1883, in Palomas.

> "... at about 7 o'clock, at J. C. Summer's saloon, on the plaza, William Martin, son of Mrs. Martin, of Mesilla, a young man under 20 years of age was lounging near the table when Dutch Charley came in. Young Martin immediately called him a vile name, and asked him why he had shot his friend Rivera. Dutch Charlie, who was unarmed, said he had not done the shooting. Hardly waiting for a reply, Martin drew his six shooter and fired two shots at him, neither taking effect... Dutch Charley ran out of the door, and Martin followed, firing twice, when Charlie fell. One ball took effect in the side and the other just under the left nipple. He died almost instantly." [47]

Martin fled, but was but was caught in 1886, convicted of murder, and sentenced to seven years in the New Mexico penitentiary.[48]

Leverson, Montague Richard. Born in March 2, 1830, in London. Leverson graduated from the University of London in 1852 and went to work as a patent attorney. He published his first book in 1854, "Copyrights and Patents, of Property in Thought." He came to the United States in January, 1867. He was admitted to the New York bar the next year. On October 22, 1869, he gave evidence before a special committee of the U.S. House about naturalization fraud. He testified that he had witnessed a Judge Barnard approve multiple batches of fraudulent naturalizations, "110 to 150, even 200 at once." At the time, he said about himself that:

> "...his attention had been specially devoted to what may be termed the philosophy of legislation; he was a disciple of Jeremy Bentham, the great father of the modern school of legislation, and had had the benefit of the personal teaching of John Stuart Mill and William Ellis"[49]

In 1872, Leverson purchased a large ranch near Lockspur, Colorado. He was in New Mexico in 1878 to sell "the finest blooded and most thorough-bred (Jersey) bulls ever brought to this country." Why he traveled to Lincoln is unknown, but he was probably there to sell bulls. The Santa Fe newspaper was running regular ads by Leverson about his bulls in both English and Spanish. Leverson was with McSween when he arrived in Lincoln on the day Sheriff Brady and Hindman were killed (April 1, 1878) and was an outraged witness to the events that followed. In 1893, Leverson obtained a medical degree from Baltimore Medical College. He became a vociferous anti-vaccination advocate and germ theory denier. He wrote several strident anti-Louis Pasteur books. In 1900, he returned to England and regained his British Citizenship. He died September 26, 1925, in London. During his lifetime he published at least 47 works, several which remain in print today.[50]

Long, Jack "John." Known variously as Frank Rivers, Barney Longmont, John Mont, and Frank Ridden. Long arrived in Lincoln in 1876 and went to work for John S. Chisum as a cowhand. He said he had hanged a man in Arizona. He was appointed deputy by Sheriff Mathews. He was in the posse that chased and killed Tunstall. He was indicted for killing Tunstall, but his murder charge was dropped when he pled Governor Lew Wallace's amnesty. He was walking down the street in Lincoln with Sheriff Brady when Brady and Hindman were killed and he was wounded slightly. He served as Dolan's best man at Dolan's wedding to Charles Fritz 's daughter Caroline on July 13, 1879. Long left New Mexico for locations unknown a year or so after Dolan's wedding.[51]

Longwell, James J. Born in 1849 in Gettysburg, Pennsylvania. His family home was near enough to the site of the Battle of Gettysburg, July 1, 1863, that he and his mother were able to witness much of the battle from their upstairs windows. After the battle, they helped care for the wounded. He and his mother were present at the Gettysburg Cemetery on November 18, 1863, when President Lincoln delivered the Gettysburg Address. According to Longwell, Lincoln patted him on head. At 17, Longwell moved to the "southwest." He later moved to New Mexico and became an express rider, carrying the U.S. Mail between Santa Fe and Mesilla.

When Dolan was in Mesilla trying to convince Emilie Fritz to swear out an arrest warrant for McSween, for stealing Emil Fritz's insurance proceeds, Longwell, a Dolan employee, was the person that brought Dolan the news that McSween had left for St. Louis. When McSween was taken under guard to Mesilla to appear before Judge Bristol, Longwell was present during the hearing (so he could report to Dolan). When Dolan returned to Lincoln with Bristol's writ of attachment for Tunstall's property, Longwell was deputized by Sheriff Brady and put in charge of the five men occupying the store.

Longwell moved to El Paso in 1888 and went to work for the El Paso Transfer Company. In 1903, he bought the company and renamed it the Longwell Transfer Company. Longwell died March 25, 1936, in El Paso.[52]

Martinez, Atanacio. The author has found nothing on Martinez's life, other than his role as Lincoln constable in 1878. According to his statement to Angel, Martinez was a mason by trade. On February 20, 1878, Martinez deputized Billy and Fred Waite to arrest the men named as Tunstall's killers in the warrant issued the previous day by Justice of the Peace Wilson. When Martinez, Billy, and Waite attempted to arrest the men, they were themselves arrested by Sheriff Brady. Martinez was held for several hours, and Billy and Waite were held for 30 hours. All three men had their arms confiscated. On February 21, 1878, Martinez, still trying to arrest Tunstall's killers, searched the Murphy-Dolan store and arrested John H. Riley. Martinez was backed up in his search by a detachment of soldiers from Fort Stanton.

Mathews, Jacob Basil. Born May 5, 1847, in Woodbury, Tennessee. Mathews fought for the Union during the Civil War, enlisting at 16 in the 5th Tennessee Cavalry Regiment. He came to New Mexico in 1867 attracted by news of a gold strike near Elizabethtown. After mining for several years, he moved to Lincoln and worked briefly for Murphy. With a partner, he began ranching at a site that later became the town of Roswell. After selling out at Roswell and ranching for a while on the Rio Penasco, he moved to Lincoln.

When Murphy retired and Dolan took over his business, Mathews was brought in as a secret partner. Appointed by Sheriff Brady as a deputy, Mathews led the posse that confiscated Tunstall's cattle at his ranch and provoked Tunstall's fatal effort to flee to Lincoln with his horses. Mathew permitted Dolan to select the members of the chase posse that murdered Tunstall. Mathews was one of the deputies walking down the street in Lincoln with Sheriff Brady when Brady and Hindman were killed by shots fired from behind Tunstall's corral wall. Mathews testified against Billy in his trial for killing Sheriff Brady and was a member of the posse that conducted Billy to Fort Stanton after the trial and turned him over to Sheriff Garrett for hanging in Lincoln. In 1893, Mathews moved to Roswell. He died June 3, 1904.[53]

McCloskey, William. There is no certain background data on McCloskey. He may have been born in 1830 in Pennsylvania. In 1875, McCloskey was working for Mescalero Apache Agent Major W. D. Crothers. Crothers was charged with stealing and McCloskey testified against him. By 1878, McCloskey was working for Tunstall. On February 17, 1878, after Mathews' first attempt to attach the cattle at Tunstall's ranch, McCloskey was sent to tell the second posse that they could round up Tunstall's cattle without hindrance. McCloskey was a member of the posse that arrested Morton and Baker. He was killed March 9, 1878, when Morton and Baker attempted to escape.[54]

McSween, Alexander Anderson. Born in 1843 on Prince Edward Island in Canada. Susan McSween, in an interview in 1927, gave this account of his early life:

> "He was a wonderful orator and a fine writer. When a young man, he wrote for sixteen prominent journals. After his death a cousin of his, a member of Parliament from Canada, wrote me and told me McSwain [sic] was chosen from a family of five boys as the most intelligent one. He was writing for magazines when he was sixteen years of age. He was born at Charlottetown, Prince Edward Island. I met him in 1870 at Pekin, Illinois. He was stopping at a hotel there and I was stopping with some friends of mine. He was in the parlor writing. I was there telling an old grandmother about the Indians, as I had been down near Indian Territory. He overheard me, and that evening he met me and got to joking and kind of flirting. He seemed to have two minds, as he would write and talk at the same time. The next morning he came and said he was going to Emporia on business."

"I got a little note from him after he was gone, but did not answer it. In two weeks he came back. We engaged in repartee, and I gave him as good as he gave. We married in '73 at Atchison, Kansas. He had no money. He was not a lawyer then, but a minister. After we were engaged, he said he wanted to study for some other profession before we got married, He said he wanted to go to Washington University at St. Louis. He was detained and got there some two weeks after it opened. The Dean did not take him that late, and he told the Dean that he could catch up. He left disconsolate, but then had a letter from the Dean. It said that he had decided he would take him in, as he felt that he could catch up with the work. He went back, and caught up, but he nearly killed himself. He ruined his health. He came to Atchison, where I was going to a convent. We married and lived at Eureka, Kansas, about a year and then started out here. We married August 23, and then left Eureka in September of the next year. McSwain practiced law in Eureka." [55]

A marriage license shows McSween and Susan were married August 13, 1873. They moved to Lincoln on March 3, 1875. On October 29, 1876, McSween met Tunstall in Santa Fe, which began their close friendship and later business association. McSween was killed attempting to flee his burning house on July 19, 1878, during the last day of the war in Lincoln.[56]

McSween, Susannah Ellen "Susan." She always gave her maiden name as Homer, but it actually was Hummer. Born December 30, 1845, in Adams County, Pennsylvania. She was raised as a Dunkard, a sect of the German Baptist Brethren. The denomination mandated conservative dress and banned the use of alcohol and tobacco. In 1863, a party of Confederate forces on their way to what would become the Battle of Gettysburg raided the Hummer farm, demanding food supplies and stealing two horses. When the battle began, the family took what shelter they could. They were close enough to the battle to experience house-rattling cannon fire. Following the battle, Susan ran away from home. The next ten years of her life are a mystery. She appears in April, 1873, in Eureka, Kansas. On August 13, 1873, she married Alexander Anderson McSween using the name Sue E. Homer. Two years after McSween's murder, she married George L. Barber. In 1885, they acquired the Three Rivers Ranch. The couple divorced on October 16, 1892. Following the divorce, Susan retained ownership of the Three Rivers Ranch. She sold it in 1917 to Albert Fall and moved to White Oaks, where she died January 3, 1931.[57]

Middleton, John. Born about 1865 in Tennessee. Middleton began working for Tunstall October 20, 1877. He was riding with Tunstall when Tunstall was killed. He was one of the men behind Tunstall's corral wall when Sheriff Brady was killed and was indicted for the killing. He was at Blazer's Mill when Buckshot Roberts was killed. One of Roberts' shots struck Middleton in the chest. Middleton died of smallpox on November 19, 1882, at San Lorenzo. In a deathbed confession, he said he had killed two men in Texas. The newspaper reporting his death wrote:

"For this last murder the state of Texas offered a reward of $1200 for his capture, dead or alive, and before dying he advised those around him to take his body to the Lone Star state, to earn that reward; but nobody seemed anxious to take the trouble of taking a small pox corpse along the road for the sake of blood money." [58]

Grave of Jose Francisco Montaño, Lincoln Cemetery, Lincoln, New Mexico. 2015 photo.

Montaño, Jose Francisco. Born January 27, 1834, near Albuquerque. When the Civil War started, Montaño enlisted in the Union forces July 2, 1861. He served in the First NM Infantry and First NM Cavalry. He mustered out of the army at Lincoln on July 31, 1864. By at least 1873, he owned a store in the Lincoln. When McSween needed bondsmen to post bail on his charge of embezzling Emil Fritz's insurance proceeds, Montaño put up $1,000. After he was physically threatened by Sheriff Brady for being one of McSween's bondsmen, he withdrew the bond offer. Montaño died November 10, 1902, in Lincoln.

Morton, William Scott "Buck." Born in 1856 in Charlotte County, Virginia. By early 1877, Morton was in Lincoln working for Murphy and Dolan as their ranch foreman. He was selected by Mathews to lead the chase posse ordered after Tunstall. Morton and Tom Hill reached Tunstall ahead of the other posse members. Morton shot Tunstall in the breast; Hill shot him in the head. Then Morton shot Tunstall's horse. Morton was arrested for Tunstall's murder by a posse led by Richard Brewer using warrants issued by Justice of the Peace Wilson. While being taken to Lincoln on March 9, 1878, Morton tried to escape and was shot and killed.[59]

Murphy, Lawrence Gustave. Born in 1831 in Ireland. By the age of 17, Murphy was in New York where he enlisted in the U.S. Army. He served two terms and was discharged a few days after the Civil War began. He travelled to New Mexico and joined the New Mexico Volunteers and served for one year, was out for a few months, then reenlisted. For a while, during his last tour, he served under Sheriff Brady at Fort Stanton. In April, 1866, he was made commander of Fort Stanton. In late 1866, he left military service and opened a brewery and store in Lincoln with Emil Fritz as a partner. In April, 1869, they hired Dolan as a clerk. Their business, which was essentially a monopoly, did well. In 1874, they built a large, two-story store in Lincoln that became known as "The House." That building later became the Lincoln County Courthouse. Murphy died October 20, 1878, in a Santa Fe hospital.[60]

Newcomb, John B. Born about 1830 in Ohio. Newcomb moved to Lincoln in 1867. In 1875, he ran for Lincoln County Sheriff as a Democrat and was defeated (the Murphy-Dolan faction were Republicans). In 1877, he took up an abandoned ranch homestead on the Ruidoso River near San Patricio. Newcomb was one of the five men that recovered Tunstall's body and returned it to McSween's house in Lincoln (the other men were Florencio Gonzales, Lazar Gallegos, Roman Barregon, and Patricio Trujillo). Newcomb served on the coroner's jury that ruled on the killing. In 1894, he was elected Lincoln County Commissioner as a Democrat. By 1898, he had moved to White Oaks. Newcomb died some time after 1903.[61]

Olinger, John Wallace. Born May 3, 1849, in Delphi, Indiana. While a child, Olinger's family moved to Delaware, Iowa, then in 1858 to Mound City, Kansas. John's father died in 1861. In 1862, after the start of the Civil War, according to Eve Ball, John and his younger brother Robert became "bushwackers." Bushwackers were anti-Union guerrillas. They were captured by Union soldiers and ordered executed, but reprieved at the last moment because of their youth. In 1865, their widowed mother remarried. By 1875, the family had moved to Seven Rivers, New Mexico, and acquired a cattle ranch.

John was one of the men that went to Tunstall's ranch with Deputy Mathews to attach his cattle. He was in the posse led by Morton that chased after and killed Tunstall. In his statement to Angel he says he was one of the men that laid out the body. He says he may have heard the two shots fired from Tunstall's revolver, and that he examined the revolver and found two shells in the chambers. He claims he did not see Tunstall's hat and no one put it under Tunstall's horse's head.

John was one of the men that formed a self-appointed posse of "Seven River Warriors" to avenge the death of Sheriff Brady. Frank McNab was killed by that "posse" on April 29, 1878. Brother Robert was killed by Billy the Kid April 28, 1881, when Billy

Grave of George Warden Peppin, Lincoln Cemetery, Lincoln, New Mexico. 2015 photo.

escaped from the Lincoln jail. Shortly after that, John left New Mexico. By 1885, he was married and living in Kansas. By 1910, according to the census of that year, he had moved to Arizona. By 1920, he was living alone in Los Angeles, California. He died in Van Nuys, California, of pneumonia, February 25, 1940.[62]

Patron, Juan Batista. Born November 20, 1852, in Santa Fe, New Mexico. Juan was educated at Santa Fe's St. Michael's School (founded by Archbishop Lamy in 1859). In 1870, the Patron family moved to Lincoln. On December 20, 1873, Juan's father was killed at a baile (dance). The killing happened when a large group of men led by brothers Sam, Merritt, and Tom Horrell burst into the dance hall and began shooting at everyone present. This was the cumulating act of the "Horrell War," an armed conflict between the Horrell family and Hispanics living in Lincoln. On September 15, 1875, Juan and John Riley got into an argument on the street in front of the Torreón in Lincoln. While Juan was turned away, Riley shot him in the back. Riley claimed self-defense and was not charged. In 1877, Juan was elected to the Territorial Assembly. He was elected speaker of the Assembly.

Patron moved to Puerto de Luna in 1879. Patron was killed there on April 9, 1884, by Michael Maney. After drinking together all day, the two got into an argument, apparently provoked by Juan. Juan drew on Maney, but his gun got snagged in his trousers. Before Juan could get his gun untangled, Maney shot him. Juan was buried beneath the vestibule of the Puerto de Luna Catholic Church.[63]

Peppin, George Warden. Born in 1838 in Chittenden County, Vermont. Peppin was a California Column veteran, having joined the Fifth Regiment of the California Infantry at he start of the Civil War. He was mustered out at Mesilla in November, 1864. Trained as a stone mason, he moved to Lincoln and built several of the town's buildings, including McSween's house and the two-story Murphy-Dolan store that later became the Lincoln Courthouse. He was appointed deputy sheriff by Brady and was with Brady when Brady and Hindman were killed. He was appointed Lincoln County sheriff on June 14, 1878, by Governor Axtell at the recommendation of Rynerson. He was removed as sheriff in February, 1879. In later years, he worked as a mason, Fort Stanton butcher, deputy, and, for a while, Lincoln jailor. Peppin died January 14, 1909.[64]

Perry, Samuel B (not Samuel R. as given by Angel). Born July 31, 1844, in Mississippi. Perry, who ranched in the Seven Rivers area, was with the posse that chased after and killed Tunstall. According to his testimony to Angel, he was one of he men who laid out Tunstall's body. He also testified that he was the person who placed Tunstall's revolver next to his body. In 1879, Perry killed Frank Wheeler near Hillsboro in a fight over the sale of some cattle. Perry was tried for the killing and acquitted. After leaving Seven Rivers, Perry established a ranch in a canyon east of Ruidoso that is now known as Perry Canyon. Perry was killed November 7, 1901, when he fell off a wagon he was driving and got his head snagged in the wagon's wheels.[65]

Purington, George Augustus. Born July 21, 1837, at Athens, Ohio. Purington was attending Western Reserve College when the Civil War opened. He left school and enlisted in the 19th Regiment Ohio Volunteer Infantry on April 22, 1861. During the war he was promoted to brevet major for distinguished service. He was appointed commander of Fort Stanton in 1877. He was replaced as fort commander by Colonel Dudley on April 5,

Grave of Samuel B. Perry, Sixteen Springs Cemetery, Otero County, New Mexico.
2009 photo.

1878. After leaving New Mexico, he served as commander of Fort Thomas in Arizona, then as commander of Forts Stockton, Ringgold, and McIntosh in Texas. He retired from the Army July 17, 1895. Purington died May 31, 1896, at Metropolis, Illinois.[66]

Riley, John Henry. Born May 12, 1850, on the Island of Valencia, Ireland. Riley came to the United States at age 12. By 1874, he was living in Lincoln, working for Murphy. Two years later he was made a Murphy partner. Just before Tunstall was killed, Riley accidently exposed Rynerson's personal letter to him and Dolan explicitly ordering violence against McSween and Tunstall. In 1878, he became post trader at Fort Bliss. In 1882, he moved to Las Cruces and acquired a large ranch on the western slope of the Organ Mountains. He moved to Denver in 1893 and became highly successful financially, buying and selling large ranches in Colorado and New Mexico. Riley died February 10, 1916, of pneumonia.[67]

Roberts, Andrew L. "Buckshot." Alias Bill Williams. Sometimes identified as O. L. Roberts. Birth unknown. He fought for the Confederacy during the Civil War. He got the nickname "Buckshot" from a load of buckshot he had taken in his right arm. His immobilized right arm left him unable to lift a rifle to his shoulder. Just prior to his killing at Blazer's Mill by Bowdre, he sold a small ranch. He was at Blazer's Mill on the fateful day of his killing, April 4, 1878, because the payment for the ranch was to be mailed to him there. He was buried in Blazer's Mill cemetery.[68] (For details on his burial and how his grave location was rediscovered, see *"The Trial of Billy the Kid"* by the author.)

Rynerson, William Logan. Born February 22, 1828, in Mercer County, Kentucky. In 1852, he travelled to California as one of the thousands attracted there by the gold discoveries. When the Civil War started, he enlisted in the First California Infantry, attaining the rank of Lieutenant Colonel. He was mustered out at Mesilla in November, 1866. He was elected to the Territorial Assembly in November, 1867, as a Republican. His election was disputed by the Democrats. When the legislative session opened, Rynerson introduced a resolution condemning Territorial Supreme Court Justice John P. Slough, who was a Democratic member of the Assembly. The two met in the billiard room of the Exchange Hotel in Santa Fe on December 14, 1867. Slough insulted Rynerson, calling him *"a son of a bitch and thief"* and suggesting that he wear a collar inscribed *"I am Heath's dog"* (Heath was Republican leader). The next day Slough and Rynerson met in the hotel's bar. Following a confrontation, Rynerson fatally shot Slough with a concealed derringer (Slough did not know he was armed). Rynerson was tried for the killing and acquitted on the ground of self-defense.

During the events covered in Angel's Report, Rynerson was District Attorney of the Third Judicial District. By refusing to accept McSween's bond for the charge of embezzling Emil Fritz's insurance proceeds, he initiated the chain of events that led to Tunstall's killing. He was an unprincipled supporter of the Murphy-Dolan faction, as was shown in his letter to *"Friends Riley and Dolan"* that was accidentally left in McSween's house by John Riley. He died September 26, 1893, in Las Cruces.[69]

Scholand, Emilie. See Fritz, Luise Marie Emilie.

Schurz, Carl Christian. Born March 2, 1829, in the Kingdom of Prussia's Rhine Province. In 1848, he graduated from the University of Bonn. Inspired by the example of the French Revolution, he joined a German revolutionary group fighting to free Germany from Prussian sovereignty. After participating in several engagements with Prussian forces, he and other German revolutionaries seized the fortress of Rastatt in Baden. When

Grave of David Pugh Shield, Masonic Cemetery, Las Vegas, New Mexico. 2010 photo.

the Prussians took the fort, Schurz succeeded in escaping, narrowly escaping execution. He fled to Switzerland, and eventually to London.

In July, 1852, Schurz immigrated to the United States. Strongly anti-slavery, he joined the Republican Party in 1857. In 1860, he supported Lincoln for president. When Lincoln won the presidency, Schurz was appointed U.S. ambassador to Spain. After the Civil War began, Schurz's diplomacy succeeded in keeping Spain from entering the war in support of the Confederacy. He returned to the United States in 1862 and joined the Union army. In 1863, he was promoted to major general. In 1868, he was elected to the United States Senate from Missouri. In 1877, he was appointed Secretary of the Interior by President Hayes, and served to the end of Hayes' term. Schurz died May 14, 1906, in New York City.[70]

Scurlock, Josiah Gordon "Doc." Born January 11, 1849, in Talaposa, Alabama. Scurlock studied medicine in New Orleans. After a brief visit to Mexico in 1869, he travelled to Lincoln and began working for John Chisum. On September 2, 1876, he killed his friend Mike Herkins when his gun accidentally discharged. He married José Herrera's daughter Antonia Miguela October 19, 1876. He left New Mexico after the Lincoln 5-day war. The 1880 census shows him living at the LX Ranch headquarters on the Canadian River in Potter County Texas. After living in various cities in Texas, including Vernon, Cleburn, and Granbury, he moved to Eastland, Texas, in 1919. Throughout his life, he had a deep passion for writing. He wrote poems and book reviews. He joined the Theosophical Society. Scurlock died July 25, 1929, and was buried in Eastland, Texas.[71]

Sherman, John E. Jr. Born September 4, 1847, in Mansfield, Ohio. Sherman was the nephew of Civil War General William Tecumseh Sherman. Prior to his arrival in New Mexico, he worked for a law firm owned by Ulysses S. Grant, Jr., President Grant's son. He was appointed N.M. Territorial Marshal in March, 1876. Governor Axtell, in a letter to C. P. Huntington, wrote about Sherman:

> *"John Sherman has a nephew here who is an imbecile – drunken fraud with no ability and not even business honesty and yet he is kept in an important position – one of the most important – U.S. Marshall (sic)."* [72]

By 1879, Sherman's professional and personal reputation was in a deep slide. In July, 1879, *Newman's Thirty-Four* reported:

> *"The indications seem to point unmistakably to the early removal of John Sherman, Jr., U.S. Marshal for this Territory. Serious charges have been made against him by the press almost from the beginning of his term of office, and the grand jury for this county at the term of court just closed has presented his case to the public and to the authorities in Washington in such a light as to compel his immediate removal, provided the powers that be are not determined to ignore the demands of justice, as has been done in former cases of a similar nature."* [73]

Sherman resigned as U.S. Marshal on March 2, 1882, leaving behind office debts of $12,784.30 in 389 different accounts. After leaving New Mexico, he moved to Washington, D.C. and reentered the banking field. Sherman died May 31, 1890.[74]

Shield, David Pugh (mistakenly given as Shields in most sources). Born December 5, 1835, in Reynoldsburg, Ohio. Shield married Elizabeth Hummer, Susan McSween's sister, November 11, 1859. He enlisted in the Missouri Militia in July, 1863, and was discharged in July, 1865. He joined the Missouri bar in 1866. In 1877, he, Elizabeth, and their three children moved to Lincoln. Shield formed a law partnership with McSween and bought one wing of his Lincoln home. Shield was in Santa Fe on business when McSween was killed and never returned to Lincoln (the house was burned down!). He set up a law practice in Las Vegas. In 1884, he was appointed San Miguel County Judge. Shield died March 6, 1888, in Las Vegas.[75]

Smith, George Washington. Born March 11, 1837, in Virginia. Smith joined the 13th Pennsylvania Volunteer Infantry August 5, 1861, about three months after the Civil War began. He fought in the Battle of Chicamauga and was promoted to brevet lieutenant colonel for gallant and meritorious service in the Battle of Jonesboro. Smith resigned in 1866, but reentered the Army in 1873 as a second-lieutenant in the 9th Cavalry and was assigned to Fort Stanton. On April 1, 1878, the day Brady and Hindman were killed, Smith, leading a detachment of 25 men, at the instigation of Sheriff Peppin, arrested McSween, Widenmann, George Robinson, George Washington, and David Shield. The arrests were vigorously protested by attorney Montague Leverson, who was present, as Peppin had no legal papers to make the arrest. McSween and the others, afraid to be left in the custody of Peppin, got Colonel Purington, Smith's superior officer, to permit them to be taken to Fort Stanton so as to not be left in the Lincoln jail. On August 19, 1881, Smith and five other men were killed at Gavilan Canyon in an encounter with Mescalero Apaches led by Chief Nana.[76]

Thornton, Edward. Born July 13, 1817, in London. Thornton entered the British diplomatic service in 1842. In 1845, he was British attaché to the government of Mexico. In that capacity, he helped the U.S. and Mexico negotiate peace after the Mexican American War. On leaving Mexico in 1852, he served in Argentina, Uraguay, and Brazil. While in Brazil, he militarily supported Brazil in its war with Paraguay. Some sources say he was the cause of the Paraguayan War, which resulted in the death of 90% of the Paraguayan population. In 1867, he was appointed British Ambassador to the United States, and served until 1881. He was knighted in 1870. Thornton died January 26, 1906, in London.[77]

Tunstall, John Henry. Born March 6, 1853, in London, England. Tunstall left England on August 18, 1872. His destination was Victoria, Canada. He arrived September 26, 1872. He got there by way of New York and San Francisco. His father with a partner had established a branch of their mercantile business in Victoria and Tunstall was sent there to learn the business. On February 18, 1876, he left Victoria for California. His goal was to make a fortune by establishing a sheep business. After investigating opportunities in California, he decided land was cheaper in New Mexico and business prospects were better. He left California August 14, 1876, for Santa Fe. In Santa Fe, he met Robert Widenmann, who convinced him that Lincoln, New Mexico, offered the golden opportunities he was seeking.

Tunstall arrived in Lincoln November 6, 1876, and, with his father's money, began building his empire. He acquired the Casey ranch on the Rio Feliz and stocked it with cattle and horses. (Robert Casey "homesteaded" the ranch, but failed to file ownership papers. After Casey's death, his widow, lacking legal ownership, was forced off the land.) Tunstall opened a general store and bank across the street from Murphy's store, enraging Murphy and Dolan and initiating the financial conflict that exploded into the Lincoln County War. Tunstall was murdered by Buck Morton and Tom Hill February 18, 1878. (For an account of how the site where Tunstall was killed was rediscovered and marked by a monument, see *"The Trial of Billy the Kid"* by the author.) [78]

VanSickle, George W.. Born about 1847. VanSickle moved to Lincoln prior to 1866. At the time he gave his statement to Angel, he had a ranch 35 miles from Lincoln on the road to Las Vegas. He testified to the tyrannical physical and financial oppression of the Murphy-Dolan faction before Tunstall arrived in Lincoln, and to their crookedness after-wards. In March, 1883, he sold his Lincoln ranch. In 1887, he was living in Las Cruces and working as a road supervisor. VanSickle died in December, 1888, at La Luz. [79]

Waite, Frederick Tecumseh "Fred." Born September 23, 1853, at Fort Arbuckle, Indian Nation, now Chickasaw Nation, Oklahoma. Waite was maybe the best-educated man in Lincoln. As a graduate of Mound City Commercial College, St. Louis, Missouri, he had what would be called a Master's Degree in Business Administration today. He arrived in Lincoln in the fall of 1877, probably first taking a job as a cowhand with John Chisum and then signing on with Tunstall. Waite was at Tunstall's ranch when Deputy Sheriff Mathews rode up with his posse and attempted to confiscate Tunstall's livestock. Mathews backed off after that first confrontation, but came back later with more men. Convinced that Mathews' real goal was to murder him, Tunstall abandoned his ranch, taking only his string of beloved horses. Tunstall asked Waite to drive a wagon of supplies to Lincoln while he, Billy, Widenmann, Brewer, and Middleton herded the horses. By that quirk of fate, Waite was not with Tunstall when he was murdered. After leaving Lincoln, Waite returned to his family home in Himmonoah, Chickasaw Nation, Oklahoma. He was elected to the Chickasaw House of Representatives and later to the Chickasaw Senate. He was the leading candidate for president of the Nation when he died September 24, 1895. [80]

Wallace, Lewis "Lew." Born April 10, 1827, in Brookville, Indiana. By 1849, Wallace was practicing law. He was a Mexican-American and Civil War veteran. In the Civil War he attained the rank of major general. Beginning May 12, 1865, Wallace served as a judge on the military commission that convicted eight persons of murdering, conspiring to murder, and/or aiding the murder of President Abraham Lincoln. He was appointed New Mexico Governor on September 3, 1878. He arrived in Santa Fe 24 days later. On November 13, 1878, he issued a proclamation that extended amnesty to everyone in Lincoln County for any crime committed between two specified dates, except those who had been indicted already. On March 15, 1878, Billy wrote Wallace and asked for a secret meeting. Wallace agreed and they met March 17, 1879, at J.P. Wilson's home. Billy lived up to his end of the agreement that they made in the meeting. Wallace did not. Wallace resigned the governorship on March 17, 1881. He died February 15, 1905.

Widenmann, Robert Adolph. Born January 24, 1852, in Ann Arbor, Michigan. Widenmann's early life is obscure. He was in Santa Fe by August, 1876, when he met Tunstall. Although Tunstall liked and trusted him immediately, he told Tunstall only lies about his background. Widenmann followed Tunstall to Lincoln a few months after their Santa Fe meeting. He was with Tunstall at his Rio Feliz ranch when Deputy Mathews' posse attempted to confiscate Tunstall's livestock. He was riding with Billy, Richard Brewer, and John Middleton when Tunstall fled to Lincoln with his horses and was murdered. He was behind Tunstall's corral wall with Billy when Sheriff Brady was shot. Afterwards, he claimed he was there only to feed Tunstall's dog and he saw and knew nothing of the shooting. He left New Mexico in October, 1878. In early 1879, Tunstall's father paid his expenses to travel to London, where he lived with (off) the family for six months. The ostensible purpose for the visit was to help Tunstall's father pursue legal action for his son's unjustified death. Widenmann's real purpose was to share in any financial settlement the Tunstalls received. Nothing came of Tunstall senior's efforts to obtain compensation for Tunstall's death. On Widenmann's return to the U.S., he settled in Nanuet, New York. In November, 1881, he married Albertine Seiler-Lemke. Sometime after 1920, he moved to Haverstraw, now Stoney Point, New York, where he died April 15, 1930.[81]

Wilson, John B. Born about 1821 in Tennessee. Wilson's real name was Green Wilson. In January, 1875, he asked the Territorial legislature to change his name to Juan Bautista Wilson. The request was refused. On March 16, 1876, the *Daily New Mexican* reported:

> *"Since the 14th, Judge Wilson signed all his mandates John B. Wilson instead of Green Wilson."* [82]

Wilson said he took John B. Wilson as a baptismal name in Albuquerque on January 20, 1859. The Ealys always called him Mr. Green. When Tunstall was murdered, Wilson, as Justice of the Peace, issued arrest warrants for James J. Dolan, J. Conovar (Cochrane), Frank Baker, Jessie Evans, Tom Hill, George Davis, O. L. Roberts, P. Gallegos, F. Green, J. Awly (Hurley), A. H. Mills, 'Dutch Charley,' Robert W. Beckwith, William Morton, George Harmon (Hindman), and Jacob. B. Mathews. The warrants were issued February 19, 1878. Constable Antonio Martinez deputized Billy and Waite to serve the warrants. On March 3, 1878, Governor Axtell nullified Wilson's J.P. office, effectively delegalizing the warrants, claiming that Wilson's appointment was illegal because he had not been elected. That was a lie as Axtell himself had signed the law that permitted a J.P. to be appointed to fill a vacancy.

When Sheriff Brady and Deputy Hindman were killed by bullets from behind Tunstall's corral wall, Wilson was hit in the buttocks by a stray bullet. The unlawful removal of Wilson by Governor Axtell did not sit well with Lincoln residents. He was elected to the office on June 15, 1878. In 1882, the *Las Vegas Gazette* reported that Wilson owned *"a large part of the town of Lincoln."* Wilson died in 1897.[83]

Here are the dates of the most important events related to the Angel Report.

- 1843 – Alexander A. McSween born on Prince Edward Island in Canada
- May 28, 1845 – Frank Warner Angel born in Watertown, New York
- March 6, 1853 – John Henry Tunstall born in London, England
- December, 1859 – William Henry McCarty (Billy the Kid) born in New York City
- Summer, 1866 – Lawrence G. Murphy moves to Lincoln and opens L. G. Murphy & Co.
- July 2, 1868 – Angel receives BA degree from City College of New York
- 1869 – Angel admitted to bar in New York
- July 12, 1871 – Mercantile Life Insurance Company of New York sells $10,000 life insurance policy #1058 to Emil Fritz
- February, 1872 – Thomas B. Catron appointed U.S Attorney for New Mexico
- August 13, 1873 – Alexander A. McSween and Susannah Ellen Hummer married in Eureka, Kansas
- June 26, 1874 – Emil Fritz dies in Germany at parent's home
- March 3, 1875 – McSween and Susan McSween arrive in Lincoln County for first time
- March 18, 1875 – Angel marries Sadie Wilcox
- January 19, 1876 – William Rynerson appointed Lincoln County District Attorney by Governor Axtell
- February 18, 1876 – John H. Tunstall leaves Victoria, B.C, Canada, for United States
- October 29, 1876 – McSween meets Tunstall in Santa Fe
- November 6, 1876 – Tunstall arrives in Lincoln, New Mexico
- November 7, 1876 – William Brady elected sheriff
- December 12, 1876 – McSween arrives back in Lincoln from New York trip
- February 14, 1877 – John B. Wilson appointed Justice of the Peace by County Commissioners
- March 14, 1877 – James Dolan acquires Murphy & Co. (the "house") store and business
- April 24, 1877 – Tunstall establishes his ranch on the Rio Feliz
- June 2, 1877 – Construction of Tunstall's store in Lincoln begins
- September 17, 1877 – Evans, Baker, Hill, and Davis steal horses from McSween and Tunatall
- September 21, 1877 – A posse consisting of Richard Brewer, Charles Bowdre, and Doc Scurlock confront Baker, Evans, Hill, and Davis at Shedd's Ranch

- September 22, 1877 – Brewer, Bowdre, and Scurlock stay at Corn Exchange Hotel in Mesilla
- October 17, 1877 – Evans, Baker, Hill, and Davis arrested at Seven Rivers by Sheriff Brady
- November 16, 1877 – Evans, Baker, Hill, and Davis escape from Lincoln jail
- December 18, 1877 – McSween, wife, and John S. Chisum leave Lincoln for St. Louis, Missouri
- December 21, 1877 – Emilie Scholand swears out a warrant against McSween for embezzlement
- December 24, 1877 – McSween and Chisum arrested at Las Vegas

- January 4, 1878 – McSween leaves Las Vegas under arrest in custody of Adolph Barrier and Antonio Campos
- January 9, 1878 – McSween arrives in Lincoln under arrest
- January 17, 1878 – Tunstall writes letter on county taxes to *Mesilla Valley Independent*
- January 21, 1878 – McSween party leave for Mesilla
- January 26, 1878 – McSween party arrive in Mesilla
- February 2, 1878 – McSween hearing held at Judge Warren Bristol's house
- February 4, 1878 – McSween hearing in Mesilla ends
- February 5, 1878 – McSween camps at Shedd's Ranch on way home to Lincoln
- February 6, 1878 – Dolan tries to get into a gunfight with McSween party
- February 7, 1878 – Judge Bristol issues write of attachment on McSween and Tunstall's property
- February 8, 1878 – Dolan arrives in Lincoln with writ of attachment.
- February 9, 1878 – Sheriff Brady attaches Tunstall's store
- February 10, 1878 – Sheriff Brady attaches McSween's house
- February 11, 1878 – McSween, Tunstall, and party arrive in Lincoln. The same day he arranges bail bond for $34,500 and sends it by registered letter to Rynerson
- February 13, 1878 – First visit to Tunstall ranch by Sheriff Brady's posse
- February 14, 1878 – Rynerson writes letter to *"Friends Riley and Dolan"*
- February 17, 1878 – Tunstall arrives at his ranch
- February 18, 1878 – Tunstall party flees his ranch and Tunstall is murdered
- February 19, 1878 – Dr. Taylor Ealy and family arrive in Lincoln
- February 19, 1878 – Tunstall's body taken to McSween's house
- February 19, 1878 – Coroner's jury meets over Tunstall's body
- February 19, 1878 – Wilson issues arrest warrants for Tunstall's killers
- February 19, 1878 – Wilson issues arrest warrant for Brady for stealing from Tunstall's store
- February 19, 1878 – Residents gather at McSween's house to protest Tunstall's killing
- February 20, 1878 – Tunstall's body embalmed
- February 20, 1878 – Constable Atanacio Martinez, Billy the Kid, and Fred Waite attempt to arrest Sheriff Brady and possemen and get arrested themselves
- February 22, 1878 – Tunstall's funeral held at McSween's house
- February 22, 1878 – Citizens' meeting in McSween's house – petition started
- February 23, 1878 – Tunstall buried just outside of and behind his horse corral

- February 23, 1878 – Robert Widenmann supported by soldiers searches Dolan's store
- February 23, 1878 – Widenmann takes possession of Tunstall's store from James Longwell
- February 26, 1878 – Widenmann writes Sir Edward Thornton, British Ambassador
- March 7, 1878 – Buck Morton, Frank Baker, and William McCloskey arrested by posse led by Brewer
- March 9, 1878 – Governor Samuel Axtell arrives in Lincoln and issues proclamation *"removing"* Wilson as JP and *"nullifying"* his arrest warrants
- March 9, 1878 – Morton, Baker, and McClosky killed
- March 29, 1878 – Barrier stops guarding McSween and returns to his home in Las Vegas
- March 31, 1878 – Billy and companions enter Lincoln and hide in Tunstall's horse corral
- April 1, 1878 – Sheriff Brady and Deputy George Hindman killed by firing from Tunstall's corral
- April 2, 1878 – Colonel Nathan Dudley arrives at Fort Stanton
- April 3, 1878 – McSween taken to Fort Stanton under arrest
- April 4, 1878 – Brewer and Buckshot Roberts killed at Blazer's Mill
- April 5, 1878 – Colonel Dudley takes command of Fort Stanton
- April 7, 1878 – Third District Court term opens in Lincoln
- April 8, 1878 – John Copeland appointed Lincoln Sheriff
- April 15, 1878 – Frank Warner Angel appointed Special Agent (best guess)
- April 18, 1878 – Grand jury returns indictments, including against Billy for the killing of Brady and Roberts
- April 22, 1878 – McSween exonerated of Fritz embezzlement charge by grand jury
- April 29, 1878 – Frank McNab killed and James Saunders wounded in an ambush
- May 4, 1878 – Angel registers at Exchange Hotel in Santa Fe
- May 12, 1878 – Angel writes anonymous letter to *Las Vegas Gazette*
- May 14, 1878 – Angel begins taking sworn statements
- May 30, 1878 – George Peppin appointed Lincoln Sheriff
- June 8, 1878 – *Las Vegas Gazette* reports that Angel is at Fort Stanton *"busily engaged in investigating."*
- June 15, 1878 – Wilson elected Justice of the Peace, thereby regaining the office he "lost" after Governor Axtell illegally removed him in his proclamation
- July 15, 1878 – First day of 5-day War in Lincoln
- July 19, 1878 – Last day of 5-day War. McSween house burned and four men killed.
- July 27, 1878 – *Las Vegas Gazette* publishes sarcastic editorial on Angel
- August 11, 1878 – Angel presents interrogatories to Governor Axtell
- August 14, 1878 – Angel leaves New Mexico for New York
- August 17, 1878 – *Las Vegas Gazette* reports it has obtained a copy of Angel's interrogatories
- August 17, 1878 – Angel arrives in Las Cruces. *Las Vegas Gazette* gives his NY address as 62 Liberty Street, NY, NY P.O. Box 746. Publishes sarcastic editorial calling Angel *"the most important fune who has ever visited New Mexico."*
- August 18, 1878 – *Albuquerque Review* reports on Angel's efforts favorably
- August 24, 1878 – Angel arrives home in New York

- August 24, 1878 – *Las Vegas Gazette* publishes a critical review of Angel. *"His pretensions are too vast to be thoroughly understood by the ordinary mind."*
- August 24, 1878 – *Grant County Herald* publishes a critical review of Angel's actions
- August 24, 1878 – *Mesilla News* republishes *Las Vegas Gazette* article
- August 31, 1878 – *Mesilla Valley Independent* publishes article praising Angel
- August 31, 1878 – *Grant County Herald* publishes Angel's interrogatories for Governor Axtell
- August 31, 1878 – Axtell writes *Mesilla News* responding to Angel's interrogatories
- August 31, 1878 – Angel meets with Secretary of the Interior Carl Schurz in Washington D.C. and gives him a verbal report on his investigations
- September 3, 1878 – Secretary Schurz meets with President Hayes and presents the results of Angel's investigations to Hayes
- September 4, 1878 – Axtell removed as governor and replaced by Lew Wallace
- September 7, 1878 – *Las Vegas Gazette* publishes editorial pronouncing Angel's visit a failure
- September 12, 1878 – Angel meets with Lew Wallace in Washington D.C. and gives him a notebook containing Angel's evaluations of various persons he met
- September 21, 1878 – *Las Vegas Gazette* complains that Angel left New Mexico before Governor Axtell had enough time to reply to his charges
- September 28, 1878 – *Las Vegas Gazette* states that Angel had no desire to deal rightly with officials
- September 30, 1878 – Wallace arrives in Santa Fe to take over governorship
- October 5, 1878 – *Santa Fe New Mexican* criticizes Angel
- October 3, 1878 – Angel submits written Tunstall report to Attorney General Devens
- October 10, 1878 – Thomas B. Catron resigns a New Mexico Attorney General
- October 20, 1878 – Lawrence Murphy dies in a Santa Fe hospital
- October 29, 1878 - Angel appointed Assistant U.S. Attorney at Brooklyn, New York (Eastern District)
- November 13. 1978 – Wallace issues amnesty proclamation

- March 17, 1879 – Billy meets with Wallace at J.P. Wilson's house

- April 16, 1879 – Dudley Court of Inquiry begins at Fort Stanton

- September 19, 1881 – President James A. Garfield assassinated by Charles J. Guiteau
- September 19, 1881 – Chester A. Arthur sworn in as 21st U.S. President

- April 25, 1885 – British Government requests U.S. Government seek compensation for Tunstall's death and loss of property
- June 1, 1885 – U.S. Government denies British Government compensation request

- February 12, 1886 – Angel resigns as US Assistant District Attorney

- December 5, 1894 – Angel admitted to practice before U.S. Supreme Court

- April 23, 1895 – Angel defends Samuel E. Anymar, accused of embezzling $20,000 from the National Shoe and Leather Bank

- March 15, 1906 – Angel dies in Jersey City, New Jersey, at age 61

Notes

2 - Genesis of the "Angel Report"

1. Don Cline, *Antrim and Billy* (Creative Publishing Co., 1990), pp 44-47.

2. Cline, *Antrim and Billy*, p 49.

3. Cline, *Antrim and Billy*, p 59.

4. *Mining Life*, September 19, 1874.

5. *Arizona Republic* (Phoenix), Dec.30, 1951.

6. *Las Vegas Gazette*, Dec. 28, 1880

1. Lincoln County at the time was about the same size as Ohio. It contained an estimated 2,000 residents.

2. Alexander A. McSween, letter to Lawrence Lapoint, March 24, 1878, Fulton Papers, Special Collections, UA.

3. Eve Ball, ed., Lily Klasner, *My Girlhood Among Outlaws* (University of Arizona Press, 1988), p 274.

4. *Cimarron News and Press*, April 2, 1878.

5. George Peppin, affidavit on Tunstall store, April 18, 1878, Mary Daniels Taylor Papers, Archives and Special Collections, NMSU.

6. The Desert Land Act passed Congress on March 3, 1877.

7. Quoted in Frederick W. Nolan, *The Lincoln County War*, Revised Edition (Sunstone Press, 2009), p 180.

8. Quoted in Frederick W. Nolan, *The Life and Death of John Henry Tunstall* (University of New Mexico Press, 1965), p 264.

9. Susan McSween interview, J. Evetts Haley, August 16, 1927, Mullin Collection, J. Evetts Haley History Center.

10. *Mesilla Valley Independent*, March 30, 1878.

11. Mary R. Ealy, letter to Maurice G. Fulton, undated, Herman B. Weisner Papers, Archives and Special Collections, NMSU.

12. Mary R. Ealy, letter to Maurice G. Fulton, undated, Herman B. Weisner Papers, Archives and Special Collections, NMSU.

13. Quoted in Nolan, *The Lincoln County War*, p 206.

14. Quoted in Nolan, *The Lincoln County War*, p 206.

15. *Cimarron News and Press*, April 11, 1878

16. Letter Widenman to Tunstall's father, quoted in Nolan, *The Lincoln County War*, pp 210-211.

17. Quoted in Nolan, *The Lincoln County War*, p 215.

18. *Mesilla Valley Independent*, Oct. 27, 1877

19. *Cimarron News and Press*, April 11, 1878.

20. *Albuquerque Review*, March 30, 1878

21. Lee Scott Theisen, *Frank Warner Angel's Notes on New Mexico Territory*, Vol 26, No. 4, Winter, 1976, pp 333-370.

22. *Santa Fe Weekly New Mexican*, May 4, 1878.

23. *Las Vegas Gazette*, May 18, 1878

24. *Las Vegas Gazette*, May 18, 1878.

25. *Las Vegas Gazette*, June 8, 1878.

26. *Las Vegas Gazette*, June 8, 1878.

27. *Santa Fe New Mexican*, August 17, 1878.

28. *Las Vegas Gazette*, August 24, 1878.

29. *Grant County Herald*, August 24, 1878.

30. *Las Vegas Gazette*, Aug 17, 1878.

31. *Mesilla News*, Aug 24, 1878.

32. *Grant County Herald*, Aug 31, 1878.

33. *Mesilla Valley Independent*, August 31, 1878.

34. Theisen, *"Frank Warner Angel's Notes on New Mexico Territory,"* pp 333-370,

35. Theisen, *"Frank Warner Angel's Notes on New Mexico Territory,"* pp 333-370.

36. *Brooklyn Daily Eagle*, February 14, 1886.

37. *New York Times*, August 21, 1878.

38. Samuel B. Axtell, letter to Collis P. Huntington, August 12, 1878, Governor Samuel B. Axtell Papers, (Photocopies. Originals Housed at Syracuse University Library), New Mexico State Records Center & Archives, Serial #13896, Collection 1959-084, Folder #5, 1878.

39. Carl C. Schurz, letter to Rutherford B. Hayes, August 31, 1878, Rutherford B. Hayes Presidential Library & Museums.

40. Carl C. Schurz, letter to Rutherford B. Hayes, August 31, 1878, Rutherford B. Hayes Presidential Library & Museums.

41. *Reading Times* (Reading PA), September 4, 1878.

42. Theisen, *"Frank Warner Angel's Notes on New Mexico Territory,"* pp 333-370,

43. Theisen, *"Frank Warner Angel's Notes on New Mexico Territory,"* pp 333-370.

44. Samuel B. Axtell, letter to Collis P. Huntington, September 19, 1878, Governor Samuel B. Axtell Papers, (Photocopies. Originals Housed at Syracuse University Library), New Mexico State Records Center & Archives, Serial #13896, Collection 1959-084, Folder #5, 1878.

45. Shulz, letter to General Lewis Wallace, September 11, 1878, Lew Wallace Collection, Indiana Historical Society.

46. *Las Vegas Gazette*, Sept. 14, 1878.

47. *Santa Fe New Mexican*, Sept. 14, 1878.

48. Axtell served as Chief Justice from August, 1882, to May, 1885.

49. *Mesilla Valley Independent*, December 21, 1878.

3 - Governor Axtell's Interrogatories

1. *Grant County Herald*, August 31, 1878.

2. Theisen, *"Frank Warner Angel's Notes on New Mexico Territory,"* pp 333-370

3. *Grant County Herald*, August 24, 1878.

4. *Mesilla News*, Aug 31, 1878.

5. *Las Vegas Gazette*, January 12, 1878.

6. *Albuquerque Review*, January 26, 1878.

7. *Cimarron News and Press*, April 11, 1878.

8. *Cimarron News and Press*, April 25, 1878.

9. Samuel B. Axtell, letter to Collis P. Huntington, September 19, 1878, Governor Samuel B. Axtell Papers, (Photocopies. Originals Housed at Syracuse University Library), New Mexico State Records Center & Archives, Serial #13896, Collection 1959-084, Folder #5, 1878.

4 - Angel's Charges Against Governor Axtell

1. Frank Warner Angel Report, Interior Department Papers 1850-1907, RG 60, NARA; Lewis A Ketring Papers, Archives and Special Collections, NMSU; Lewis A Ketring Papers, Archives and Special Collections, NMSU; Consolidated Clippings File, Frank Angel Report, Archives and Special Collections, NMSU.

5 - Witness Statements

1. Frank Warner Angel Report, Interior Department Papers 1850-1907, RG 60, NARA; Lewis A Ketring Papers, Archives and Special Collections, NMSU; Lewis A Ketring Papers, Archives and Special Collections, NMSU; Consolidated Clippings File, Frank Angel Report, Archives and Special Collections, NMSU.

6 - Letters

1. Frank Warner Angel Report, Interior Department Papers 1850-1907, RG 60, NARA; Lewis A Ketring Papers, Archives and Special Collections, NMSU; Lewis A Ketring Papers, Archives and Special Collections, NMSU; Consolidated Clippings File, Frank Angel Report, Archives and Special Collections, NMSU.

7 - Attempt to Destroy the Report

1. *Las Vegas Gazette*, August 7, 1878; *Las Vegas Gazette*, August 28, 1878; *Santa Fe Weekly New Mexican*, October 5, 1878.

2. Frederick W. Nolan, *A Sidelight on the Tunstall Murder*, New Mexico Historical Review, Vol. 31, No. 3, July, 1956, p 219.

3. Nolan, *A Sidelight on the Tunstall Murder*, p 222.

4. Nolan, *A Sidelight on the Tunstall Murder*, p 222.

5. *Brooklyn Daily Eagle*, February 1, 1897.

6. Quoted in Norman Cleaveland, *The Great New Mexico Cover-Up,* Southern New Mexico Historical Review, Summer, No. 5, 1975, p 8.

7. Quoted in Cleaveland, *The Great New Mexico Cover-Up*, p 8.

9. Quoted in Cleaveland, *The Great New Mexico Cover-Up*, p 8.

10. Quoted in Cleaveland, *The Great New Mexico Cover-Up*, p 8.

11. Cleaveland, *The Great New Mexico Cover-Up*, p 6.

12. Nolan, *A Sidelight on the Tunstall Murder*, pp 206-222.

Appendix A – Cast of Characters

1. *New York Times*, July 3, 1868; *The Brooklyn Union*, October 10, 1878; *Brooklyn Daily Eagle*, February 2, 1886; *Brooklyn Daily Eagle*, March 16, 1906.

2. Don Cline, *Antrim and Billy* (Creative Publishing Co., 1990), pp 44-47.

3. Cline, *Antrim and Billy*, p 49.

4. Cline, *Antrim and Billy*, p 59.

5. *Mining Life*, September 19, 1874.

6. *Arizona Republic* (Phoenix), Dec.30, 1951.

7. David G. Thomas, *The Trial of Billy the Kid*, (Doc45 Publishing, 2020), pp 172-178.

8. *Santa Fe Weekly New Mexican*, February 15, 1879; *Leavenworth Times*, November 24, 1882; *New York Times*, April 25, 1914.

9. *Reading Times* (Reading PA), September 4, 1878; *Santa Fe New Mexican*, August 7, 1891.

10. *Mesilla Valley Independent*, September 29, 1877.

11. Quoted in Nolan, *The Life and Death of John Henry Tunstall*, pp 243-244.

12. Jeff Burton, ed., Philip J. Rasch, *They Fought for "The House,"* English Westerners' Society (The English Westerners' Society, 1971); *Las Vegas Gazette*, March 16, 1878; *Mesilla Valley Independent*, March 16, 1878; *Santa Fe Weekly New Mexican*, April 4, 1878.

13. *Las Vegas Gazette*, July 28, 1877.

14. *Las Vegas Gazette*, May 7, 1878.

15. *El Paso Herald*, October 14, 1901; Inmate File 76049318, Records of the Bureau of Prisons, 1870-2009, RG 129, NARA.

16. Dudley Court of Inquiry Records, report to Act. Asst. Adjutant General, July 20, 1878, Letters Received by the Office of the Adjutant General, 1871-1880, RG 153, NARA; Jeff Burton, *They Fought for "The House."*

17. Rich Eastwood, *Nuestras Madres, A Story of Lincoln County New Mexico* (Creative Space Independent Publishing, no date), pp 89, 92.

18. *Las Vegas Gazette*, April 6, 1873; *Mesilla Valley Independent*, May 18, 1878; Jeff Burton, *They Fought for "The House."*

19, Donald R. Lavash, *Sheriff William Brady, Tragic Hero of the Lincoln County War* (Sunstone Press, 1986).

20. *Lincoln County Leader*, August 2, 1884; *Rio Grande Republican*, January 18, 1890; *Mesilla Valley Democrat*, January 21, 1890.

21. Bill O'Neal, *Henry Brown The Outlaw-Marshal* (Creative Publishing Co, 1980).

22. *Santa Fe Weekly New Mexican*, September 9, 1868; *Santa Fe New Mexican*, January 14, 1869; *Santa Fe New Mexican*, February 12, 1872.

23. *Las Vegas Gazette*, November 27, 1875; *Santa Fe New Mexican Review*, December 12, 1884.

24. Dan L. Thrapp, *Encyclopedia of Frontier Biography: A-F*, Vol 1, (Univ. of Nebraska Press, 1991) p 321; Exhibit 11, Dudley Court of Inquiry Records, RG 153, NARA.

25. *Tri-Weekly Herald* (Marshall, TX), May 25, 1880; *Galveston Daily News*, July 9, 1880.

26. https://en.wikipedia.org/wiki/Carl_Schurz, accessed November 5, 2021.

27. *Santa Fe Weekly New Mexican*, July 26, 1879; *Santa Fe Daily New Mexican*, March 2, 1898; *"Flying H Ranch,"* National Register of Historic Places, 85003633, NARA.

28. Ruth R. Ealy, "Medical Missionary," *New Mexico Magazine*, March, 1954.

29. *Santa Fe New Mexican*, December 18, 1891; *Albuquerque Journal*, June 23, 1907.

30. Frank Clifford, *Deep Trails in the Old West, A Frontier Memoir* (University of Oklahoma Press, 2011), pp 272-273; *Santa Fe New Mexican*, Oct. 17, 1877.

31. *Kansas Daily Commonwealth* (Topeka, KS), Nov. 11, 1871; Grady E. McCright and James H. Powell, *Jesse Evans: Lincoln County Badman* (Creative Publishing Company, 1983); *Santa Fe Weekly New Mexican*, Feb. 1, 1876.

32. https://en.wikipedia.org/wiki/William_M._Evarts, accessed November 12, 2021.

33. Nolan, *The Lincoln County War*, p 462.

34. Nolan, *The Lincoln County War*, p 462.

35. Nolan, *The Lincoln County War*, pp 462-463.

36. Mark Wimberly, Peter Eidenbach, and Julio Betancourt, *"Canon del Perro, A History of Dog Canyon,"* (Human Systems Research, Inc, Tularosa NM, 1978).

37. *The Eagle* (Silver City NM), April 3, 1895; *Western Liberal* (Lordsburg NM), June 14, 1895.

38. Burial Register, Post Cemetery, Fort Bayard, New Mexico, Records of the Office of the Quartermaster General, RG92, NARA, p 16.

39. J. Evetts Haley, notes on G. Gauss, undated, Panhandle Plains Historical Museum Research Center (PPHMRC).

40. Eve Ball, *"Don Florencio of Lincoln County,"* True West, November, 1981; *Santa Fe Weekly New Mexican*, September 28, 1875; *Santa Fe New Mexican*, September 3, 1883.

41. Philip J. Rasch, *The Men at Fort Stanton*, English Westerners' Society (The English Westerners' Society, 1961).

42. https://en.wikipedia.org/wiki/Rutherford_B._Hayes, accessed September 5, 2021.

43. Burton, *They Fought for "The House."*

44. Lily Klasner, *My Girlhood Among Outlaws* (University of Arizona Press, 1972), pp 153-154.

45. 1885 Dona Ana County Census Records, taken June 9, 1885.

46. Burton, *They Fought for "The House;"* *Las Vegas Gazette*, January 27, 1885; *Lincoln County Leader*, March 21, 1885.

47. Burton, *They Fought for "The House;"* *Rio Grande Republican*, December 8, 1883.

48. *Rio Grande Republican*, May 1, 1886.

49. *New York Election Frauds*, House of Representatives Report No. 31, February 23, 1869, pp 119-120

50. *Santa Fe Weekly New Mexican*, January 19, 1878; https://en.wikipedia.org/wiki/Montague_Leverson, accessed September 15, 2021.

51. Burton,*They Fought for "The House."*

52. *The Southwesterner*, July 1, 1966; *El Paso Times*, July 14, 1888; *El Paso Herald-Post*, March 25, 1936.

53. Elvis E. Fleming, *J. B. "Billy" Mathews, Biography of a Lincoln County Deputy* (Yucca Free Press, 1999); *Roswell Register*, June 10, 1904; Burton, *They Fought for "The House."*

54. *Santa Fe Weekly New Mexican*, May 4, 1878.

55. Susan E. Barber, letter to J. Evetts Haley, August 16, 1927, Panhandle Plains Historical Museum Research Center (PPHMRC).

56. Robert N. Mullin, ed., *Maurice G. Fulton's History of the Lincoln County War* (University of Arizona Press, 1968).

57. Kathleen P. Chamberlain, *In the Shadow of Billy the Kid* (University of New Mexico Press, 2013); Nolan, *The Lincoln County War*.

58. *Silver City Enterprise*, December 7, 1882.

59. *Las Vegas Gazette*, March 16, 1878; *Mesilla Valley Independent*, March 16, 1878.

60. Thrapp, *Encyclopedia of Frontier Biography: G-O*, Vol 2, (Univ. of Nebraska Press, 1991), p 1035.

61. *Santa Fe New Mexican*, June 9, 1875; *Mesilla Valley Independent*, December 22, 1877; *White Oaks Eagle*, July 25, 1895; Roman Barregon, letter to J. Evetts Haley, August 12, 1927, Panhandle Plains Historical Museum Research Center (PPHMRC).

62. George Olinger, *"John Wallace Olinger, His Life, His Ancestors, and His Descendants,"* unpublished manuscript, 2010.

63. Paul L. Tsompanas, *Juan Patron, A Fallen Star in the Days of Billy the Kid* (Belle Isle Books, 2013).

64. George W. Peppin statement, Exhibit 8, Dudley Court of Inquiry Records, NARA; *Lincoln County Leader* (White Oaks, NM), March 29, 1884; *White Oaks Eagle* (White Oaks, NM), Jan. 20, 1898.

65. *Rio Grande Republican*, October 3, 1882; Burton, *They Fought for "The House."*

66. Philip J. Rasch, *The Men at Fort Stanton*, English Westerners' Society (The English Westerners' Society, 1961); Thrapp, *Encyclopedia of Frontier Biography: P-Z*, Vol 3, p 1179.

67. Burton, *They Fought for "The House."*

68. Burton, *They Fought for "The House."*

69. Gary L. Roberts, *Death Comes for the Chief Justice* (University Press of Colorado, 1990); Darlis A. Miller, *William Logan Rynerson in New Mexico, 1862-1893*, New Mexico Historical Review, Vol. 48, No. 2, April, 1973, p 101-130; *Rio Grande Republican*, September 26, 1893.

70. https://en.wikipedia.org/wiki/Carl_Schurz, accessed November 5, 2021.

71. Philip J. Rasch, Joseph E. Buckbee, and Karl K. Kline, "*'Doc' Scurlock, Man of Many Parts*," Outlaw Gazette, Vol. XII, No. 1, Nov., 1999, pp 23-24.

72. Theisen, ed., *Frank Warner Angel's Notes on New Mexico Territory*, 1878, Arizona and the West, Winter, Vol 18, No 4, 1976.

73. *Newman's Thirty-Four*, July 2, 1879.

74. *Santa Fe New Mexican*, Feb. 19, 1884; *Cleveland Plain Dealer*, June 3, 1890.

75. *Las Vegas Gazette*, August 24, 1878; *Lincoln County Leader* (White Oaks), March 24, 1888; Nolan, *The Lincoln County War*, p 486.

76. Rasch, *The Men at Fort Stanton*.

77. https://en.wikipedia.org/wiki/Edward_Thornton,_2nd_Count_of_Cacilhas, accessed December 3, 2021.

78. Nolan, *The Lincoln County War*, p 76-102.

79. *Lincoln County Leader*, July 19, 1884; *Lincoln County Leader*, December 29, 1888.

80. Waite Mike Tower, *The Outlaw Statesman, the Life and Times of Fred Tecumseh Waite* (Authorhouse, 2007).

81. Nolan, *The Lincoln County War*, pp 428-433.

82. *Santa Fe New Mexican*, January 4, 1875.

83. *Santa Fe New Mexican*, March 16, 1876; John B. Wilson testimony, Dudley Court of Inquiry Records, NARA.

Index

Doc45 Publications

Killing Pat Garrett, The Wild West's Most Famous Lawman - Murder or Self-Defense?

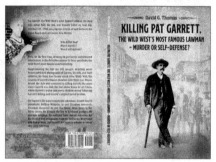

Pat Garrett, the Wild West's most famous lawman – the man who killed Billy the Kid – was himself killed on leap day, February 29, 1908, on a barren stretch of road between his Home Ranch and Las Cruces, New Mexico.

- Who killed him?
- Was it murder?
- Was it self-defense?

No biographer of Garrett has been able to answer these questions. All have expressed opinions. None have presented evidence that would stand up in a court of law. Here, for the first time, drawing on newly discovered information, is the definitive answer to the Wild West's most famous unsolved killing.

Supplementing the text are 102 images, including six of Garrett and his family which have never been published before. It has been 50 years since a new photo of Garrett was published, and no photos of his children have ever been published.

Garrett's life has been extensively researched. Yet, the author was able to uncover an enormous amount of new information. He had access to over 80 letters that Garrett wrote to his wife. He discovered a multitude of new documents and details concerning Garrett's killing, the events surrounding it, and the personal life of the man who was placed on trial for killing Garrett.

- The true actions of "Deacon Jim" Miller, a professional killer, who was in Las Cruces the day Garrett was killed.
- The place on the now abandoned old road to Las Cruces where Garrett was killed.
- The coroner's jury report on Garrett's death, lost for over 100 years.
- Garrett's original burial location.
- The sworn courtroom testimony of the only witness to Garrett's killing.
- The policeman who provided the decisive evidence in the trial of the man accused of murdering Garrett.
- The location of Garrett's Rock House and Home Ranches.
- New family details: Garrett had a four-month-old daughter the day he killed Billy the Kid. She died tragically at 15. Another daughter was blinded by a well-intended eye treatment; a son was paralyzed by childhood polio; and Pat Garrett, Jr., named after his father, lost his right leg to amputation at age 12.

Garrett's life was a remarkable adventure. He met two United States presidents: President William McKinley, Jr. and President Theodore Roosevelt. President Roosevelt he met five times, three times in the White House. He brought the law to hardened gunmen. He oversaw hangings. His national fame was so extensive the day he died that newspapers from the East to the West Coast only had to write "Pat Garrett" for readers to know to whom they were referring.

2020 Will Rogers Medallion Award Finalist for Excellence in Western Media
2020 Independent Press Award Distinguished Favorite, Historical Biography
2019 Best Book Awards Finalist, United States History
2019 Best Indie Book Notable 100 Award Winner.

Doc45 Publications

La Posta – From the Founding of Mesilla, to Corn Exchange Hotel, to Billy the Kid Museum, to Famous Landmark, David G. Thomas, paperback, 118 pages, 59 photos, e-book available.

"For someone who grew up in the area of Mesilla, it's nice to have a well-researched book about the area – and the giant photographs don't hurt either.... And the thing I was most excited to see is a photo of the hotel registry where the name of "William Bonney" is scrawled on the page.... There is some debate as to whether or not Billy the Kid really signed the book, which the author goes into, but what would Billy the Kid history be without a little controversy?" –Billy the Kid Outlaw Gang Newsletter, Winter, 2013.

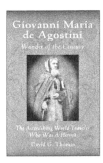

Giovanni Maria de Agostini, Wonder of The Century – The Astonishing World Traveler Who Was A Hermit, David G. Thomas, paperback, 208 pages, 59 photos, 19 maps, e-book available.

"David G. Thomas has finally pulled back the veil of obscurity that long shrouded one of the most enduring mysteries in New Mexico's long history to reveal the true story of the Hermit, Giovanni Maria de Agostini. ...Thomas has once again proven himself a master history detective. Of particular interest is the information about the Hermit's life in Brazil, which closely parallels his remarkable experience in New Mexico, and required extensive research in Portuguese sources. Thomas's efforts make it possible to understand this deeply religious man." – Rick Hendricks, New Mexico State Historian

Screen With A Voice - A History of Moving Pictures in Las Cruces, New Mexico, David G. Thomas, paperback, 194 pages, 102 photos, e-book available.

The first projected moving pictures were shown in Las Cruces 110 years ago. Who exhibited those movies? What movies were shown? Since projected moving pictures were invented in 1896, why did it take ten years for the first movie exhibition to reach Las Cruces? Who opened the first theater in town? Where was it located? These questions began the history of moving pictures in Las Cruces, and they are answered in this book. But so are the events and stories that follow.

There have been 21 movie theaters in Las Cruces – all but three or four are forgotten. They are unremembered no longer. And one, especially, the Airdome Theater which opened in 1914, deserves to be known by all movie historians – it was an automobile drive-in theater, the invention of the concept, two decades before movie history declares the drive-in was invented.

Billy the Kid's Grave – A History of the Wild West's Most Famous Death Marker, David G. Thomas, paperback, 154 pages, 65 photos.

"Quien es?"

The answer to this incautious question – "Who is it?" – was a bullet to the heart.

That bullet – fired by Lincoln County Sheriff Patrick F. Garrett from a .40-44 caliber single action Colt pistol – ended the life of Billy the Kid, real name William Henry McCarty.

But death – ordinarily so final – only fueled the public's fascination with Billy the Kid. What events led to Billy's killing? Was it inevitable? Was a woman involved? If so, who was she? Why has Billy's gravestone become the most famous – and most visited – Western death marker? Is Billy really buried in his grave? Is the grave in the right location?

These questions – and many others – are answered in this book.

Doc45 Publications

The Stolen Pinkerton Reports of the Colonel Albert J. Fountain Murder Investigation, David G. Thomas, editor, paperback, 194 pages, 28 photos.

The abduction and apparent murder of Colonel Albert J. and Henry Fountain on February 1, 1896, shocked and outraged the citizens of New Mexico. It was not the killing of Colonel Fountain, a Union Civil War veteran and a prominent New Mexico attorney, which roused the physical disgust of the citizenry - after all, it was not unknown for distinguished men to be killed. It was the cold-blooded murder of his eight-year-old son which provoked the public outcry and revulsion.

The evidence indicated that although Colonel Albert J. Fountain was killed during the ambush, his son was taken alive, and only killed the next day.

The public was left without answers to the questions:

- Who ambushed and killed Colonel Fountain?
- Who was willing to kill his young son in cold-blood after holding him captive for 24 hours?

The case was never solved. Two men were eventually tried for and acquitted of the crime.

The case file for the crime contains almost no information. There are no trial transcripts or witness testimonies. The only reports that exist today of the investigation of the case are these Pinkerton Reports, which were commissioned by the Territorial Governor, and then stolen from his office four months after the murders. These Reports, now recovered, are published here.

These Reports are important historical documents, not only for what they reveal about the Fountain murders, but also as a fascinating window into how the most famous professional detective agency in the United States in the 1890s - the Pinkerton Detective Agency - went about investigating a murder, at a time when scientific forensic evidence was virtually non-existent.

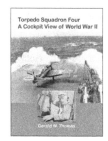

Torpedo Squadron Four – A Cockpit View of World War II, Gerald W. Thomas, paperback, 280 pages, 209 photos, e-book available.

"This book contains more first-person accounts than I have seen in several years. ...we can feel the emotion... tempered by the daily losses that characterized this final stage of the war in the Pacific. All in all, one of the best books on the Pacific War I have seen lately." – Naval Aviation News, Fall 2011.

The Trial of Billy the Kid

This book is about Billy the Kid's trial for murder, and the events leading to that trial. The result of Billy's trial sealed his fate. And yet Billy's trial is the least written about, and until this book, the least known event of Billy's adult life.

Prior biographies have provided extensive — and fascinating — details on Billy's life, but they supply only a few paragraphs on Billy's trial. Just the bare facts: time, place, names, result.

Billy's trial the most important event in Billy's life. You may respond that his death is more important — it is in anyone's life! That is true, in an existential sense, but the events that lead to one's death at a particular place and time, the cause of one's death, override the importance of one's actual death. Those events are determinative. Without those events, one does not die then and there. If Billy had escaped death on July 14, 1881, and went on to live out more of his life, that escape and not his trial would probably be the most important event of Billy's life.

The information presented here has been unknown until now. This book makes it possible to answer these previously unanswerable questions:

- What were the governing Territorial laws?
- What were the charges against Billy?
- Was there a trial transcript and what happened to it?
- What kind of defense did Billy present?
- Did Billy testify in his own defense?
- Did Billy have witnesses standing for him?
- Who testified against him for the prosecution?
- What was the jury like?
- What action by the trial judge virtually guaranteed his conviction?
- What legal grounds did he have to appeal his verdict?
- Was the trial fair?

Supplementing the text are 132 photos, including many photos never published before.